MODERN HUMANITIES RESEARCH ASSOCIATION
LIBRARY OF MEDIEVAL WELSH LITERATURE

General Editors
NERYS ANN JONES
ERICH POPPE

HISTORICAL TEXTS FROM MEDIEVAL WALES

Edited by
Patricia Williams

LIBRARY OF MEDIEVAL WELSH LITERATURE

Already Published

Welsh Court Poems*
edited by Rhian M. Andrews (2007)

Selections from Ystorya Bown o Hamtwn*
edited by Erich Poppe and Regine Reck (2009)

Early Welsh Gnomic and Nature Poetry
edited by Nicolas Jacobs (2012)

Forthcoming

Hystoria Gweryddon yr Almaen:
The Middle Welsh Life of St Ursula and the 11,000 Virgins
edited by Jane Cartwright (2013)

Medieval Welsh Political Poetry
edited by Helen Fulton (2013)

A Selection of Early Welsh Saga Poems
edited by Jenny Rowland (2013)

* (available from University of Wales Press)

HISTORICAL TEXTS FROM MEDIEVAL WALES

Edited by
Patricia Williams

MODERN HUMANITIES RESEARCH ASSOCIATION
2012

Published by

The Modern Humanities Research Association,
1 Carlton House Terrace
London SW1Y 5AF

First published 2012

ISBN (hardback) 978-1-907322-60-0
ISBN (paperback) 978-1-907322-69-3

Copies may be ordered from www.medwelsh.mhra.org.uk

CONTENTS

To

Mary Chris and Gwilym

in gratitiude for their friendship and support over a period of many years.

PREFACE

The purpose of this anthology is to make available to non-native speakers of Welsh, who have some knowledge of Middle Welsh, a selection of annotated passages which deal with Welsh history from Welsh historiographical sources, based on Latin texts. Excluded are texts such as the History-Bible *Y Bibyl Ynghymraec*, *Ystorya Dared*, the Welsh translation of *De Excidio Troiae* attributed to Dares Phrygius and anecdotes from texts of other genres, such as the law texts, medical texts and hagiographies. The selections included in this anthology range from an account of the legendary origin of Britain to the fall of the last native prince. Excerpts have been chosen from the *Brut Dingestow* version of Geoffrey of Monmouth's *Historia Regum Britanniae*, edited by Henry Lewis, from *Historia Gruffud vab Kenan*, edited by Simon Evans (together with some passages direct from MS NLW Peniarth 267), from Thomas Jones's editions of *Brut y Tywyssogyon* (MS NLW Peniarth 20 version) and *Brenhined y Saesson*. All the passages selected have been checked against the manuscript from which they were transcribed, and in some cases minor changes were made. Since the Peniarth 20 version of *Brut y Tywysogyon* is a diplomatic edition, the excerpts selected for this anthology from that work have been subjected to editorial revision.

With regard to subject matter, I have chosen what I hope is an interesting and entertaining selection of texts. So that the reader may more easily relate the passages to their wider context, I have supplied summaries of the omitted sections. With the needs of the target readership in mind, I have tried to make the notes and glossary as 'user-friendly' as possible. In quoting the Latin passages from Geoffrey's History, the reference follows the citation and Neil Wright's elegant translation; where a literal translation has been made by myself, the reference follows the citation only.

Inevitably in an anthology such as this I have made use of the work of the original editors of the texts, as well as Dr Brynley Roberts's excellent edition of *Brut y Brenhinedd*, which presents a further selection of historical texts from another manuscript source. I am hugely indebted to the invaluable advice and encouragement of Professor Erich Poppe, the University of Marburg, Germany and Dr Nerys Ann Jones, the University of Edinburgh, who invited me to undertake this work. I would also like to thank Dr Jones and Dr Regine Reck for user-testing the work on their students in the Universities of Edinburgh and Marburg respectively, and Dr Jenny Day, University of Wales Centre for

Advanced Welsh and Celtic Studies, Abersytwyth, for reading the typescript and suggesting suitable emendations. I am also grateful to Professor Gwyn Thomas, emeritus professor of Welsh, the University of Bangor, for his willingness to discuss and advise on obscure points of syntax, Professor Christopher Allmand, emeritus professor of Medieval History, the University of Liverpool, for reading the introduction and making valuable suggestions, Mr Einion Thomas and Ms Elen Wyn Simpson, University of Bangor Archives, for directing me to the correct sources for information on place-names, Dr Rhian Andrews, formerly of Queen's University Belfast, my cousin Jeffrey Alton and in particular Dennis Hartley, the University of Liverpool, for advice and help with the preparation of the maps, Professor D.A. Price Evans, emeritus professor of Medicine, the University of Liverpool, for the interest he has shown in the work and for his generous donation, Nan Hughes Parry, and my daughters, Lowri and Carys, for proofreading parts of the typescript and helping to index the glossary. Finally I would like to thank Gerard Lowe, publishing manager MHRA for his help in guiding this book through the publishing process. Any errors are entirely my own.

Principal Names associated with HRB

(For Modern Welsh and English forms, see Index of Place names)

Principal Names associated with BT, BS and HGK

KEY

KEINT	region
Caer	town
Hauren	river / island

(For Modern Welsh and English forms, see Index of Place names)

INTRODUCTION

Medieval writers of historical texts had a far less objective approach to their data than that which we expect from modern historians. Although they would sometimes name certain authorities as the source of their information, they would make little or no attempt to check the accuracy of their facts and figures, often blurring the line of demarcation between myth, legend and history. In the fourteenth-century bardic grammars a knowledge of *ystoryav*, 'tales' and 'histories',[1] is listed together with ancient verse and poetry as one of the three essential ingredients of *cyfarwyddyd*, 'the art of story telling'.[2] In western medieval literature in general there is a close connection between *historia* (historical truth) and *fabula* (fiction) and it is interesting to see that in the Latin colophon to the Irish native tale *Táin Bó Cúailnge* (The Cattle-Raid of Cooley)[3] the scribe recognised that there could be a conflict between the two genres:

> *Sed ego qui scripsi hanc historiam aut verius fabulam quibusdam fidem in hac historia aut fabula non accommodo. Quaedam enim ibi sunt praestrigia demonum, quaedam autem figmenta poetica, quaedam similia uero, quaedam non, quaedam ad delectionem stultorum.*[4]

> [But I who have written this story, or rather this fable, do not trust certain things in this *historia* or *fabula*. For some things there are delusions of demons, others poetic inventions, some resemble the truth, others do not, some are for the delectations of fools.][5]

This conflict was likewise noted by Isidore of Seville (*c.* 560–636), Bishop of Seville and one of the great scholars of the early Middle Ages, who drew a triple distinction between histories (*historiae*), plausible narratives (*argumenta*), and fables (*fabulae*):

> Histories are true deeds that have happened, plausible narrations are things that, even if they have not happened, nevertheless could happen, and fables are things that have not happened and cannot happen, because they are contrary to nature.[6]

Centuries earlier, Thucydides (c. 460 B.C.–395 B.C.), Greek historian and author of the *History of the Peloponnesian War*, had also discussed the difference between his own approach to history (which was to draw inferences from reported data) and that of poets and popular historians, who respectively embellished the facts

---

[1] For a more detailed discussion and definition of *ystoria* see B. F. Roberts, '*Ystoria*', *BBCS* 26 (1974–76), pp. 13–20.

[2] Williams and Jones, *Gramadegau*, p. 134.

[3] Found in the 12th century manuscript known as The Book of Leinster.

[4] O'Rahilly, *Táin*, p. 136, lines 4921–25.

[5] Poppe, 'Evidence', p. 303.

[6] Isidore, *Etymologies*, Bk. 1. § xliv.5, p. 67; see also Toner, 'The Ulster Cycle', pp. 1–20.

and presented them 'with a view to making them not more truthful, but more attractive to their audiences'.[7] He admitted that he found his search for data extremely arduous, because his informants gave varying reports of the same events depending on their sympathies and their memories, and he suspected that his narrative would seem less pleasing to some listeners because it lacked an element of fiction.[8] This philosophy of history is diametrically opposite to that of Cicero (106 B.C.–43 B.C.), Roman statesman, lawyer, philosopher and generally considered one of the greatest orators of his day, who had scant regard for the truth, if it did not answer his purpose. In fact, Cicero went so far as to say that it was permissible for rhetoricians to tell lies in their historical writings, to make the account more poignant.[9] An example of his attempt to turn this concept of history into a practical reality can be read in a letter to the historian Lucius Lucceius, in which he asked him to write a subjective and adulatory account of his (Cicero's) consulship. He begged him to exaggerate his actions with more enthusiasm than the rules of history allowed, on the grounds that an account of his changing fortunes would give enormous pleasure to the reader.[10] Quintilian (c. 35–c. 100), a Roman rhetorician of Spanish origin and a great admirer of Cicero, voiced a not dissimilar view; like Aristotle, he considered *historia* to be closely related to poetry and described it as a kind of free verse (*carmen solutum*).[11] He continued by asserting that history should be shunned by the orator as its function was to tell a story, not to prove anything (*scribitur ad narrandum non ad probandum*) and was written to record events for the purpose of posterity and to gain glory for its author.

The result of regarding history as anything other than a narration of true facts is a tendency to exaggerate, particularly in the description of a battle scene, with the numbers and bravery of the antagonists overstated or understated according to the political bias of the author. Monsters, demons, magical characters, incredible feats of daring by super-heroes and cosmic phenomena feature in early histories, but as Ralph O'Connor points out in his informative article on truth-claims in the Icelandic sagas,[12] we cannot assume that what is unbelievable to a twenty-first-century reader would not have been believed by a medieval audience. He continues by stating that what would have seemed incredible even to a medieval audience might have been believed in the context of the distant past. Other characteristics of ancient and medieval histories are the inclusion of the *encomium*, an extravagant oration in praise of an individual, and the citation of speeches, which are the invention of the author rather than the actual words of the characters to whom they are attributed. It is astonishing to modern ears that

7   Thucydides, *Peleponnesian War*, ed. Blanco and Roberts, Bk. 1 §21, p. 11.
8   Ibid., Bk.1 §22, p. 11.
9   Cicero, *Brutus*, ed. Henrickson and Hubbell, Bk. XI, p. 41.
10 Cicero, *Epistolae*. ed. Williams, Vol. 1, pp. 368, 369.
11 Quintilian, *Orator's Education*, ed. Russell, Bk. X p. 268.
12 O'Connor, 'History', p. 107.

even Thucydides, who more than any other ancient historian strove to give a true and accurate report of events, admitted the following approach to speeches:

> As to the speeches of the participants, either when they were about to enter the war or after they were already in it, it has been difficult for me and for those who reported to me to remember exactly what was said. I have, therefore, written what I thought the speakers must have said given the situations they were in, while keeping as close as possible to the gist of what was actually said.[13]

All the above-mentioned characteristics are to be found in Middle Welsh historical texts, which are translations or adaptations from Latin originals.

Medieval historians were deeply influenced by Christian theology and the cultural legacy of the Roman Empire,[14] and had no inhibitions about tailoring historical events to prove a point. The Venerable Bede (c. 672–735), a Benedictine monk, regarded as the father of English history on account of his *Historia Ecclesiastica Gentis Anglorum*, 'The Ecclesiastical History of the English People', made no secret of the fact that the quality of the written word could have an impact on people's behaviour. He maintained that if history recorded the deeds of good men, the reader would be spurred on to imitate them, if it recorded the 'evil ends of wicked men', then the reader should be stimulated to avoid such perverse behaviour and pursue 'those things which he had learned to be good and pleasing in the sight of God'.[15] From this, therefore, it can be seen that historical events were used as *exempla* to prove the importance of submission to the divine will: a nation would flourish if it found favour in the eyes of God, whereas its failure to succeed was seen as a token of divine disapproval. Geoffrey of Monmouth, the well-known twelfth-century historian, stated this view very clearly towards the end of his great work, *Historia Regum Britanniae* 'History of the Kings of Britain': *Nolebat enim Deus Britones in insulam Britanniae diutius regnare* 'God did not want the Britons to rule over the island of Britain any longer'.[16]

Against this background, it is not astonishing that medieval historians should follow a methodology used in the Bible, namely establishing an individual's credentials by showing from what stock he had originated.[17] Giraldus Cambrensis, otherwise known as Gerald de Barri and Gerald of Wales, one of the greatest Latin writers to emerge from Wales in the Middle Ages, testified to the desire of the Welsh to trace their lineage and maintained that even the humblest peasant could recite a list of his ancestors dating back to the seventh generation and beyond.[18] The Irish too saw the importance of genealogy, as Donnchadh Ó'Corráin points out in connection with early Irish narrative prose:

---

[13] Thucydides, *Peleponnesian War*, Bk.1 §22, p. 11.
[14] Hanning, *Vision*, pp.1–43.
[15] Bede, *Ecclesiastical History*, p. 3.
[16] *GM*, pp. 278, 279 §205.
[17] Genesis 5.1–31; 1 Chronicles, 1–9; Matthew 1.1–16 and Luke 3.23–38.
[18] Gerald of Wales, *Journey* (trans. Thorpe), p. 251.

Tales cast in a historical mould, in which prominent roles are given to the ancestors (real or imagined) of powerful lineages, have an immediacy and a remarkable potential for the communication of ideas which might otherwise be difficult to convey.[19]

In the light of this it is understandable that a genealogical approach is employed by Geoffrey of Monmouth to prove the importance, not simply of an individual but of an entire nation, in his monumental history, which claims that the British race arose from the ashes of Troy.[20]

Historia Regum Britanniae

The most influential history, or rather pseudo-history, in the Middle Ages was undoubtedly Geoffrey of Monmouth's *Historia Regum Britanniae*. In fact, the work was so well-received that it has been preserved in no fewer than 217 manuscripts.[21] However, the title by which Geoffrey himself referred to the work was *De Gestis Britonum* 'Concerning the Deeds of the Britons' and it is this title that Reeve and Wright employed as a sub-title for their 2007 edition.[22] Although the term pseudo-history is pejorative when applied to modern history, in as much as it implies that the writer has not properly researched the subject, has not disclosed his sources or has been less than honest in the interpretation of the data, this is not so when applied to the works of medieval historians. As explained above, classical and medieval historians did not regard the verification of facts as their foremost priority. Instead, they used their material as evidence to corroborate a preconceived conclusion, namely the supremacy of their own nation, which they claimed enjoyed its exalted status as a result of divine will, rather than take the more scholarly approach of extrapolating the truth from an objective analysis of the so-called facts. The *Historia Regum Britanniae* is discussed in some detail in the introduction to the present edition, because, although written in Latin, it is the text from which the selections of the Welsh recensions included in this anthology are derived. Geoffrey's *Historia* was written during the 1130's[23] and purports to be a history of the British nation from its foundation by Brutus, grandson of the Trojan Aeneas, to its fall as a result of Saxon domination. The story of the birth of Britain echoes the classical tale of the foundation of Rome by Aeneas after his escape from the ashes of Troy and

---

[19] Ó'Corráin, 'Historical Need', p. 144.

[20] The device of using pedigrees to prove the importance of a nation had already been employed in *Historia Brittonum*, traditionally attributed to Nennius, where it was claimed that the British people descended from Brutus, grandson of Aeneas, and ultimately back to Adam. (Morris (ed.), *Nennius, British History*, §18, pp. 22, 63; Rowley, *Historia*, §18, Dumville, *Historia*, pp. 72–74). For further discussion on the authorship of HB see Dumville, 'Nennius'.

[21] For a complete list see Crick, *Historia*.

[22] See Abbreviations s.v. *GM*.

[23] Wright, *Historia* (1984), p. vii. Reeve, (*GM*, p. vii) maintains that the HRB must have been finished between 1123 and 1139.

embodies an ideal expressed in *Historia Brittonum*,[24] namely that the Britons had as glorious an ancestry as that of the ancient Romans. The work also records the development of Britain through civil strife, Roman conquest, the Saxon invasions and reaches its climax with the reign of Arthur. His rule is depicted as Britain's golden era and more space is devoted to this period than to any other. Such success, however, is short-lived; Arthur is betrayed by his nephew, deposed at the pinnacle of his success and Britain is left floundering without a strong leader. Finally the death of Cadwaladr the Blessed, A.D. 681 with which the work concludes, eradicates any hope of immediate recovery. Although Geoffrey interprets the Britons' loss of sovereignty as a result of their own degenerate behaviour, he does not leave them entirely without hope of reoccupying their kingdom. Cadwaladr was told that only when his bones were returned to Britain and displayed together with those of the other saints, which had been hidden away for fear of desecration by the pagans, would the Britons hold sway over their country again. This is clearly the source of later vaticinatory verse[25] where he is depicted, like Arthur, as the saviour who will lead the Welsh to freedom. Although none of his deeds are recorded in extant manuscripts, he must have been a formidable figure in his day and possibly spent his final years as a monk, judging from the fact that the church of Llangadwaladr in Anglesey claims him as its founder and patron saint, and churches in other parts of Wales have also been dedicated to him.[26]

Geoffrey of Monmouth

Despite the popularity of *Historia Regum Britanniae*, little is known about Geoffrey of Monmouth's personal life. He refers to himself three times in the *Historia* as Geoffrey of Monmouth; he also uses the signature *Galfridus Monemutensis*, in his capacity as witness in five official documents connected with religious foundations in and around Oxford, which have been dated to between 1129 and 1151. This nomenclature suggests that he had lived in Monmouth, even if he had not been born there. Another indication of Geoffrey's connection with Monmouth is the fact that he moves Arthur's court from the Celliwig (in Cornwall) of Welsh tradition to Caerleon-on-Usk in Monmouthshire, a town with which he was probably familiar. In a sixth document connected with religious institutions at Oxford he signs himself as *Galfridus Arthurus*, a form of signature he may have used because Arthur was his father's name, rather than because of his desire to be associated with the legendary king, to whose exploits he devoted so many pages of his history. The eminent early twentieth-century historian John Edward Lloyd suggested that Geoffrey used this title 'in the days of his obscurity',[27] before the publication of his famous work. Reeve, however,

[24] See fn. 20.
[25] Williams, *Armes Prydein*, p. 6 and Jarman, *Llyfr Du Caerfyrddin*, p. 33.
[26] Lloyd, *History*, p. 231.
[27] Lloyd, *History*, ii, p. 524.

states that 'some of the older and better manuscripts' in titles and subscriptions also call him Galfridus Artur (or Arturus) Monemutensis.[28] On the basis of this nomenclature, and considering the fact that Arthur was not a common name in Wales at that time, Lloyd suggested that Geoffrey was the son of one of the Bretons, who had settled in Monmouth during that period.[29] Further indications of his Breton origin rest on the fact that he depicts the Bretons as being far more morally upright and capable of sagacious rule than the pusillanimous Britons, who do not deserve the country founded by their ancestor Brutus. In times of crisis the leaders of Britain repeatedly turn to their fellow countrymen in 'Little Britain' for help. When requested to help the Britons rid their country of the invading Picts and Scots, Aldroenus (Aldwr), king of Brittany, refuses to act, saying that he prefers to rule his own small kingdom in liberty, rather than Britain under the yoke of slavery.[30] Likewise it is to Brittany that Cadualadrus (Cadwaladr) flees to escape the famine and plague which had beset Britain as a result of civil war,[31] but this time even Breton intervention could not save Britain from Saxon domination.

That Geoffrey lived and worked in Oxford cannot be disputed. We have the evidence of his signature on the above mentioned charters, in two of which he described himself as *magister* (master).[32] As the University of Oxford had not yet been founded, he would not have been a professor, but he may have held some sort of teaching position, possibly in the college of St. George's, in Oxford. It has been suggested that he may have been a canon in that college on the grounds that one of the charters he signed dealt with the island of Osney, which was in the parish of St George and that his friend, Archdeacon Walter, whom he frequently mentions in his work, was provost of St. George's. He was most certainly a cleric, and strange though it may seem to us today, early in 1151 he became Bishop Elect of St Asaph in North Wales, although he had not yet been ordained as a priest. In fact he was consecrated as bishop a mere week after his ordination in February 1152, but it is unlikely that he ever visited his see.[33]

The obscurity surrounding Geoffrey's life is in direct contrast to the fame of his writings. In addition to his *Historia Regum Britanniae*, which appeared in the 1130's, Geoffrey composed two other works, *The Prophecy of Merlin*, written before the *Historia* but subsequently incorporated into that work[34] and *Vita Merlini*, 'The Life of Merlin', a long poem in hexameter verse, which was composed 1150–51.[35] Geoffrey claimed to have translated *The Prophecy of Merlin*, at the request of Alexander, bishop of Lincoln, *de Britannico in Latinum*, 'from

---

[28] *GM*, p. vii.
[29] Lloyd, *History*, ii, pp. 523–24.
[30] *GM*, pp. 116–17; *BrD*, p. 85.
[31] *GM*, pp. 278–79; *BrD*, pp. 205–06.
[32] Geoffrey of Monmouth, *History* (trans. Thorpe), pp. 11–12.
[33] Lloyd, *History*, ii, pp. 524–25.
[34] *GM*, pp. 144–59.
[35] Clark, *Vita*. Facsimile by Mary F. E. K. Jones, http://www.geocities.com/branwaedd/merlini.html

British into Latin',[36] but he did not indicate the identity of his British source. His final work, *Vita Merlini*, which Geoffrey dedicated to a later bishop of Lincoln, Robert de Chesney, who had been one of the canons of St. George's in Oxford, is a further indication of Geoffrey's connection with that establishment.

Geoffrey's Sources

The only work acknowledged by Geoffrey as the source of his material for the *Historia* is 'an ancient book in the British language', which he claims had been given to him by his friend Walter, archdeacon of Oxford, and which he had subsequently translated into Latin. This assertion, however, should be viewed with caution, for as Brynley F. Roberts points out, 'The mangled version of Geoffrey's closing reference to Walter's ancient book . . . led to its being taken as Geoffrey's source. . . and gave it unwarranted, and misleading, authority.[37] Nevertheless, the identification of this source book has been the subject of keen debate among scholars. Did it originate in Wales or Brittany? Was it a medieval reader's digest (no longer extant) of the works of earlier historians, such as Gildas[38] and Bede, who are quoted by Geoffrey in the prologue to the *Historia*?[39] Did it even exist outside Geoffrey's fertile imagination? Lloyd was positive that 'no Welsh composition existed which could be reasonably looked upon as the original, or even the groundwork, of the *History of the Kings of Britain*'.[40] However the fact that it is no longer extant does not mean that it never existed, and when one considers that more medieval manuscripts perished than survived, the loss of Walter's 'ancient book' would not be remarkable. Brynley F. Roberts suggests that it may have had a real existence as a book of genealogies, but does not claim that it was Geoffrey's only, or even most important, source.[41] Anton Griscom voiced the opinion that this 'ancient book' may be latent in other editions of the *Historia*, which, although admittedly post Galfredian, could have incorporated material which pre-dated Geoffrey.[42] Two of the Welsh versions contained in manuscripts listed by Griscom[43] were published in the *Myvyrian Archaeology of Wales* under the titles *Brut Tysilio* and *Brut Gruffudd ab Arthur*.[44] The former was once considered to be a copy of the *vetutissimus liber* 'the ancient book', which Geoffrey had claimed as his source and the latter to be a translation

---

[36]   *GM*, p. 142.
[37]   See *Celtic Culture*, Vol. 1, 298–99.
[38]   Gildas was a sixth- century monk and author of *De Excidio et Conquestu Britanniae*, 'On the Ruin and Conquest of Britain'.
[39]   *GM*, pp. 4, 5.
[40]   Lloyd, *History*, ii, p. 526.
[41]   B. F. Roberts, *Brut y Brenhinedd*, p. xviii.
[42]   Griscom, *Historia*, pp. 99–147.
[43]   Ibid., pp. 586–99.
[44]   The *Myvyrian Archaeology of Wales* is an anthology of verse and prose texts published in 1870 by a group of successful London Welshmen interested in making Welsh literature more accessible to a wider audience. See also B. F. Roberts, *Brut Tysilio*.

of Geoffrey's Latin text, but both in fact are now thought to have derived from the *Historia*.[45]

The publication of a variant version of the *Historia* by Jacob Hammer[46] gave rise to yet another theory about the source of Geoffrey's work. Hammer was of the opinion that this variant, which omits the references to Walter and his 'ancient book', was an adaptation of the *Historia* by some other contemporary author, even though Geoffrey's name appears in the colophon. Robert A. Caldwell, however, proposed that this variant version preceded the standard text and was later polished and revised to become the standard version of the Historia, which is now known as the Vulgate.[47] The implication of this assertion is that if this variant version really was the work of an author other than Geoffrey and earlier than the standard text, this could be the 'ancient book' itself. These views have been dsicussed by subsequent critics, such as Pierre Gallois, who rejected the theory that the Variant predated the Vulgate,[48] Hans-Erich Keller, who, like Caldwall, believed the Variant antedated the standard text[49] and R. William Leckie, who considered the Variant to be a later recension compiled sometime between 1138 and 1155.[50] Their views are succinctly summed up by Neil Wright, who nevertheless finds their theories defective.[51]

A closer examination of the wording in the Arthurian section of Geoffrey's *Historia*, where there is a second reference to Walter's involvement in the composition of this extraordinary book suggests another interpretation. After stating his wish not to comment on the treachery of Arthur's nephew Modred, Geoffrey announces that he will describe the battle which ensued between them, following the account given *in praefato Britannico sermone* 'in the aforementioned discourse', which he had 'heard' from Walter of Oxford.[52] It is significant that Geoffrey refers to his source material here as *sermo*, which suggests an oral rather than a written account,[53] a possibility further reinforced by his choice of the verb *audiuit* 'heard'. One of the meanings of *liber* is 'list' or 'catalogue' and it was used in this sense by Cicero in his second speech against

---

[45] Jones, Thomas, 'Historical Writing in Medieval Welsh', *Scottish Studies*, 12 (1968), 15–27. p. 16; BrD, p. xviii.

[46] Geoffrey of Monmouth, *Historia*, ed. Hammer, p. 17.

[47] John J. Parry and Robert A Caldwell 'Geoffrey of Monmouth' in Loomis, *Arthurian*, pp. 72–93 (87). The paragraphs in which the Variant Version of the Historia is discussed have been added by Caldwell and should not be attributed to Parry (see editor's note, p. 72). For a discussion on Geoffrey's sources, see also Geoffrey of Monmouth, *The History of the Kings of Britain* trans. Lewis Thorne (Harmondsworth, 1988), 14–19.

[48] P. Gallais, '*La Variant Version* de l'*Historia Regum Brittaniae* et le *Brut* de Wace', *Romania* 86 (1966), pp. 103–26.

[49] H. Keller, 'Wace et Geoffrey de Monmouth: problème ed la chronologie es sources', *Romania* 98 (1977), pp. 379–89.

[50] R. W. Leckie, *The Passage of Dominion: Geoffrey of Monmouth and the Periodization of Insular History in the Twelfth Century,* (Toronto, 1981).

[51] Wright, *Historia* (1988), pp. xi–xvi.

[52] GM, p. 249.

[53] L&S, pp. 1679–80.

Verres,[54] in which he mentioned a letter he had seen *in litterarum allatarum libris*, 'in the catalogues of letters received'.[55] That being so, could it be that the 'ancient book' was no more than a list of manuscript sources or material remembered from oral tradition, transmitted to Geoffrey by Walter in conversation? And not only in conversation; for in the Dedication to the *Historia* he refers to tales of ancient heroes 'proclaimed by many people as if they had been entertainingly and memorably written down'.[56] This confirms Brynley F. Roberts's assertion that much of the material on which Geoffrey based his *Historia* was drawn from an oral tradition, which is difficult to trace, as well as from literary sources easier to identify, since they would be drawn from the prescribed works that an educated man in the Middle Ages would be expected to have read — the Bible, Classical Literature, histories, genealogies and contemporary romance.[57] There are indications in the *Historia* that Geoffrey was familiar with all these works: not only does he make a specific reference to the historians Gildas and Bede in the prologue to his *Historia*, but the nomenclature of that work in general further indicates that Geoffrey was familiar with the genealogies and the list of the Cities and Marvels of Britain contained in the *Historia Brittonum* in BL MS. Harley 3859.[58] In fact, Reeve cites these works as 'sources beyond dispute';[59] but there are indications that Geoffrey was also familiar with Welsh tradition.[60] For example, the tripartite division of Britain, is reminiscent of the Welsh passion for triadic grouping,[61] which Geoffrey seemed to have been aware of as a rhetorical device, even though Rachel Bromwich maintained that there was no evidence to suggest that Geoffrey had direct knowledge of the Triads themselves.[62] According to Geoffrey, on the death of Brutus, the founder of Britain, the country was divided among his three sons, who gave their names to the area each had inherited:

> *A Locrinus, canys hynhaf oed, a gymerth y rann berued o'r enys, yr honn a elwir Lloegyr o'e enw ef; ac y kymerth Kamber o'r tu arall y Hauren, yr hon a elwir o'e env ef Kymry; ac y kymerth Albanactus y gogled, yr hon a elwis ynteu o'e enw ef yr Alban.*[63]

> [And Locrinus, because he was the eldest, took the central part of the island, which is called Lloegr [England] after his name, and Camber took the other side of the Severn, which is called Cymru [Wales] after his name, and Albanactus took the north which he too called after his own name, Yr Alban [Scotland].]

---

54 A Roman magistrate (*c.* 120 BC — 43 BC), notorious for his misgovernment of Sicily.
55 Page, *Verrine*, p. 20. See also L&S, p. 1058.
56 *GM*, pp. 4–5; *BrD*, p. 1.
57 Roberts, *Brut y Brenhinedd*, p. xv.
58 Morris, *Nennius*, pp, 41–42, 81–84, Rowley, *Historia*, pp. 64–73.
59 *GM*, p. lvii.
60 B. F. Roberts, *Brut y Brenhinedd*, pp. xv-xxi.
61 The best example of this is an index of legendary characters listed in groups of three known as *Trioedd Ynys Prydein*. For a brief description of the Triads, see Stephens, *New Companion*, pp. 735–36.
62 Bromwich, *Trioedd*, pp. lxxix-lxxx.
63 See text p. 4 below.

Another example of a knowledge of the Welsh tales is to be seen the names of Arthur's companions: Beduerus and Kaius correspond to Bedwyr and Cai; and Gualuainus is possibly the Welsh Gwalchmai, while Arthur's sword Caliburnus corresponds to Caledfwlch, his spear Ron to Rongomyniad, his shield Pridwen to his ship Prydwen in the native tale *Culhwch ac Olwen*.[64] Furthermore, the account of his encounter with Ritho, the giant of Mount Aravius, who boasted of the number of kings he had killed by wearing a cloak made of their beards, is reminiscent of Welsh folklore[65]. That Geoffrey takes the trouble to mention Ritho's obsession with cutting off the beards of his victims also suggests a familiarity with the Welsh oath, *mefl ar dy farf*, 'shame on your beard', an expression which frequently occurs in the Welsh tales and a possible cause of litigation, for according to the Welsh laws a woman could not with impunity wish a blemish on her husband's beard, as this would be tantamount to casting aspersions on his virility.[66] Nevertheless, his portrayal of Medrawd (Modred), Arthur's nephew, is a departure from tradition. Geoffrey himself seems to be the source of vilifying him as a *sceleratissimus proditor* 'an infamous traitor',[67] for in medieval Welsh poetry Medrawd (Modred) is the epitome of valour and courtesy.[68] Geoffrey was the first to claim that Medrawd (Modred) was responsible for Arthur's death in the Battle of Mount Camlan. This may be a result of Geoffrey's personal interpretation of a comment in the *Annales Cambriae* (Welsh Annals) in BL MS. Harley 3859, under the year 537, *Gueith Camlann in qua Arthur et Medraut corruerunt*. 'The battle of Camlan, in which Arthur and Medrawd fell'.[69] The only information given in the annal is that Arthur and Medrawd fell in that battle; there is no indication whether they were fighting on the same or on opposite sides, but the mere mention would have been enough for Geoffrey to weave an elaborate tale. Since it would have been unthinkable for as great a leader as Arthur to have been vanquished by anyone or anything other than treachery, this brief annal suggested to Geoffrey a means of safeguarding Arthur's reputation by introducing Medrawd as the villain.[70] Maybe Geoffrey knew of the special relationship in primitive societies, known as avunculate,[71] between a man and his sister's son, who would be his heir, rather than his own son, and from this seed of knowledge could not resist the temptation of presenting a dramatically tragic ending by the vilification of the nephew. As Brynley F. Roberts writes, 'A man of Geoffrey's imagination would

---

[64] Bromwich and Evans, *Culhwch*, lines 159–60 and 938.
[65] Grooms, *Giants*, pp. 214–15.
[66] Wiliam, *Iorwerth*, p. 28; Jenkins, *The Law*, 52–53.
[67] GM, pp. 248–49; BrD, pp. 182.
[68] Padel, *Arthur*, pp. 113–15. For examples of the court poets comparing their patrons favourably to Medrawd, see *CBT I* poem 3.25–26, *CBT II* poem 25.43, *CBT IV* poem 9.23–24.
[69] Morris, *Nennius*, pp. 45 and 85.
[70] Loomis, *Arthurian*, p. 85.
[71] See Ó Cathasaigh, 'Sister's son'.

have had no difficulty in combining and adapting these different sources and creating a story from a mere record of a name'.[72]

Geoffrey's purpose

Geoffrey's avowed objective in writing the *Historia* was to fill a gap in British history which had been left by Gildas and Bede, who, he claimed, had ignored the kings who reigned in Britain before the Incarnation of Christ. He maintained that as the deeds of these early kings had been preserved in the memory of many people, he felt it was his duty to record them in writing. This could well be no more than a literary convention, for in the Preface to the *Historia Brittonum* the author claimed to have undertaken the task of preserving in writing the history of the Britons from whatever sources he could find, *quia nullam peritiam habuerunt neque ullam commemorationem in libris posuerunt doctores*, 'for the scholars (i.e. of the isle of Britain) had no skill, and set down no record in books'.[73] This is reminiscent of the Roman historian Livy's preface to his *Ab Urbe Condita* 'From the foundation of the City', where he stated that his purpose was to commemorate the deeds of the foremost people of the world, neither affirming nor refuting the ancient traditions of the Romans, which were adorned with poetic legend rather than based on trustworthy proofs.[74] To Livy the importance of history, whether based on actual or poetic truth, was that it gave examples and warnings, so that the reader could learn about the men and the policies through which the empire was established and how, through the relaxation of discipline and the moral code, it deteriorated to the point when they 'could endure neither their vices nor their cure'.[75] Whether Geoffrey was simply following a literary convention in stating his professed purpose or not, he certainly shared the same philosophy of history as the author of *Historia Brittonum*, Gildas, Bede, and Livy, who used historical events as *exempla* to prove respectively the omnipotence of God or the might of Rome.

Geoffrey's underlying purpose was, therefore, more subtle than his avowed intent. He did not simply aim at filling an omission in the nation's historiography but at using his recorded material to prove a point. He is not the first to take this pragmatic view of history. Isidore, many centuries earlier, had claimed that one of the functions of recording past events was the instruction of the present,[76] and, as Erich Poppe points out in a discussion on medieval Irish genealogy and hagiography 'these works about the past met the needs of their present, and were adapted accordingly'.[77] Geoffrey, in his opening chapter, describes the island of

---

[72] B. F. Roberts, *Brut y Brenhinedd*, pp. xiv-xv.

[73] Morris, *Nennius*, §1, pp. 9, 50. According to another version, the author claims to be making an attempt 'to deliver the few remaining ears of corn about past happenings, seeing that an ample crop has been snatched away already by the hostile reapers of foreign nations': see Rowley, *Historia*, §1.

[74] Livy, *Books I-II*, trans. Foster, p. 2.

[75] Ibid. pp. 5–7.

[76] Isidore *Etymologies*, Bk.1. § xliii, p. 67.

[77] Poppe, 'Evidence', p. 306.

Britain and names the five races that inhabit it, namely the Normans, the Britons, the Saxons, the Picts and the Scots. Of these, he claims that the only rightful rulers are the Britons, but because of their wrongdoing and arrogance, God allowed the English, the Picts and the Scots to oppress them. It is significant that he does not name the Normans as oppressors; it would not have been politically expedient to champion the Welsh claim to sovereignty rather than that of the ruling class. Throughout this work Geoffrey stresses the unity of Britain and the view that power can only be invested in one ruler. When Caduallo (Cadwallawn) considers granting the crown of Northumberland to Edwinus (Edwin) he is warned by his nephew Brianus (Breint Hir) of the possible consequences of sharing power with outsiders. Heeding this advice, he refuses Edwin's request on the grounds that it was contrary to the custom of the land that there should be more than one crowned king.[78] Reconciling this view of sovereignty with political reality must have been a dilemma for Geoffrey. It has been suggested that the dedication of his work to both Robert Earl of Gloucester (c. 1090–1147) and Waleran of Beaumont, Count of Meulan (1104–1166) is symbolic of his divided loyalty. Robert was the illegitimate son of Henry I and a half brother to Matilda, now Countess of Anjou, whom Henry had designated as his heir. Therefore by dedicating his book to Robert, Geoffrey showed his support for Matilda, but when Stephen, rather than Matilda, inherited the throne, Geoffrey revealed his changed allegiance by adding a second dedication to Waleran, 1104 -1166, son of Robert de Beaumont and twin brother to Robert Earl of Leicester, who was Stephen's particular favourite.[79] In the version of the *Historia* contained in Bern, Burgerbibliothek MS. 568 Stephen himself was also added to the list of dedicatees. In fact an overall scrutiny of the extant manuscripts has revealed five different forms of dedication.[80] Such variation suggests that scholars may have attached too much significance to these multiple dedications, which could have been added or removed in the course of textual transmission.

In the opening chapters of the *Historia* Geoffrey gave the British nation as prestigious an origin as that of Rome and concluded by showing how the Britons' loss of sovereignty had occurred partly through Cadwaladr's debilitating illness, which caused him to lose control of his realm, and partly through natural disasters, which killed off a vast proportion of the population. These disasters — famine and pestilence, reminiscent of the biblical plagues of Israel — Geoffrey interpreted as divine retribution against a degenerate nation. King Cadwaladr fled to Brittany, lamenting the fact that his country, which had never been defeated by a succession of enemies, was now left barren by the wrath of God and that, as a result of his people's crimes, the coast was now clear for Saxon

---

[78] *GM*, pp. 264–65; *BrD*, p. 195.
[79] Loomis, *Arthurian*, p. 80.
[80] *GM*, pp. ix-x.

invasions.[81] Cadwaladr's death heralded the end of the British nation, for his successors failed in their resistance against the invading Saxons.

> *Barbarie etiam irrepente iam non uocabuntur Britones sed Gualenses, uocabulum siue a Gualone duce eorum siue a Galaes regina siue a barbarie trahentes.*[82]

> [As the foreigners encroached upon them, they were no longer called 'Britons' but 'Welsh', this word deriving either from their leader, Gualo or from their Queen Galaes, or else from their being so alienated from their native culture.]

The Welsh version of the *Historia* in the Dingestow Court manuscript (NLW 5266B) is very brief and simply states, *Ac o hynny allan ny elwit vynt yn Urytanyeit, namyn yn Gymry,*[83] 'And henceforth they were not called Britons but Welsh', omitting any explanation of the changed nomenclature. The author of the Latin version, however, saw a parallel between the name *Gualenses*, 'Welsh', derived from the Anglo-Saxon *waelisc*, which means 'foreign', and the Latin epithet *barbarus*. Just as *barbarus* in Latin referred to anyone who was not Greek or Roman, so 'Welsh' became an epithet for those who were not of Saxon origin. To be treated as foreigners in their own land was the Britons' punishment for their profligate lifestyle; the English, on the other hand, behaved more wisely and gained dominance over the whole island. Nevertheless the Britons were not left entirely without hope of eventual recovery. Cadwaladr was assured by an angelic voice that one day the British people would be rewarded for its faithfulness and would achieve independence once again, when the appointed moment arrived. This is a continuation of the returning hero motif, which had been subtly introduced with the fall of Arthur: in a contradictory phrase Arthur is said to have been 'mortally wounded' and taken to the isle of Avalon *ad sananda uulnera sua* 'so that his wounds may be healed'.[84] The absence of a reported death and burial subsequently became symbolic of the nation's hope of regaining its lost sovereignty, while the Normans could rejoice in the fact that they had succeeded in conquering a people with as illustrious a past as the ancient Romans. Geoffrey was indeed filling a historical need.

Welsh Recensions of the Historia

There are several Welsh recensions, based on Geoffrey's *Historia*, which are frequently referred to by the collective title *Brut y Brenhinedd* 'The Chronicle of

---

[81] *GM*, pp. 276–77; *BrD*, pp. 204–05.
[82] *GM*, p. 281.
[83] *BrD*, p. 208.
[84] *GM*, p. 253; see also text §37 below from *BrD*, p. 185.

the Kings'.[85] Of the earliest versions, the one contained in the Dingestow Court manuscript is considered to be the most eloquent, as it presents the content of the original without producing a literal translation. It is from this manuscript, dated by Daniel Huws to the second half of the thirteenth century,[86] that the extracts from *Brut y Brenhinedd* chosen for this anthology are taken.

Brut y Brenhinedd is in its manuscript transmission the centre piece of an historical cycle.[87] The link between it and earlier works is clearly stated in the addendum to *Y Bibyl Ynghymraec*, 'The Bible in Welsh',[88] which despite its title can be regarded as an historical text. In this work, the author traces the ancestors of the legendary Aeneas (great grandfather of Brutus, the eponymous founder of Britain, in Geoffrey's *Historia*) back to Japheth son of the biblical Noah:

> . . . A mab y hwnnw (Ericonius) vv Tros ap Ericonius. A hwnnw a edeilawd Troya, ac a'y henwis o'y henw ehun. Ac y hwnnw y bu deu vab, nyt amgen, Ylus vab Tros ac Assaracus vab Tros. Mab y Assaracus vv Capis. A mab y hwnnw vv Ancisses. A mab y hwnnw vv Eneas Ysgwydwynn. Ac am hwnnw a'u etiued y traethir yn Ystorya [y] Brut.[89]

> [And a son of his [Ericonius] was Tros son of Ericonius. And he built Troy and named it after himself. And he had two sons, none other than Ylus son of Tros ac Assaracus son of Tros. Capis was a son of Assaracus. And a son of his was Anchises. And a son of his was Aeneas of the White Shield. And it is about him and his son that an account is given in *The History of the Brut*.]

The concluding paragraph of *Y Bibyl Ynghymraec* also traces the descent of Ylus, the other son of Tros, king of Troy, through Laomedon to Priam, whose story is related in *Ystorya Daret*, 'The History of Darius'[90] a translation of the sixth century Latin text, *Historia Daretis Phrygii de Excidio Troiae*, 'Darius Phrygius's

[85] For a list of the MSS containing versions of the Welsh Chronicles, see Huws, *Medieval*, pp. 58–63. For a discussion of Gwengrvryn Evans's classification of versions of the Bruts in Rhŷs and Evans, *Text*, pp. xiii- xvi and that of J. J. Parry in 'Welsh Texts', pp. 424–31. See also B. F. Roberts, *Brut y Brenhinedd*, pp. xxv-xxxi.
[86] Huws, *Medieval*, p. 58.
[87] T. Jones, 'Historical', p. 16; B. F. Roberts, 'Historical', p. 246.
[88] *YBY*, p. 63. This edition of YBY has been transcribed from NLW, MS Peniarth 20, pp. 2–64, which has been dated by Daniel Huws (*Medieval*, p. 47) to c.1330, with the missing opening passages transcribed from BL MS Add. 31055, 111a-112a in the hand of Thomas Wiliems, Trefriw (August 1594). Thomas Jones, however, argued forcefully that this introduction once existed in Pen. 20 (*YBY*, pp. lxxxvii-lxxxviii.). YBY is an adaptation of Peter Pictaviensis's *Promptuarium Bibliae*, which in turn is a synopsis of Peter Comestor's *Historia Scholastica*, two theological texts dating to the twelfth century. The professed purpose of the work was to provide an abridged version of the most important events in sacred history for impoverished students, who could not afford to buy a quantity of history books or even the complete version of the Bible itself. This purpose is stated clearly in the introduction to one of the English versions contained in BL MS Add. 20010, but this introduction is missing from the Welsh version. Nevertheless, the *Historia Scholastica* would have been too big for individual ownership and would have been studied in monastic libraries.
[89] *YBY*, p. 63. *Ystorya [y] Brut* is a reference to Geoffrey of Monmouth's *Historia Regum Britanniae*.
[90] For a the diplomatic edition of the text in the Red Book, see Rhŷs and Evans, *Text*, pp.1–39; for diplomatic editions of all medieval recensions see also Owens, *Fersiynau*. An English translation of *Dares Phrygius* is to be found on line: http://www.theoi.com/Text/DaresPhrygius.html.

History of the Fall of Troy', which gives an account of the fall of Troy and which was used during the Middle Ages to prove the Trojan origin of many nations.[91]

> *Ylus vab Tros a vv vrenhin Troya, ac a edeilawd Ylium dinas, ac a'y henwis o'y henw ehun. Ac y hwnnw y bu vab Laomedon vab Ylus. Ac y hwnnw y bu vab Priaf, vrenhin Troya. Ac am hwnnw a'y etiued y traethir yn Ystorya Daret.*[92]

> [Ilus son of Tros was king of Troy, and built the city of Ilium, and named it after himself. And he had a son, Laomedon son of Ilus. And he had a son, Priam, king of Troy. And it is about him and his heir that an account is given in *The History of Dares*.]

Just as the concluding paragraphs of *Y Bibyl Ynghymraec* form a cyclical connection with *Brut y Brenhinedd,* so too the narrative of events following the death of Cadwaladr, with which the *Brut* ends, is continued in *Brut y Tywysogyon*, 'The Chronicle of the Princes'. This is a collective term, used to refer to the various recensions of a set of annals recording the history of Wales from the year 682 to the death of Llywelyn ap Gruffudd in 1282. Thus, these four texts, *Y Bibl Ynghymraec, Ystorya Daret, Brut y Brenhinedd* and *Brut y Tywysogyon*, encompass a history of the British people from the Creation to the end of the thirteenth century.[93]

Brut y Tywysogyon

Brut y Tywysogyon has been attributed to Caradoc of Llancarfan, no doubt as a result of the comment in the concluding paragraph of Geoffrey's *Historia*,[94] in which he transferred to Caradoc of Llancarfan the task of continuing the history of the kings of Britain, from the point where he had left off. The history of the Saxon kings, however, he entrusted to William of Malmesbury and Henry of Huntingdon, with a recommendation that the last two should say nothing about the kings of the Britons, since they did not have in their possession 'that book in the British language', discussed above. Although the Welsh version of the *Historia* in the Dingestow manuscript makes no reference to 'the ancient book', it too commissions Caradoc to undertake the task of continuing the history,[95] but there is no evidence to prove that Caradoc was the author of *Brut y Tywysogyon*. In fact Lloyd put forward a very convincing argument to show why Caradoc could not have written the Latin original or translated any of the versions of *Brut y Tywysogyon*.[96]

---

[91] For the fascination of medieval historiographers with Troy, see Federico, *New Troy.*
[92] *YBY*, p. 63.
[93] For the signifancance of this historical conspectus see Jones, 'Historical Writing', pp.16–21; J. Beverley Smith,, *The Sense of History in Medieval Wales* (Aberystwyth, 1989), pp. 7–8.
[94] This does not occur in the Cambridge University MS 1706 on which Griscom based his edtion of Geoffrey's *Historia* (p. 218) but he transferred the concluding paragraph from the Bern, Burgerbibliothek MS 568 (Griscom, *Historia*, p. 536), which was the manuscript used by Wright as the basis of his edition of the *Historia* and also included by Reeve in *GM*, pp. 280–81.
[95] *BrD*, p. 208.
[96] Lloyd, *Welsh Chronicles*, pp. 5–9.

The recensions of *Brut y Tywysogyon*[97] are translations of a lost Latin original compiled by an anonymous chronicler. It has been suggested that he could have been a Cistercian monk, probably working in the monastery of Strata Florida,[98] a place which is frequently mentioned in both the Red Book and Peniarth 20 versions of *Brut y Tywysogyon*. Not only is it the burial ground of many Welsh leaders and their families[99] but it is here too that the princes of Wales swore allegiance to Dafydd ap Llywelyn ap Iorwerth of Gwynedd in 1238.[100] Above all there is specific reference in *Brut y Tywysogyon* to *anales/annyales y vanachloc* 'the annals of the monastery' (i.e. Strata Florida), which record a remittance of half the debt owed by the monastery to king Henry III.[101]

Lloyd cited three possible sources for *Brut y Tywysogyon*:[102]
(i) the annals from the years 444 to 954 in BL MS Harley 3859, which he claims were composed in the scriptorium of St David's,
(ii) a set of annals in BL MS. Cotton Domitian A i, beginning with the Creation and continuing until the year 1288; this, too, Lloyd regarded as a St. David's document,
(iii) the annals preserved on the fly-leaves of the *Breviate of the Domesday Book*, now kept in the Public Record Office and copied *c*.1300.
The final entry, under the year 1286, refers to the burning of the buildings at the abbey of Strata Florida. This and the fact that the last fifty years form a chronicle of that abbey strongly suggest that it was compiled in Strata Florida.

Thomas Jones added another source, which had not come to light when Lloyd published *The Welsh Chronicles*, namely *The Cronica de Wallia*, a set of annals for the period 1190 –1266 with omissions for the years 1217–27, 1229, 1232, 1249–53 and 1263. This text is now kept at Exeter Cathedral Library but internal evidence suggests that it too originated in Strata Florida.[103] Thus two of the sources listed above are connected with St. David's, two with Strata Florida. Lloyd argued that the chronicle's changing focus of attention from the activities of one area to those of another indicated the source of the information. The early entries up to *c*.1100 point to documentary evidence lodged at St David's; events of 1100 — 1175 suggest a Llanbadarn source, while those from 1175 –1282 indicate that

---

[97] For a list of manuscripts containing BT, see Huws, *Medieval*, pp. 59, 60, 62.

[98] *BT (Pen. 20 trans.)*, p. xxxix.

[99] The following are reported to have died and/or been buried at Strata Florida: Cadell ap Gruffudd ap Rhys, Hywel ap Ieuaf, Einion ap Cynan, Owain ap Rhys, Hywel Sais (son of the Lord Rhys), Matilda de Breos, Rhys Ieuanc ap Gruffudd, Maelgwn ap Rhys, Owain ap Gruffudd ap Rhys, Maredudd ap Rhobert ap Llywarch, Morgan, son of the Lord Rhys, Maelgwn Ieuanc, together with his daughter Gwenllian and son Rhys, Maredudd ap Owain ap Gruffudd, Maredudd ap Gruffudd and Owain ap Maredudd ap Owain.

[100] *BT (Pen. 20 trans.)*, p. 104; *BT (Pen. 20)*, p. 197; *BT (RB)*, p. 234.

[101] *BT (Pen. 20)*, p. 203; *BT (Pen. 20 trans.)*, p. 108; *BT (RB)*, pp. 240, 241.

[102] Lloyd, *Welsh Chronicles*, pp. 14–15; see also *Celtic Culture*, vol. I, pp. 299–300.

[103] *BT (Pen. 20 trans.)*, p. xl. See also Thomas Jones, *Cronica de Wallia and Other Documents from Exeter Cathedral Library MS. 3514*. Reprinted with indexes, from *B* xii. (November, 1946), 27–44; J. Beverley Smith, 'Historical Writing in Medieval Wales: The Composition of *Brenhinedd y Saesson*, *Studia Celtica*, XLII (2008), 57–58.

the chronicler based his entries on records kept at Strata Florida. Nevertheless, Lloyd did not rule out the possibility that some of the annals could have been based on documents kept at other Cistercian houses, such as Llantarnam, Aberconwy, Basingwerk, Strata Marcella, Cwm Hir and Whitland.[104] Daniel Huws confirms that the Cistercian order encouraged the keeping of annals and was largely responsible for propagating the Welsh versions of these chronicles.[105] He maintains that the version of *Brut y Tywysogyon*, contained in NLW Peniarth 20 manuscript was from Valle Crucis and Peniarth 18 probably from Strata Florida.[106] Beverley Smith agrees that the provenance of the final entries of Peniarth 20 from 1291 to 1332 was Valle Crucis, but is of the opinion that the Latin text on which it was based was probably composed at Strata Florida.[107] Whoever the author or authors of these annals may have been, the style of *Brut y Tywysogyon* is very different from that of *Brut y Brenhinedd*, as is illustrated by the following extracts, which give an account of the death of Cadwaladr:[108]

Brut y Brenhinedd (Dingestow Version)   *Brut y Tywysogyon* (Peniarth 20 Version)

Ac ym pen yspeit wedy ymgadarnhau o'r ysgymunedic pobyl honno, coffau a wnaeth Catwaladyr ry peidyav y tymhestyl honno a'r uall a'e gyuoeth. Ac erchi porth a wnaeth y Alan urenhin Llydav y oresgyn y gyuoeth idav tracheuyn. A guedy adav porth idav o Alan, tra ytoed yn paratoi y llyghes y doeth llef o nef ar Catwaladyr y erchi idav peidyav a'e darpar, cany mynnei Duv guledychu o'r Brytanyeit ar enys Prydein hvy no hynny, eny delhei yr amser tyghetuenavl a daroganvs Myrdin rac bron Arthur. Ac erchi a wnaeth y llef y Catwaladyr mynet hyt yn Ruuein hyt ar Sergius pap, ac yno guedy darfei idav y penyt ef a riuit y rvng y rei guynuydedic.
. . . Ac yna yd ymedwis Catwaladyr Uendigeit ac yd ymvrthodes a phob peth bydavl yr caryat tragywydavl teyrnas Duv, ac yd aeth hyt yn Ruuein. Ac yna y cadarnhavs Sergius pap ef ym plith eiryf

Pedwar vgein mlyneδ a chwechant ac vn oyd oed krist pan vv varwolaeth vawr yny ynys brydein. Yn y vlwydyn honno y daeth Kadwaladyr vab Kadwallawn y brenhin dwaethaf a vv ar y Brytanyeid y Rufein ac yno y bu varw y deuδecved dyδ o galan Mei.

---

[104] Lloyd, *Welsh Chronicles*, pp. 19–20.
[105] Huws, *Medieval*, p. 12.
[106] Ibid., p. 76.
[107] J. Beverley Smith, 'Historical Writing', 82–83.
[108] *BrD*, pp. 206–07; *BT* (*Pen. 20*), p. 1.

y seint gleinnyon, ac yn y lle o deissyuyt
heint y cleuychvs, ac yn y deudecuet
dyd wedy Calan Mei yd aeth o'r byt
hvn ef y tragywydavl terynas wlat nef,
yn yr vythuet vlvydyn a phetwar ugeint
a seith gant guedy eni mab Duv o'r
arglvydes Ueir Wyry

(And a short time after that accursed people had gathered its strength once more, Cadwaladr remembered that the storm and pestilence had ceased in his own kingdom. And he asked Alan, king of Britanny, for assistance in recovering his kingdom. And after Alan had promised him his help, while he was preparing his fleet a voice from heaven begged Cadwaladr not to continue, because God did not wish the Britons to settle in the Isles of Britain until the arrival of the appointed time prophesied by Myrddin before Arthur. And the voice bade Cadwaladr to go to Rome and visit Pope Sergius, and there, after doing penance, he would be counted among the blessed. . . .

The blessed Cadwaladr then journeyed to Rome and renounced all wordly preoccupations for the everlasting love of the kingdom of heaven. And then, after Pope Sergius had confirmed him among the number of the holy saints, he was attacked by a sudden illness and on the twelfth day of the Kalends of May he departed from this life to the eternal kingdom of heaven in the seven hundred and eighty-eighth year after the son of God was born of the virgin Mary.)

(Six hundred and eighty-one was the year of Christ when there was a great mortality in the island of Britain. In that year Cadwaladr ap Cadwallon, the last king that ruled over the Britons went to Rome; and there he died on the twelfth day from the Calends of May.)

Brut y Brenhinedd is full of embellishments and euphemisms, whereas the account given in *Brut y Tywysogyon* is terse and unadorned. Nevertheless Geoffrey's theme of the lost sovereignty of Britain and Saxon supremacy was not lost on the author of *Brut y Tywysogyon*, as he also adds: *Ac o hynny allan y kolles y Brytanyeid goron teyrnas ac y kafas y Saesson hi, megis y proffwydassei Verδin wrth Wrtheyrn Wrtheneu*, 'From then on the Britons lost the crown of kingship and the Saxons obtained it, as Myrddin had prophesied to Gwrtheyrn Wrthenei'.[109] (This is a reference to Merlin's prophecy to Vortigern in *Historia Regum Britanniae*).

Editions of Brut y Tywysogyon

The three main versions of *Brut y Tywysogyon* have been edited, translated and annotated by Thomas Jones:[110]

(i) The text in the Red Book of Hergest (Oxford, MS Jesus 111), which records events in the form of annals from 682 to 1282, stops before the death of Llywelyn ap Gruffudd, the last native prince of Wales. This is defective in many places but closely resembles earlier manuscripts, namely NLW MSS Peniarth 18, Peniarth 19, Mostyn 116 and Llanstephan 172.

(ii) The text in MS Peniarth 20, which likewise covers the period 682 to 1282, including the death of Llywelyn ap Gruffudd, which is missing from the Red Book version. These annals are followed by an addendum which records events up to 1332. This continuation is an addition in a different hand from that of the main text, but like the early part, it too is a translation from the Latin.[111] The entries for the period 900–49 are missing, but Thomas Jones filled this lacuna in his edited version by transcribing the corresponding passage from the Red Book. The Peniarth MS 20 version is also represented by the texts of Mostyn MS 143, Mostyn MS 159 and Peniarth MS 213.

(iii) The text known as *Brenhinedd y Saesson*, 'The Kings of the Saxons', which is contained in BL MS Cotton Cleopatra B.v, ending with the year 1197 but continued down to 1461 in the Black Book of Basingwerk (NLW MS 7006).[112]

The extracts from *Brut y Tywysogyon* chosen for this anthology are taken from the text in Peniarth 20, which Daniel Huws dates to the fourteenth century, *c.* 1330.[113] The most noticeable difference between the text of Peniarth 20 and that of the Red Book occurs in the form of the eulogy to the Lord Rhys, after his death in 1197, which is more detailed in the former version, culminating in an encomium in Latin verse consisting of eighteen elegiac couplets, followed by

---

[109]   *BT (Pen. 20)*, p. 1; *BT (Pen. trans. 20)*, p. 1.
[110]   For details see Bibliography below.
[111]   *BT (Pen. 20 trans.)*, p. lxii.
[112]   *BS*, p. xv. For the composition of this work, see Beverley Smith, 'Historical Writing', pp. 55–86.
[113]   Huws, *Medieval*, p. 47.

another five elegiac couplets ending with a hexameter, which are said to have been composed after his burial and are an epitaph on his sepulchre.[114]

Auctorial comments such as *megys y dywedir yn y diareb Gymraec*, 'as is said in the Welsh proverb'[115] suggest that the Welsh chronicles are translations; had the original text been Welsh, such an explanation would have been unnecessary. The more concise *Brenhinedd y Saesson* on the other hand makes no mention of the proverb's source, an omission which supports Thomas Jones's theory that the compiler of *Brenhinedd y Saesson* did not use either of the two full versions of *Brut y Tywysogyon* down to the year 1197.[116] However the retention of inflected forms such as *Ambri* and *Hugone*[117] for the nominative *Amber* and *Hugo* respectively clearly indicates that *Brenhinedd y Saesson* too is a translation from Latin, but it is difficult to tell whether it is a direct translation of a Latin chronicle that combined a summary of the text from which the Red Book and Peniarth 20 versions are translated with sections from the *Annales de Wintonia*,[118] or whether it is a compilation made in Welsh from the Latin original underlying the Red Book and Peniarth 20 versions and the Winchester Annals.[119] Nevertheless, in spite of the close correspondence between the Red Book and Peniarth 20 versions of *Brut y Tywysogyon*, the difference in phraseology and sometimes content suggests that they are independent translations of different Latin originals, or at least of variant copies of a Latin original.

Less flamboyant than *Brut y Brenhinedd*, *Brut y Tywysogyon* has been described as sober and pedestrian, 'occasionally waxing eloquent but as a rule content to record the simple facts'.[120] Nevertheless Lloyd considered these annals to be 'the greatest monument of Welsh historiography in the Middle Ages'.[121] Major and minor events are recorded, the early ones very briefly, the later annals more fully. The first detailed account is the vanquishing of the usurper Rhain in 1022. The account of the Norman Conquest in 1066 implies much in its brevity. It is reported that William the Bastard, leader of the Normans, deposed Harold and won for himself the kingdom of the Saxons with victorious hand.[122] The annalist does not comment on the significance of this event or analyse the implication for the Welsh territories, which suggests that the change of dynasty in the 'kingdom of the Saxons' posed no greater threat to the Welsh princes than

---

[114]   *BT (Pen. 20 trans.)*, p. 78. In BS (pp. 192, 193) his death is recorded briefly: *Ac y bu varw Rys ap Grufud, tywyssauc deheubarth Kymre, blodeu y marchogyon, a'r gorev o'r a uu o genedyl Gymre eroet, .iiij. Kalendas Maij gwedy llawer o uudugolaythev.* (And Rhys ap Gruffudd, prince of south Wales, flower of knights and the best ever of the Welsh nation, died on the fourth day from the Calends of May after many victories.)

[115]   *BT (Pen. 20)*, pp. 15, 73; *BT (Pen. 20 trans.)*, pp. 12, 44.

[116]   *BT (Pen. 20 trans.)*, p. xxxvii.

[117]   *BS*, pp. 3, 88.

[118]   A chronicle attributed to Richard of Devizes (fl. late 12th century, a monk of St Swithin's house, Winchester.

[119]   *BT (Pen. 20 trans.)*, p. xxxvii.

[120]   Lloyd, *Welsh Chronicles*, p. 4.

[121]   Ibid., p. 21.

[122]   *BT (Pen. 20.)*, p. 20; *BT (Pen. 20 trans.)*, p. 15.

before. The implication of this bald statement is that the Norman conquest was a Saxon rather than a Welsh problem.

Occasionally an event is presented as a narrative, complete with dramatic tension and direct speech, the best known example being the violation and abduction of Nest by Owain ap Cadwgan.[123] An interesting feature of this episode is the different interpretation of Owain's actions in the account given in Peniarth 20 and that of the Red Book. In the former Owain is said to be acting at the instigation of the devil,[124] while in the latter he is inflamed with passion at the instigation of God.[125] Thomas Jones believed that the compiler of the Red Book seemed to have been averse to naming the Devil, but he had no such inhibitions in the entry for 1255, when he named the Devil as the instigator of the strife between Owain Goch and Dafydd, the sons of Gruffudd ap Llywelyn.[126] Since the Latin words for God (*deus*) and the Devil (*diabolus*) share the same initial letter, this anomaly is far more likely to reflect a faulty translation than a euphemism to avoid incurring the wrath of the Devil, particularly if the translator was working from a damaged parchment.

Accounts of historical events are sometimes punctuated by reports of natural disasters and supernatural phenomena. These are often coupled with the record of a traumatic event, implying the far-reaching significance of that event and the way in which it upset the natural order of the universe. For example, the author attributed the calamities of 1173, when many men and animals were lost, to the illicit union of the Lord Rhys (1132 –1197), ruler of the kingdom of Deheubarth in south Wales, with his niece, resulting in the birth of a son. Again twenty three years later in 1196 there was *diruawr tymhestyl o varwolaeth*, 'a mighty pestilence of mortality' throughout the whole island of Britain, which claimed among its victims the Lord Rhys; this tragedy, however, the author interpreted, not as an act of God, but as the result of the venomous powers of Fate.[127] This seems a curious assertion, as *Brut y Tywysogyon* is generally pervaded by a Christian view of history, but as the whole of this passage is so influenced by classical writing, it is understandable that the author should continue in that style, without considering the inconsistency of the statement in the wider context of the work as a whole.

The panegyric delivered on the death of certain princes or clerics is an important feature of *Brut y Tywysogyon*. These obituaries are not intended to be an accurate record of the deceased's life but follow the convention of the eulogies sung by the poets, who praise the abstract virtues of the ideal leader.[128] The

---

[123] For a biography of Nest, see Maund, *Princess Nest.*
[124] *BT (Pen. 20)*, p. 41; *BT (Pen. 20 trans.)*, p. 28.
[125] *BT (RB)*, pp. 54–55. See also *n.* 44.9 below.
[126] *BT (RB)*, pp. 246–47.
[127] *BT (Pen. 20)*, p. 139; *BT (Pen. 20 trans.)*, p. 77, see 75.2*n.*
[128] For a general overview of early Welsh poetry see Jarman and Hughes, *Guide*, pp. 11–188; Parry, *History*, pp. 1–8, 43–54ß; *Celtic Culture* (ed. Koch) s.v. *Cynfeirdd*, 536, *Cywyddwyr*, 543–48, *Gogynfeirdd*, 826–29.

qualities praised are nobility of lineage, comeliness of appearance, gentleness of manner, courage and ferocity on the battlefield, the giving of alms and penance at the hour of death. In view of this, it is astonishing that the obituary to Llywelyn the Great is so brief, considering his importance in the development of the nation in general and of Gwynedd in particular, while that of his grandson, Llywelyn the Last, is non-existent. The Red Book version of the chronicle ends early in 1282 while Llywelyn was still flourishing and harassing the south, but although Peniarth 20 continues beyond that date, his death is not described as an episode of any exceptional significance. The author of *Brenhinedd y Saesson* exercises his usual restraint in recording Llywelyn's death, but he does add, *Ac yna y bwriwyd holl Gymry y'r llawr*, 'And then all Wales was cast to the ground',[129] suggesting that he acknowledged the event as the undoubted calamity it was. There are more elaborate entries in both the fifteenth century Aberconwy Chronicle and the Annals of Worcester,[130] to the effect that the Welsh were terrified after the death of Llywelyn and gave Edward I, King of England, among other things, the crown of the famous Arthur, once king of Britain. The Aberconwy Chronicle also adds the comment, *et sic gloria Walliae et etiam Wallencium regibus et magnatibus Angliae translata est*, 'and so the glory of Wales and the Welsh was handed over to the kings and magnates of England'. Generally speaking this chronicle is pro-English in its orientation and one can only assume that it is the long-lasting influence of Geoffrey's *Historia* that caused the compiler to refer to the lost sovereignty of Britain.

In his inaugural lecture, 'The Sense of History in Medieval Wales', J. Beverley Smith draws attention to documents[131] which record the exchanges between Llywelyn ap Gruffudd and Archbishop Peckham in a diplomatic attempt to solve the hostilities between the Welsh prince and King Edward I in 1282. In these exchanges Llywelyn tries to validate his right to govern Wales by claiming descent from the legendary Camber, who, according to Geoffrey, inherited the territory known as Wales. Smith points out that in Geoffreys's tripartite allocation of Britain to the sons of Brutus, there is 'an implicit admission of the superiority of Locrinus', the eldest son, who inherits Lloegr, 'England', over Camber and Albanactus, who inherit Wales and Scotland respectively. Furthermore he maintains that Llywelyn ap Gruffudd would have been happy to allow Edward I to be heir to Locrinus as long as he, Llywelyn, was acknowledged as heir to Camber.[132] Smith also writes that Llywelyn's declarations 'provide one of the clearest expressions which we now possess of the blending of a sense of history with political necessity in medieval Wales.'[133]

---

[129] *BS*, pp. 258–59.
[130] Ellis, *Register*, p. 12; Luard, *Annales*, p. 486, quoted in Stephenson, *Aberconwy*. fn. 63. Also published on http:// www. hughes.cam.ac.uk/about/events/kathleen 2001.
[131] Martin, *Registrum*.
[132] Smith, *Sense of History*, p. 15.
[133] Ibid., p. 1.

Historia Gruffud vab Kenan

Brut y Tywysogyon is far more extravagant in its praise of Gruffudd ap Cynan than it is of Llywelyn ap Gruffudd, the last native prince of Wales. The chronicle refers to Gruffudd ap Cynan as *tywyssawc Gwyned a phenn a brenhin ac amdiffynnwr a thangnefedwr Kymru oll,* 'prince of Gwynedd and head and king and defender and pacifier of all Wales'.[134] However the report of his death in his eponymous biography *Historia Gruffud vab Kenan*[135] is much more personal. Gruffudd dies surrounded by his family, the greatest and wisest men of his kingdom, as well as distinguished clerics. He blesses his sons, just as the patriarch Jacob had blessed his sons, and is lamented by Welshmen, Irishmen and men of Denmark, just as Joshua son of Nun was lamented by the Jews. These, however, are not the only references to biblical events in *Historia Gruffud vab Kenan*: for example, Gruffudd's ancestry is traced back to Adam, son of God;[136] he is compared to the biblical King David,[137] while his liberation of Gwynedd from the hands of usurpers is compared to Judas Maccabaeus's delivery of Israel from the bondage of pagan kings.[138] The author also hopes that Gruffudd will be sustained by Christ, not by the pagan deities Diana or Apollo.[139] Indeed throughout the work his achievements are attributed to divine providence. The references to specific members of the clergy and the comparisons drawn from the Scriptures suggested to Simon Evans that the author was a Welsh cleric who was close to the centre of power in Gwynedd at that time. More specifically Evans named, as a candidate for authorship, David, who was archdeacon in Bangor in the 1160s and possibly a son of Simeon of Clynnog, also archdeacon and present at Gruffudd's deathbed.[140] Evans even suggested that Simeon himself may have been involved in the composition of the *Historia*,[141] but there is no concrete evidence to prove conclusively that either David or Simeon was the author or the translator. The omission of references to events which could have portrayed Gruffudd as champion of the church in Gwynedd has caused Nerys Ann Jones to cast doubts upon Evans's theory not only on the authorship of the *Historia* but also on the dating of it.[142]

That the *Historia* is a translation from a lost Latin original is beyond dispute,[143] but the edition of a later Latin version of it contained in NLW MS Peniarth 434 (dated 1575 to 85)[144] has shed new light on the transmission of the text. In the introduction to his edition of the Latin Life of Gruffudd ap Cynan,

[134] *BT (Pen 20)*, p. 88; *BT (Pen 20 trans.)*, p. 52.
[135] *HGrK*, p. 32–33; *MPW*, p. 83; *VGC*, 88 §§ 34, 35.
[136] *HGrK*, p. 2, 5; *MPW*, p. 54, 57; *VGC*, 54 § 3, 58 § 7.
[137] *HGrK*, pp. 8, 19, 20, 23; *MPW*, pp. 60, 71, 72, 75; *VGC* pp. 62, 74, 78 §§ 12, 22, 23, 25.
[138] *HGrK*, p. 28, *MPW*, p. 80; *VCG* 84 § 31.
[139] *HGrK*, p. 6, *MPW*, p. 58, *VCG* 58 § 8.
[140] *HGrK*, pp. ccxxviii- ccxxx, *MPW*, pp. 17–18.
[141] *HGrK*, p. ccxlix.
[142] *HGVK*, p. 152.
[143] *HGrK*, p. ccxxvii, *MPW*, p. 20.
[144] *VGC*, p. 4.

Vita Griffini Filii Conani, Paul Russell presents a convincing case for believing that this version represents a copy of the original medieval Latin life, which was the ultimate source of the thirteenth-century Middle Welsh version. He tentatively dates the VGC to 1137–48 and suggests St David's as the most likely place of composition.[145] In addition to a general closeness to the Latin original with regard to contents and structure, particularly in the concord of subject and verb (although this construction also occurs in early native texts), evidence of translation can be seen from the following stylistic features:

(i) the Latin title *Historia* is retained rather than translated to *hanes* or *buchedd*, although Russell believes that this is 'suggestive rather than central to the argument',[146]

(ii) a Latin quotation is included in Myrddin's prophecy,[147]

(iii) auctorial intrusions such as added explanations of place names are to be seen; for example. in referring to a battle in a narrow valley, the translator adds *y lle a elwir yg Kymraec Gvaet Erw neu y Tir Gwaetlyd*, 'the place which is called in Welsh the Bloody Acre or the Bloody Land'.[148] A Welsh original would have obviated the necessity for this explanation,

(iv) the translator fails to change the ablative form of the proper noun *Remo* to the expected nominative *Remus*.[149]

Nevertheless, the translator did not always slavishly follow the Latin; for example, he translated the historic present *conspicit*[150] by the preterite (simple past) *weles*,[151] which is no surprise, considering the relative scarcity of the historic present as a stylistic device in Middle Welsh prose.[152] Evans asserted that few changes were made to the text during the process of translation,[153] but the Latin text from NLW MS Peniarth 434 has revealed errors in the early transmission of the Welsh text.[154]

Historia Gruffud vab Kenan has the distinction of being the only extant biography of a lay person in the Middle Ages written in Welsh, although saints' lives abound. It opens with a report of Gruffudd's birth in Dublin to a Welsh father and Irish-Scandinavian mother, from whom he first heard of his lost patrimony in Wales. Then follows a detailed description of his pedigree, showing his distinguished lineage. An account of his efforts to recover Gwynedd, which he regarded as his rightful heritage, takes up the bulk of the *Historia*. His first

---

[145]   *VGC*, pp. 43–47.
[146]   *VGC*, p. 17.
[147]   *HGrK*, p. 5, *MPW*, p. 58.
[148]   *HGrK*, p. 9, *MPW*, p. 61.
[149]   *HGrK*, p. 4, *MPW*, p. 56.
[150]   *VGC*, p. 72 § 22.
[151]   *HGrK*, p. 18, *MPW* p. 71.
[152]   Poppe, Review, p. 262.
[153]   *HGrK*, p. ccxxvii.
[154]   *VGC*, pp. 42–43.

encounter is against the usurper Trahaearn,[155] whom he defeats in the battle of Gwaed Erw with the help of men from Gwynedd and the Norman baron, Robert of Rhuddlan. Shortly afterwards Gruffudd attacks Rhuddlan castle, in spite of the assistance previously given to him by its occupant, but because of rivalry between some of his Welsh and Irish supporters, Gruffudd is defeated in the battle of Bron-yr-Erw and forced to return to Ireland. Undeterred by this setback he returns to claim his kingdom once more, but again because of the treachery of his followers he suffers a further defeat and returns to Ireland. The Norman barons take advantage of the unrest in Gwynedd and launch a successful attack against that land: *A honno vu y bla gentaf a dyvodyat agarw y Nordmannyeit yn gentaf y daear Wyned, wedy eu dyvodyat y Loegyr*, 'and that was the first plague and fierce arrival of the Normans first to the land of Gwynedd after their arrival in England.'[156] After a further period of exile in Ireland, Gruffudd returns with a fleet of Scandinavians, Irish and Welsh from Porthlarc (Port Láirge, Waterford) and lands in Porth Clais near the bishopric of Menevia (St David's). Here he forms an alliance with Rhys ap Tewdwr, King of Deheubarth, and together they are victorious in the famous battle of Mynydd Carn. But again success is shortlived and Gruffudd is betrayed by one of his own men, a certain Meirion Goch, to two Norman barons, Hugh of Rhuddlan and Hugh of Shrewsbury, who imprison him in Chester for twelve years. There is some confusion about the length of his incarceration, as it is reported in a later section that he was rescued after spending sixteen years in prison.[157] The rest of the *Historia* recounts Gruffudd's numerous attempts to regain control of Gwynedd, which after many setbacks he eventually succeeds in doing. By turning to diplomacy as a means to the end, he makes peace with Henry I, King of England, who grants him the territories of Llŷn, Eifionydd and Arllechwedd. From then on Gruffudd prospers and governs successfully, forging a friendly relationship with Henry, King of England, Murchadh, King of Ireland and the kings of the islands of Denmark.[158] In his old age he retires from earthly power to lead a godly life and donates much of his wealth to churches in Wales and Ireland and even to the monasteries of Chester and Shrewsbury. The *Historia* ends with a very personal account of Gruffudd's deathbed scene, where he is attended by his family and priests. It is unlikely, however, that the unknown author of HGK was personally acquainted with Gruffudd or his wife, Angharad, as he cites as his source of information about their personal appearance, Gruffudd's *kedemeithon gvahanredaul* 'special friends' and *doethyon y kyuoeth* 'the wise men of the kingdom'. Consequently the

---

[155] K. L. Maund argues that there is no independent evidence to corroborate this; see Maund, *Ireland*, p. 83.

[156] *HGrK*, p. 13, *MPW*, p. 65.

[157] Lloyd (*History*, ii, pp. 390, n. 109, 403–04) thought that Gruffudd had escaped by 1094 and that his re-appearance gave renewed impetus to the men of Môn and Arfon in their struggle against the Normans. This, however, is disputed by Maund, who believes that Gruffudd's involvement in the 1094 rebellion was less than that suggested in the *Historia*. She also argues that he did not escape from captivity until the mid- to late-1090's, (Maund, *Ireland*, p. 84).

[158] *HGrK*, p. 30, *MPW*, p. 81.

portrayals are stereotypical rather than graphic descriptions based on personal observation.

Simon Evans argued convincingly that the purpose of the *Historia* was to elevate the status of the kings of Gwynedd and consolidate the rights of those who held power over the kingdom. Consequently it presents an idealised portrait of its subject, more akin to hagiography than to modern biography;[159] with only the sections which are corroborated by other sources to be regarded as authentic. Evans rejected Arthur Jones's contention that the *Historia* was 'written to amuse as well as instruct',[160] but saw the work as a piece of political propaganda that would publicise the supremacy of Gwynedd not only to its rivals but also to an audience outside the confines of Wales.[161] Russell, however, believes that the Welsh version of the *Historia* is more focused on Gwynedd than is the Latin version,[162] and Nerys Ann Jones likewise maintains that the Welsh translation of the *Historia* was probably intended for a Vendotian audience.[163] Thomas Charles-Edwards has suggested that the *Historia* was written to try to legitimise Gruffudd's claims to the kingship of Gwynedd, as his position was untenable according to the laws of inheritance.[164] He writes, 'The Life of Gruffudd ap Cynan is far from unique in applying the ordinary law of inheritance to royal succession, but it agrees rather with the poetry, frequently propagandist in nature, than with the law.'[165]

By considering the general ambience of the text and by matching internal references to the political events of the period, Evans suggested three possible dates for the composition of this work:

(i) the period immediately following Gruffudd's death in 1137,

(ii) the year 1157 when his son Owain Gwynedd was forced to pay homage to Henry II,

(iii) sometime between the death of his wife Angharad in 1162 and the death of his son in 1170.

He failed, however, to adjudicate decisively in favour of any one of these dates.[166]

Lloyd too dated the *Historia* to the twelfth century and suggested that it was composed with the consent of his son Owain Gwynedd. He also regarded the text as a reasonably reliable source for events of the period in which it was set, in spite of some inaccuracies and exaggerations.[167] Maund, however, takes a

---

[159]   *HGrK*, pp. ccxli- ccxliii.
[160]   *HGrK*, p ccxliii; see also Arthur Jones, A. *The History of Gruffydd ap Cynan* (Manchester, 1910), p. 28.
[161]   *HGrK*, p. ccxliii; *MPW*, p. 18.
[162]   *VGC*, p. 44.
[163]   Maund, 'Gruffudd', p. 156.
[164]   Charles-Edwards, *Early Irish*, pp. 220–24. See also Maund, 'Gruffudd', pp. 109–16. See also Maund, *Ireland*, p. 83.
[165]   Maund, *Ireland*, p. 295. See also Williams, 'Meilyr', pp. 165–86.
[166]   *HGrK*, pp. ccxliii-ccxlix.
[167]   Lloyd, *History*, ii, p. 379.

different view. She argues for a later date, on the grounds that if the purpose
of the biography was to establish Gruffudd's claim to be the legitimate ruler
of Gwynedd, one would have expected it to have focused more on his later
achievements, which would have been within living memory, rather than on
his early life. She even goes so far as to speculate that it could belong to the
reign of Llywelyn ap Iorwerth (1200–1240), who like his great-grandfather,
Gruffudd ap Cynan, had to overcome many obstacles to establish himself as
a legitimate ruler.[168] As further evidence to support her suggestion of a later
date for the *Historia* than that which had been previously assumed, she uses
the reference to *Guilim Gledyf Hir*,[169] (William Longsword) whom she argues is
William Longéspee, earl of Salisbury and illegitimate son of Henry II, warden
of the Welsh March from 1208 and commander in King John's Welsh and Irish
expeditions of 1210–12,[170] rather than William Rufus, son of the Conqueror and
king of England 1087–1100, as suggested by Evans.[171]

The text of *Historia Gruffud vab Kenan* used in this anthology has been
transcribed from NLW MS Peniarth 17, pp. 1–16, which has been dated by
Daniel Huws to the second half of the 13th century.[172] The missing section at
the end has been transcribed from NLW Peniarth 267, pp. 373–86, which is a
product of the 17th century and was copied by John Jones (copyist and collector
of manuscripts from the mansion of Gellilyfdy in the ancient parish of Ysgeifiog
in what is now Flintshire, north east Wales) during the time of his imprisonment
in London (1635–41).[173] He wrote at the start of the *Historia* that he had copied
it from a book in the possession of Sir Risiart Gwynn of Gwydyr, which had
been borrowed by his great grandfather from his (John Jones's) grandfather, Sion
ap William ap Sion. The *Historia* has also been preserved in a number of later
manuscripts listed by Evans in his edition of the work, all of which are deemed
to have been copied from a different original than that used by the copyist of
Peniarth 17.[174]

Orthography

As one would expect in a selection of texts from different manuscripts the
orthography of the texts in this collection varies considerably. The same
graphemes and digraphs as those found in the ModW alphabet are used,[175]
with the addition of <k>, <j> and <v>. The graphemes <k> and <j> are listed

---

[168]   Maund, *Ireland*, pp. 173–74.
[169]   *HGrK*, p. 4.
[170]   Maund, *Ireland*, pp. 174–75.
[171]   *HGrK*, p. 53.
[172]   Huws, *Medieval*, pp. 58, 75.
[173]   Ibid., p. 153.
[174]   A full survey of the manuscripts containing the *Historia* is given in *HGrK*, pp. ccli–cclxxxiv, and
        a detailed discussion of the Latin manuscripts which form the basis of *The Medieval Latin Life of
        Gruffudd ap Cynan* is to be found in Paul Russell's edition of that work, *VGC*, pp. 3–15.
[175]   The Modern Welsh alphabet is given at the beginning of the Glossary.

in the glossary under <c> and <i> respectively; <v> is more complicated as it represents the phonemes /v/, /ɨ/ and /u/. Those graphemes which have a different phonetic value from that of standard ModW are discussed below. In the case of graphemes with a very high frequency of occurrence only a small sample is listed. The discussion is confined to lexemes which occur in the present selection of texts taken from *Brut Dingestow* [*BD*] (Dingestow Court Manuscript), *Brut y Tywysogyon* [*BT*] (MS Peniarth 20) and *Historia Gruffud vab Kenan* [*HGK*] (MSS Peniarth 17 and 267); the excerpt from *Brenhinedd y Saesson* is too small to be significant. A study of the orthography of the complete manuscripts is outside the ambit of this work. The location of the examples in the text can be found by consulting the glossary.

Consonants[176]

<b> <p>

The graphemes <b> and <p> generally have the same value initially as in modern English standard orthography, but sometimes <p> represents the phoneme /b/ both medially and finally: *cyffelypit, yspryt,* (*BD*) *dosparth, drycysprydawl, pap* (*BT*) *archescopty, atep, doethinap* (*HGrK*).

<c> <k> < g>

<c> and <k> share the same phonetic value, namely /k/; <c> is usually employed before <a> and <o> , whereas <k> is employed before <e> < i> <y> <u> <w>, but there are examples of <k> as well as <c> before <a>, (e.g. *kadarnhau* and *cadarnhau*). <g> usually has the phonetic value /g/; however <c> and <k> occur for /g/ medially in the following examples: (*arch*)*escob, datcanu, escor, racrymhaa* (< *rac* + *grymhaa*), *yscol* (*BD*), *datkanadwy, tervyscu, yskrin* (*BT*) and *archescopty, escop, racdav, yscrin* (*HGK*). The only examples of intervocalic <c> and <k> = /g/ are *drycysprydawl* and *gwasgaredicyon*; all the other examples of medial <c> and <k> occur after <s> or a plosive. The graphemes <c> and <k> = /g/ occur finally in the following examples: *amlwc, carrec, dreic, dysc, ehedec, Pasc, rac, rvysc, teyrnwisc* (*BD*) *cic, dec, drwc, duc, gwarthec,* (*BT*) *bonhedic, gureic, goruc, gwydelec* (*HGK*); <c> also occurs regularly for <g> in the endings –*awc* and –*ic* in all three texts, the only exception being *kyssygredig* (in the section of *HGK* from Peniarth 267). There is one example of <g> representing <c>, namely *ieuang* (*BT*). In addition, <g> sometimes represents /ŋ/ in medial and final position, as in *agheu, agheuavl, aghyvrwys, kyghoret, kyghorwyr, egylyon, llogheu, llyg(h)es, tagnheuedus, ethrykyg, yg* (*BD*), *kyghorwr, kyghoruynna, gyllwg, rwg* (*BT*).

<ch>

<ch> usually has the phonetic value /χ/ in all texts, but in *BD* there are two examples of <hc> representing /χ/, namely *cohc* and *merhc*. There is also one

---

[176]   See *GMW* §§9–17.

possible example of <h> representing <ch>, namely *goruleheu* for *gorflychau*, but it may be a scribal error. In Peniarth 267, which contains the final sections of *Historia Gruffudd vab Kenan* /χ/ is represented by <c> underdotted. This has been transcribed in the present work as <ch>, following Simon Evans's practice in his edition.

<d> <ḍ> <δ> <t> <th>

The grapheme <d> can represent:

(i) /d/ initially, medially and finally in all three manuscripts, e.g. *da, damunav, damwein, adeilat, bryd, clod, diwyrnavd, goruod, pryd* (BD), *dala, dangos, darystwng, brodyr, amod, bod, byd, deuδecved, gweled, gwlad, myned* (BT), *damunet, danhed, dechrynv, kedymdeitheon, dywedynt, guahanredaul, huaudel* (HGK) .

(ii) /δ/ initially, as lenited form of /d/, as well as medially and finally in all three manuscripts, e.g. *lladassant, bluyd, lladawd, boned* (BD and BT respectively); *bedin, dydyeu* (HGK).

In the Peniarth 20 manuscript, however, the symbol <q3> is employed in addition to <d> to denote the phoneme /δ/ in medial and final position. In the first part of the manuscript (ff. 65r to 89r) <q3> is used exclusively for /δ/, but from f. 89r <d> is also employed to represent /δ/. In those sections where <q3> represents /δ/, the grapheme <d> is employed regularly for the phoneme /d/, but where <d> is used for /δ/ the grapheme <t> is usually employed for /d/, although examples of <d> occur also.[177] In his diplomatic edition Thomas Jones has substituted <q3> with the symbol /δ/, e.g. *blwyδyn, blyneδ, deuδecved, dynesawδ, yδ*, a practice followed in the present edition. In Peniarth 267 /δ/ is represented by <ḍ>; it occurs initially in lenited forms, e.g. *y diwed dydieu*; medially as in *adfet, digwydedigaeth, eidaw, idi, udunt, rodes* and finally as in *brenhined, kyffelyprwyd, diwed, dyd, herwyd, oed, yd*. In Simon Evans's edition of *Historia Gruffudd vab Kenan* underdotted <d> has been transcribed as Modern Welsh <dd>, but as <d> in the present edition, to be consistent with the practice employed in the other passages included in this collection.

The grapheme <t> in final position usually represents the phoneme /d/, e.g. *calet* (BD), *cannyat* (BT), *kerdet* (HGK). There are also a few examples of <t> = /δ/: *dothoet , etyuet, hanoet, lladavt, medhavt* (BD) and *breit* (HGK).

In MS Pen. 267 <t> is employed to represent /θ/, e.g. *doetaf, kywoet, portloed, plit, drygerfertasant, part*. In Evans's edition of HGK this grapheme is transcribed as <th>, a practice employed in the present anthology.

Both <t> and <th> occur medially in *gantav, ganthaw, genthi, gantunt, gantwynt, ganthunt*. In a discussion of Middle Welsh dialects from a phonetic perspective, Peter Wynn Thomas[178] explains the difference between <t> and <th> as a dialectal variation. The interesting point about the <t>/<th> variation here, however, is that it occurs within the same text, which could be explained

---

[177] *BT (Pen. 20)*, pp. xvii-xviii.
[178] Thomas, 'Middle Welsh', pp. 18–21; *id.,*, 'Cysylltiadau', pp. 62–65.

as an example of interference by an amanuensis who spoke a different dialect from that of the translator, whose work he was copying. Note the variation in the personalised forms of *gan* in the various manuscripts:

BD	BT	HGK
gantav	*ganthaw*	*ganthav*
ganthav	*genthi*	
gantunt	*ganthunt*	
ganthunt	*gantwynt*	

Paul Russell in his discussion of graphic variants,[179] however, argues that 'in general medieval Welsh scribes notoriously found the Welsh fricative /θ/ difficult to spell, writing *t*, *th*, *ht*, and *tt*, and even *s* or *sh*; it was one of the last spellings to settle down into its recognisable modern shape of *th*.'

<f> <ff> <ph>

In initial position the voiceless fricative /f/ is represented by both <f> and <ff> in all MSS; however <f> has a higher frequency in *BD* and *HGK*: *ford, fydlavn, fryd(y)eu*. Medially <ff> is always represented by <ff> in all three texts: k*affael*, *kyffroi, kyffes*, but in *BD* there is an example of <f> = /f/: *darfei*. <f> also represents the voiced fricative /v/ both medially and finally: *cyfnessaf, nachaf* (*BD*) *digyfoethi, kefynderw* (*BT*) *afruyd, bonhedicaf* (*HGK*). In the selections of this anthology there is only one example of initial <ph> which is not a mutation of /p/: *phioleu* (*BD*).

<l> <ll>

The graphemes <l> <ll> usually represent /l/ and /λ/ respectively; however there are examples of <ll> = /l/: *callon* (*BD*), *amrauaellyon, hwyllyeu* (*HGK*) and <l> = /λ/: *ar glan y lynn*, (*BD*). In Peniarth 267 <l> is employed to represent the phoneme /λ/, e.g. *al̦aur, hol̦*, but transcribed as <ll> in the current edition, following the practice of Simon Evans in his edition of *Historia Gruffudd vab Kenan*.

<r>

<r> represents both <r> and <rh>, e.g. **rac, ran(n), rodi.** In the sections of *Historia Gruffudd vab Kenan* from Peniarth 267 <r> is underdotted in the manuscript, but transcribed in Simon Evan's edition as <rh>. In this edition, however, it is transcribed as <r>, which is consistent with the practice employed in the other selections included in this collection.

---

[179] Russell, 'Medieval Scribes', p. 81.

Vowels and Semi-vowels[180]

<a>

This grapheme nearly always has the value /a/; however occasionally <a> interchanges with <y>: *achuanec, achuanegu, adoed, damunav, damunedic* (*BD*), *manachloc* (*BT*), *damunet, manegi* (*HGK*). The reverse occurs in *ynyalwch* for *anialwch* (*BT*).

<e>

Usually <e> = /e/ or /ɛ/, but it frequently represents:
(i) <y> with phonic value (a) /i/: *reeni* (*HGK*), *e* pref. pron., and *'e* inf. pron. (*BD* and *HGK*), *ehun / ehvn, ehunein*, (*BD, HGK* and *BT*), (b) /ɨ/ as in *ket* (*BD*) and *kedymdeithas* (*BD* and *HGK*), *henne* (*HGK* and *BT*), but more especially (c) /ə/ which has the highest frquency of occurrence in *HGK*: *bedin, kemryt, kentaf, e* /*er* (def. art., pre-verbal part.), *em-, ema, en, end-, enteu, eny, henne, menych, menyd* etc. It also occurs in *BD*: *eman, enys, menegi* etc. and *BT*: *kefnitherw, direbud, en, eno, odena.*

The reverse <y> for <e> occurs in *ynnill* for *ennill* (*HGK*) and *yr* for *er* (*BD*). There may have been early confusion between the sounds of <e> and <y>, but from the middle of the thirteenth century <y> becomes more common.[181]
(ii) <i> / <y> with phonic value (a) /i/ as in *ell* (*BD*), *'e* infix. pron. and prep. (*BD* and *HGK*), (b) /j/ *kedymdeitheon* (*HGK*).
There is also a very small number of examples of <e> representing what may be variant forms, rather than graphic representations of the same sound:
(i) <a> as in *edeilat, egylyon, ethrylith, llewenyd* (*BD*), *ebostol* (*BT*).
(ii) <o> as in *efferen* (*BD*), *effeirieit* (*BT*), *effeiryeid* (*HGK*).

<i> <y>

<i> and <y> commomly represent /i/ and /j/ in all three texts, but <y> has the highest frequency of occurrence in *BD*.
(i) /i/ *caredyc, kymeredyc, dyal, dyllat, dynas, dyruawr, dywet, hy, hythev, nyth, oblegyt, onys, ryth* (*BD*), *ryeni, megys* (*HGK*) *ydaw, gwedy, llyaws, perys* (*BT*).
(ii) /j/ *yarll, yavn, caryat, medyamt, molyant, taryan* (*BD*); *esgeiryeu, vnyaun, caryatwraged*, (*HGK*); *keinnyawc, keissyawd, gogonyant, medylyaw* (*BT*). *an(n)-yan, anyanavl, aryant* occur in both *BD* and *BT*.
<i> sometimes has the phonic value
(i) <I>, e.g. *ewyllis*, (*BD*), *goresgin*,[182] *llwith*, (*BT*) *kyffelip* (*HGK*).
(ii) /ə/ *miui* (*BD*), *gorchyvigwyr, tywis(s)auc* (*BT*), *mivi* (*HGK*).
<y> represents ModW <e> in *mywn* in *BD, HGK* and *BT*.

---

[180]   See *GMW* 1–8.
[181]   *GMW* § 1.
[182]   Nevertheless *goresgyn* occurs more frequently.

<u> <v> <w>

The graphemes <u> and <v> can represent the phonemes /v/ /ɨ/[183] and /u/ in all three texts, while <w> represents /u/, mainly in *BT*, and very rarely /v/. There are no examples of <w> = /ɨ/.

<u> represents the following phonemes:

(i) /v/ mainly in medial position in all three texts e.g. *diruavr* /*diruaur*/ *diruawr*; occasionally in initial position, e.g. ***ual*** (*BD* and *HGK* only) and never in final position, where it **/v/** is represented by <f>.

(ii) /ɨ/ medially and finally in all three texts, e.g. *anrydedus*, *cladu*, *kyrchu*, *aelodeu*; initially it occurs in *BD* and *HGK* only, e.g. ***un***, ***urdas*** (*BD*), ***uchof***, (sic) ***ugeint*** (*HGK*). There are no examples in *BT.*

(iii) /u/ (vocalic and semi-vocalic) initially in *BD* and *HGK* only, e.g. ***urth***, ***urthav***; medially *braud*, (*BD* and *BT*), *caur* (*HGK*), *guedi* (*BD* and *HGK*). *BT* however prefers <*gw-*>. In the section of *HGK* from Peniarth 267 vocalic /u/ is underdotted: *muyaf*, *irau*, *gur*, *oleu*. However, it is transcribed as simple <u> in the present edition.

<v> represents the phonemes:

(i) /v/ usually in medial position as in *kyvoedyon* (*BD*), *dwyvron* (*BT*), *darvot* (*HGK*); occasionally in initial position, as in ***val*** in all three texts. It never occurs in final position.

(ii) /ɨ/ occasionally in initial, medial and final position, e.g. ***vn*** (*BD* and *HGK*), ***vwch*** (BT), ***vgein*** (*BD* and *BT*) ***bvdugolaetheu***, *kynnvllus* (*HGK*); *yntev* (BD), *kyvarvv*, ***ev*** (*BT*), *dechrynv*, *esgynnv* (*HGK*).

(iii) /u/ frequently in medial position, especially in *BD*, e.g. *bvyt* (*BD*) and in final position in *BD* only, e.g. *assv*, *yv*, *llav*, *marv*.

<w> represents:

(i) /u/ mostly in medial position e.g. *kelwyd* (*BD*), *kyuyawn* (*BT*),*gwreig*(HGK); it also occurs initially as in ***wyneb***, ***wynep*** (*BT* and *HGK*), ***wrth*** (all three texts) and finally *kyuryw* (*BD*), *marw* (*BT* and *HGK*).

(ii) /v/ initially in two examples only, ***wu*** 'fu' and ***wuy*** 'mwy', both lenited forms of <b>, and <m> respectively.[184] There are a few further examples in medial position in *BD* and *HGK*: *kywarsangedic*, *kywersengir*, *kywoeth* and possibly *diawul*. In final position /v/ is represented by the voiced fricative <f> (see above).

The main distinguishing feature of the orthography of the selections taken from the manuscripts discussed above is the preference of *BD* for the grapheme <y> to represent the phoneme /i/ and <v> instead of <w> to represent the phoneme /u/, whereas *BT* prefers <w> and *HGrK* <u>. An analysis of the three

183 The graphemes <u> and <v> can be pronounced as /ɨ/ or /i/ depending on their geographical distribution, but as that is outside the orbit of this edition, the symbol /ɨ/ is used here in order to differentiate it from the phonemes /v/ and /u/.

184 For a full discusion of <w> for /vu/ see Russell, 'Medieval Scribes', pp. 90–91.

texts, however, shows that orthographic variations of the same lexeme occur not only between manuscripts but also within the same mausucript.

Initial Mutations[185]

1. Lenition

As one would expect in the case of texts chosen from different manuscripts, there is considerable orthographic inconsistency in the notation of mutations. Visible recognition of lenition is impossible in the case of the grapheme <d>: since <d> represents /ð/ as well as /d/, it cannot be proved whether the mutation would have been indicated or not, e.g. *ef a adeylwys* **d***ynas* (9–10), *o'e* **d***ewynyon* (13). In the Peniarth 267 section of *HGrK* lenited <d> is shown by underdotting the grapheme, e.g. *hanner y* **d***a* (857), *yn y diwed dydyeu* (855), *wedy y dyd ef* (859), *Kymry a Gwydyl a gwyr Denmarc yntwy a* **d***rygyrferthassant o* **d***igwyddedygaeth Gruffud vrenhin* (860–1). In this edition, however, in the interests of consistency with the other passages, the underdotting has been omitted and it has been transcribed simply as <d>.

The grapheme <t> is also problematic, since it represents not only /t/ but also /d/and /ð/. Note the inconsistencies in its employment: *heb tat* (191–2, 236) but *heb* **d***at* (203), *y tat ef* (12) but *y* **d***ad ef* (628), *y terynas* (59) but *y deyrnas* (370–1). There is also an inconsistency in the use of the lenited and unlenited forms of the prepositions *tros* /*dros* and *trvy*/*drvy*. *BD* has a preference for the unlenited forms, whereas the lenited forms have a higher frequency in *BT*.

In the examples quoted below lenition is not noted orthographically, but lexemes with initial <d> are not included, as the phonic value of that grapheme is uncertain.

(i) In all three texts the most frequent non-indication of lenition occurs in the object of the conjugated verb, but since lenition of the object is not obligatory in MW,[186] perhaps not too much importance can be attributed to these examples:

> *Ac yna y kymerth Guendoleu* **ll***ywodraeth y tyrnas* (79)
> *a ryd* **c***anhorthwy* (270–1)
> *A hwnnw a gynhelis* **p***ennaduryaeth ar y Brytanyeid* (585–6)
> *ef a gymyrth* **g***ureic* (730)
> *ef a gynnvllus* **ll***ynges* (771–2)
> *yn y vlwydyn honno y kynnhelis yr Arglwyd Rys ap Gruffud* **ll***ys . . . yn Aberteiui* (867–8)

(ii) In *BD* and *HGK bot* is rarely mutated when introducing a noun clause:

> *mi a brofaf arnadunt* **bot** *yn gelwyd a dywedassant'* (238–9)
> *gvypvn i* **bot** *tat idav ef* (222)

---

[185]   See *GMW* §§18–23.
[186]   *GMW* § 21

y ouyn idav a allei hynny **bot** yn wir (224)
a chvynav urthav ef en benhaf . . . **bot** estravn genedloed en argluydi ar y
dadaul deyrnas (746–7)

but examples occur where lenition is indicated:

wynt a dywedassant **vot** y vorvyn yn veychavc ar vab a ladei y vam a'y tat
(15)
klybot a wnaeth Ywein **vod** Nest . . . yn y dywededic kastell (605–6)
a mynegi ydaw **vot** yn well ganthunt eu llad yn ryuel dros eu rydit nogyt
diodef eu sathru yn andylyedus y gan estronyon (1026–8)

(iii) Sometimes lenition of the initial consonant of a feminine noun and adjective
following the definite article is not indicated:

y **t**yrnas (79)
y **p**obyl (118)

(iv) Inversion of adj and noun requires a mutation of the initial letter of the noun
but this is not always indicated:

yr ysgymun **p**obyl (honno) (177)
y tragywydavl **t**eyrnas (562)

(v) Lenition usually occurs after the numeral *deu*, but there are examples where
it is not indicated:

ar tal y deu **g**lin (147–8)
deu **c**an (417)

(vi) There is occasional non-indication of lenition after certain prepositions
which are usually followed by a mutated consonant:

A llawer a syrthvs yna o **p**ob parth (169)
mab heb **t**at idav (191–2)
ar **g**lan y lynn (256)
yn llavn o **p**aganyeit arvavc (482)
vrth **c**ladu (510)
y **p**avb (524)
a dan **p**ymp brenhin (590)

(vii) Sometimes lenition is not indicated after the adverbial and predicative *yn*:

yn **p**ymp ran (592)
megys yn **t**rwydet (770)

2. Nasalisation[187]

(a) The orthographic notation of the nasal mutation after the preposition *y/
yn* in the thirteenth century manuscripts which contain *BD* and *HGK* shows a

---

[187] See *GMW* §§25–26.

remarkable consistency, in that the mutation of the noun is not shown, although *yn > yg* or *ym* depending on the quality of the consonant which follows, e.g.,

> *yg* (= *yng*) + <k, g> as in *yg Kernyw, yg Caer Uudei, yg glan y mor* (*BD*); *yg*
> *kymvt, yg Gwydelec* (*HGK*)
> *em/ym* + <b, p> as in *ym pen y trydyd dyd* (*BD*); *em bruyder* (*HGK*)
> yn/*en* + <d, t> as in *en ty, yn Duw* (*HGK*)

Even in compound prepositions, the nasalisation of the nominal element is not shown, e.g. *ymplith* (*BD* and *HGK*). These prepositions are sometimes written as two separate words, as in *ym pen* (*BD*) and *yg kylch* (*HGK*). However in the later Peniarth 267 manuscript, which contains the concluding sections of *Historia Gruffudd vab Kenan*, there is an attempt to show nasalisation, e.g. *y Mangor*, but without the repetition of graphemes, (e.g. **ym** *Mangor*), which happened in a later orthographic notation.[188]

Peniarth 20 which contains *BT* employs different orthographic ways of denoting nasalisation after the preposition *yn*:
(i) *yg* + <k>, as in *ygKaer Loyw, ygKeredigyawn*, where the mutation of the initial consonant of the dependent noun is not shown, but *ygHeredigyawn* also occurs, which represents the pronunciation, again without the repetition of graphemes, which developed later, (e.g. *yng Ngheredigiawn*).
(ii) *yg* + *g, as in yGwyned*, where the <g> is not doubled but assimilated into the preposition. The pronunciation is as Modern Welsh *yng Ngwynedd* but without the graphic representation of the double nasal.
(iii) In compound prepositions the noun is attached to the preceding preposition and the nasalisation clearly shown, e.g. *yghylch, yghysswllt, yghyfrwg*. The pioneering early twentieth-century grammarian John Morris-Jones explains this by asserting that the nasal is wholly unaccented.[189]
(b) In *BD* and *HGK* <k> remains in its radical form after *vy*, which appears in the form *vyg* to represent a nasal mutation, e.g. *uyg kyghor, vyg kyuoeth*, whereas in *BT* the full nasalisation is shown, e.g., *vyghael*. John Morris-Jones maintains that the joining of noun and pronoun occurred because of prejudice against initial <ng>, which was finally overcome in the 1620 translation of the Bible.[190] It is difficult to tell whether the nasal is represented in *vy glinyeu* (*HGK*), whereas <b> and <d, > are fully nasalised in the following examples from *BD*: *rac y* **mron** *i* (where *y* represents a variant of *vy*), *vy* **newinyon**.

Editorial Method

Opinion differs about editorial methods ranging from the conservative stance that any form of interference is unacceptable to the more liberal principle of

[188]   For a full discussion of the orthographic representation of the nasal following *yn* and *vy* see
        Watkins, 'Arddodiad'.
[189]   Morris-Jones, *Welsh Grammar*, p. 175.
[190]   Ibid., p. 174.

making the text as intelligible as possible to the reader. A different approach is needed in editing a text for the exclusive benefit of other scholars from that followed when the objective is to make a text accessible to a wider readership. Since the purpose of this edition is to make some Middle Welsh historical texts comprehensible to students, a diplomatic edition was not an option. Although printed works edited by others (see Preface) have been used, all the texts in this collection have been checked against the manuscripts from which they have been transcribed and a few minor changes made.

As far as it was practical to do so, the original orthography has been preserved but in the selections of *Historia Guffudd vab Kenan* from Peniarth 267 the practice of D. Simon Evans in dealing with the underdotted graphemes <c> and <t> has been followed and they have been transcribed as <ch> and <th> respectively. Evans also notated <ṛ> as <rh>, but in the interests of consistency with the rest of the selections in this anthology this grapheme has been transcribed simply as <r>. For the same reason Evans's notation of <ḍ> as Modern Welsh <dd> has been rejected and it has been transcribed simply as <d>. Peniarth 267 employs <ḷ> to represent the phoneme /λ/ but again in the interests of orthographic consistency, in this edition it is transcribed as <ll>. Also the vocalic /ṵ/ of Peniarth 267 is transcribed here simply as <u>.

The excerpts of *Brut y Tywysogyon* from Peniarth 20 have been transcribed as faithfully to the manuscript as possible, but for the sake of clarity certain changes have been made. The spelling is that of the manuscript and has not been modernised, but where there was a mark indicating abbreviation in the mansucript, the missing abbreviated grapheme has been supplied in the transcript, (e.g. *hyny* with a nasal stroke over the first <y> has been transcribed as *hynny*). Where the grapheme <z> is employed in the manuscript to indicate <r>, it has been transcribed as <r>. Where the special symbol <q3> is employed for the phoneme /δ/ Thomas Jones's notation has been followed and it has been substituted with /δ/, e.g. *blwyδyn, blyneδ, deuδecved, dynesawδ, yδ* rather than *blwyq3yn, blyneq3, deuq3ecved, dynesawq3, yq3*, since this could cause confusion to the reader.

The capitalization of words, paragraphing and punctuation throughout are editorial.

BIRTH OF BRITAIN

The passages which follow are selected from one of the Welsh versions of Geoffrey of Monmouth's Historia Regum Britanniae, *contained in the Dingestow Court manuscript, dated to the second half of the thirteenth century. Following the origin tale in the* Historia Brittonum, *Geoffrey attempts to give the Britons as illustrious an origin as that of the ancient Romans by claiming their descent from Brutus, grandson of Aeneas, who after his flight from the ruins of Troy, rebuilt a kingdom in Italy. Just as Aeneas had been advised by his divine mother to sail to a western land, so too was Brutus told by the goddess Diana to settle in an island beyond France. After his arrival in this island, then called Albion, he cultivated it and renamed it Britain after himself.*

From Lewis, *Brut Dingestow*, I 3–4, 16; II 1, 4–5; III 20 with significant variants noted from the following manuscripts; The Red Book of Hergest (RB), Havod 1 and 2 (H1, H2), Llanstephan 1 (Ll1).

The Early Years of Brutus

Eneas Yscvydwyn, gvedy daruot ymladeu Tro a dystryw y gaer, a foes ac Ascanius y vab y gyd ac ef, ac a doethant ar longeu hyd yg gvlad yr Eydal, yr hon a elwir yr avrhon gvlad Ruuein. Ac yn yr amser hunnv yd oed Latinus yn vrenhyn yn yr Eydal, y gvr a arvolles Eneas yn anrydedus. Ac yna gvedi gveled o Turn vrenhyn Rutyl hynny, kyghoruynnu a llydyav a   5
oruc, ac ymlad ac ef. A goruod a wnaeth Eneas a llad Turn vrenhyn Rutyl, a chaffael yr Eydal a Lauynya merch Latinus yn wreyc ydaw. Ac yna gvedy ymlenwy dyewed buched Eneas, Ascanius y vab ynteu a wnaethbvyt yn vrenhyn. A gvedy dyrchauael Ascanius ar vrenhynavl gyvoeth, ef a adeylwys[1] dynas ar avon Tyberys. A mab a anet ydav ac y dodet arnav   10
Syluyus. A'i gvas hvnnv, gvedy ymrody y ledradavl odyneb, gorderchu a oruc nyth y Lauynya a'y beychogy. A gvedy gveled o Ascanius y tat ef hynny, erchy a wnaeth o'e dewynyon dywedvyt ydav pvy a'r veychogassey y vorvyn. A gvedy dewynav onadunt a chaffael gvybot dyheurvyd o'r peth hvnnv, wynt a dywedassant vot y vorvyn yn veychavc ar vab a ladei y vam   15
a'y tat. A gvedy darfey ydav treyglav llawer o wladoed y dayar, o'r dywet y dav ar ulaenwed goruchelder anryded. Ac ny thvyllws eu dewyndabaeth vynt, canys doeth eu devyndabaeth. Ac yna gvedy dyuot oet y'r vorvyn y escor ar y theuydle[2] y bu varv. Ac yuelly y lladavd y vam. A'r mab a rodet ar uaeth, ac y dodet Brutus arnav.   20

---

[1] MS *adeylvylaws.*
[2] H1 *y ar y etiued*; H2 and *MA* 476b 9 *ar y thevytle, TBRB* 42.2 *ar ei thevyd wely*; see *BrD* p. 209.

A gvedy meythryn y mab a'e uod yn bymtheg mluyd, dywyrnavd yd
oet y gvas[3] yn hely yn kanlyn y tat. Ac val yd oydynt yuelly nachaf carw
y[4] kerdet hep eu llav. Sef a oruc Brutus anelu bva ac ellvng saeth, ac yn
keyssyav llad y carw y gvant y tat a'r saeth a dan y vron, ac y bu varv.

25 Ac yvelly y lladavt y tat. A gvedy marv y tat o'r ergyd hvnnv y deholes
gvyr yr Eydal Brutus, canyd oet teylvng gantunt kymrut yn vrenhyn
arnadunt gvr a wneley kyulauan gymeynt a llad y vam a'e tat. A gvedy y
dehol yd aeth ynteu hyd y Groec, ac y gveles gvelygord o etyuet Helenus
uab Pryaf yg keythywet adan Pandrasus vrenhyn Groec. Pyrr uab Achel

30 a dugassey y genedyl honno gantav gvedy dystryw Tro yn dyal y tat, ac
a'y gvarchayssey yg keythywet yg kyhyt a hynny o amser. Ac yna gvedy
adnabot o Brutus y genedyl, trygyav a wnaeth y gyd ac vynt. Ac yn y lle
gvedy kyneuynau Brutus ac ymadnabot a phawb ohanav, kymeynt wu
y davn yn eu plyth yny oet garedyc a chymeredyc y gan y brenhyned a'r

35 tywyssogyon yn wuy no neb o'e gyvoedyon. A hynny a oet ydav o'e bryd
a'e devred a'e haelder a'e daeony a'e vylwryaeth a'e glod. A sef achavs oet
hynny, doethaf oet ymplyth y doethon, dewrhaf ymplyth y rei ymladgar.
Ac ygyd a hynny, pa beth bynnac a damweyney ydav nac eur nac aryant
na meyrch na dyllat, hynny oll a rodey ef o'e gyduarchogyon ac y bavb

40 o'r a'e mynhey y gantav. A gvedy ehedec y glod tros wladoet Groec yd
ymgynullyssant atav pavb o'r a hanoet o genedyl Tro o bob lle hyd yd
oet teruyneu Groec, ac erchy ydav ef bot yn dywyssavc arnadunt, ac eu
rydhau o geythywet gvyr Groec.

Brutus settles in Britain

A'r amser hvnnv y gelwit hi y Wenn Ynys, a diffeith oed eithyr ychydic o
45 kevri yn y kyuanhedu. Tec hagen oed y hansavd o auonoed tec a physgavt
yndunt, a choedyd a bvystuiled gvyllt yndunt yn amhyl. A bodlavn
uuant y'r lle vrth bressvylav yndav. A gvedy gvelet o'r kevri wynt yn
damgylchynu yr enys, fo a wnaeth y kevri yg gogoueu y mynyded. Ac
yna gan ganhyat Brutus y rannvyt yr enys ac y dechreuyt diwyllyav y
50 tired ac adeilat tei, ac yn ychydyc o amser guneuthur dyruawr gyuanhed
arnei. Ac y mynnvys Brutus galv yr enys o'e enw ef Brytaen, a'r genedyl yn
Vrytannyeit. Ac o hynny allan yr yeith, a elwyt kyn no hynny yeith Tro,
neu ynteu Kam Roec, a elwit gvedy hynny Brytannec.

The division of the kingdom on Brutus's death

Ac yna, guedy kyweiryav pob peth ar hyt yr enys yn tagnheuedus ac adeylat
55 y gaer a'r dinas, kysgu a wnaeth Brutus gan y wreic. A thri meyb a anet
ydav ohenei, sef oed eu henw, Locrinus, Kamber, Albanactus. Ac ympen

---

[3]   MS *y gvas* added above.
[4]   MS <n> has been added after 'y' in a later hand.

y petwared vlwydyn ar ugeint guedy y dyuodedygaeth y enys Prydein y
bu uarv Brutus ac y cladwyt yn y gaer a adeilassei ehun yn anrydedus. Ac
yna y rannvt[5] y teyrnas y rung y ueibyon ynteu. A Locrinus, canys hynhaf
oed, a gymerth y rann berued o'r enys, yr honn a elwir Lloegyr o'e enw   60
ef; ac y kymerth Kamber o'r tu arall y Hauren, yr hon a elwir o'e env ef
Kymry; ac y kymerth Albanactus y gogled, yr hon a elwis ynteu o'e enw
ef yr Alban. A gvedy eu bot yuelly yn tagnheuedus trvy hir amser y doeth
Humyr urenhyn Dunavt[6] a llyges ganthav hyt yr Alban. A guedy ymlad
ac Albanactus, y lad a cymhell y bobyl ar fo hyt ar Locrinus.   65

The Naming of the Severn

*After avenging his brother, Locrinus falls in love with the beautiful Esyllt, one
of his captives, to the annoyance of his prospective father-in-law Corineus.*

Ac y kysgvs Locrinus gan Wendoleu[7] merch Corineus. Ac yr hynny
ny leihavys caryat Essyllt ganthav, namyn y gossot y myvn daearty yn
Llundein, ac annvyleyt ydav y'v gvassanaethu yn dirgel[8] ac y'v gvarchadv.
Ac yno y deuei ynteu yn gudyavc attei hi. Ac y uelly y bu yn mynychau
attei seith mlyned heb vybot y neb eithyr y anvylyeit, namyn yn rith   70
gvneuthur aberth y'r dwyweu yd aei yno. A beychogi a gauas Essyllt,
a merch a uu idi, ac ar honno y dodet Hauren. A beychogi a gauas
Guendoleu, a mab a anet idi hitheu, ac ar hvnnv y dodet Madavc, ac y
rodet ar Corineus y hendat ar uaeth.

Ac ym pen yspeit guedy marv Corineus, ymadav a wnaeth a Guendoleu,   75
a dyrchauael Essyllt yn urenhynes. A llidyav a wnaeth Guendoleu eithyr
mod, a mynet hyt yg Kernyw a chynullav y llu mvyhaf a allvys y ryuelu
ar Locrinus. Ac yg glan yr auon a elwir Sturam ymgyfaruot, ac o ergyt
saeth llad Locrinus. Ac yna y kymerth Guendoleu llywodraeth y tyrnas,
ac mal yd oed engirolaeth Corineus y that, erchi bodi Essyllt a'e merch   80
yn yr auon hono, ac y dodet ar yr auon Hauren o env y uorvyn yr hynny
hyt hediw.

The Naming of London and the Succession of Casswallon

Ac yn ol Manogan y doeth Beli Mavr y uab ynteu, a deu ugein mlyned y
bu urenhin yn enys Prydein. Ac y hvnnv y bu tri meib, Llud a Chaswallavn
a Nynnyav. A guedy marv Beli Mavr, yna y gunaethpvyt Llud y mab   85
hynaf ydav yn urenhin, y gvr a uu guedy hynny[9] ogonedus ac adeilavdyr

---

[5]   Inserted in the left margin of the manuscript in the original hand.
[6]   *MA* 483a 38 *Humyr brenyn Hunawt*; H1 *Humyr vrenhin hunawt*
[7]   Final <u> is a later addition in red.
[8]   H1 *yn rinyawc*.
[9]   Inserted in the margin of the manuscript.

kaeroed a dinassoed, ac a atnewydhavys muryoed Llundein a'e thyroed.
A chet bei llaver ydav o dinassoed ereill, hvnnv eissoes a garei yn wy no'r
vn, ac vrth hynny y gelwit Caer Lud. A guedy hynny trvy lygru y henv y
90 gelwit Llundein. A phan vu uarv y cladvyt yn Llundein ger llav y porth a
elwir etwa o'e env ef Porth Llud yg Kymraec, ac yn Saesnec Ludysgat. A
deu uab oed idav, Auarvy a Theneuan. A phan uu uarv Llud nyt oed oet
arnunt ual y gellit eu gwneuthur yn urenhin. Ac wrth hynny y gunaethpvt
Caswallavn eu hewythyr yn urenhin. Ac ymdyrchauael a wnaeth ynteu o
95 haelder a daeoni yny oed y uolyant tros y tyrnassoed pellaf, ac vrth hynny
y cauas ynteu uot yn urenhin. Ac eissoes herwyd y warder, ny mynnvs
ef uot y meibyon yn dirann o'r tyrnas, namyn rodi y Auarvy Llundein a
yarllaeth Geint, ac y Teneuan yarllaeth Gernyw. Ac ydav ynteu coron y
tyrnas.

GWRTHEYRN (VORTIGERN)

*After the departure of the Romans, Britain is assailed by new enemies, the
Picts and the Scots. The Britons make an appeal to their fellow-countrymen
in Brittany, who come to their aid in defeating the enemy and Custennyn
(Constantine), brother of the king of Brittany is enthroned as king. His
treacherous death at the hands of a Pict causes a problem of succession.*

From Lewis, *Brut Dingestow*, VI 6–7, 12; VI 16–19; VII 3.

Gwrtheyrn plots to seize the kingship

100 Ac yna guedy llad Custennyn Uendigeit y kyuodes anundeb y rvng
guyrda y teyrnas am wneuthur brenhin. Canys rei a uynnynt guneuthur
Emreis Wledic yn urenhin, ereill a uynnei Vthur Pen Dragon, ereill a
uynnynt wneuthur un oc eu kenedyl. Ac o'r diwed, guedy na duunynt
ar hynn, sef a wnaeth Gortheyrn Gortheneu — yarll oed hvnnv ar Went
105 ac Ergyng a Yeuas — vrth geissyav y urenhinaeth idav ehun o'r diwed,
mynet hyt yg Kaer Wynt yn y lle yd oed Constans yn uynach — y mab
hynhaf y Gustennyn Uendigeit oed hvnnv — a dywedut vrthav ual hyn:
'Constans,' heb ef, 'dy tat ti y syd uarv, a'th urodyr y syd ry yeueinc vrth
wneuthur brenhin onadunt. Ac ny welaf innheu o'th lin ditheu a allo
110 bot yn urenhin. Ac vrth hynny, o bydy ditheu vrth gyghor ac achuanegu
kyuoeth a medyant y minheu ar y urenhinaeth, minheu a ymchuelaf
vyneb y bobyl a'r kyuoeth parth ac attat titheu, ac a baraf dy dynnu o'r abit
hvnnv ket boet gvrthvyneb gan yr urdas, a'th wneuthur yn urenhin.' A
phan gigleu Constans yr ymadrawd hvnnv, llawenhau yn uavr a wnaeth,
115 ac adav trvy aruoll rodi idav pob peth o'r a uynhei, ac na wnelhei dim
o'r urenhinaeth namyn vrth y gyghor. A'e gymryt a wnaeth Gortheyrn
Gortheneu a['e] tennu yn diannot o'r uynechtit a'e wisgav o urenhinavl

dillat, a dyuot ac ef hyt yn Llundein, ac yna o ureid cahel canhyat y pobyl
o'e dyrchauael yn urenhin. Ac yn yr amser hvnnv marv uuassei Kuhelyn
archescob Llundein, ac vrth hynny ny chaffat un escob a gymerei arnav 120
y gyssegru ynteu wrth ry tynnu o'r creuyd. Ac eissyoes yr hynny nyt
ebryuygvs Gortheyrn y gueithret hvnnv, namyn mynet ehun[10] yn lle
escob, a chymryt coron y teyrnas a'e dodi am ben Constans, ac y uelly y
urdav yn urenhin.

A guedy dyrchauael Constans yn urenhin y rodes ynteu holl lyvodraeth 125
y teyrnas yn llav Gortheyrn, ac ehun heuyt a ymrodes ym pob peth
vrth y gyghor. Canys amgen dysc a dyscassei ef yn y clavstyr no llywyav
brenhinaeth. A guedy caffael o Gortheyrn medyant kymeint a hvnnv yn y
lav, medylyav a oruc pa ansavd y gallei caffael ehun y urenhinaeth, canys
hynny yd oed yn y damunav ac yn y ystrywav o'e holl dihewyt. Damwein 130
truan heuyt ry daroed, yr uarv hynaf guyr y teyrnas a'e chyghorwyr
yn llwyr, megys nat oed un gur mor arbennic a Gortheyrn, a megys
meibyon oed pavb o wyrda y teyrnas oll y vrthav ynteu. Ac euo a gaffei
anryded pavb onadunt hwy, canys ef a uedei y kyghor. A guedy guelet o
Ortheyrn y uot yn caffael pob peth vrth y ewyllys, medylyav a wnaeth o'e 135
holl ethrylith pa wed y gallei diot Constans uynach o'r urenhinaeth a'e
chymrut idav ehun.

Gwrtheyrn and Rhonwen

*Having established himself as king, Gwrtheyrn soon faces a new difficulty by
the arrival of three shiploads of Saxons under the leadership of Hengist and
Horsa. Gwrtheyrn decides to use them to his own advantage and offers them
rewards in return for help in warding off an attack from the Picts. Hengist,
however, wishes for greater prizes. Using scaremongering tactics, he reminds
Gwrtheyrn of his unpopularity and warns him of an alleged plot to crown
one of Constans's young sons in his place. Hearing this, Gwrtheyrn readily
agrees to Hengist's suggestions that he should send envoys to bring more
reinforcements from Germany. They also bring with them Hengist's daughter
Rhonwen, with whom Gwrtheyrn makes a disastrous marriage.*

Ac ymchuelut a wnaeth y kennadeu o Germania a deunav llong ganthunt
yn llavn o etholedigyon uarchogyon aruavc, a merch Heingyst ganthunt,
sef oed y henv hi Ronwen. Ac nid oed yr eil a gyffelypit idi rac y theccet. 140
A guedy dyuot y niuer hvnnv, sef a wnaeth Heingyst guahavd Gortheyrn
y edrych yr adeilat deissyuyt yr[11] wnathoedyt ac y edrych y marchogyon

---

[10] MS *mynent* with a line beneath the second <n>; *ehun* is inserted above the line
[11] MS *yr a wnathoedyt* with *a* crossed out.

newyd dyuot. A guedy dyuot y brenhin yno a niuer bychan[12] ganthav,
moli a wnaeth y gueith newyd, a chymryt y marchogyon newyd dyuot
145   yn wyr idav. A guedy daruot udunt bvyta o urenhinavl anregyon, nachaf
y uorwyn yn dyuot o'r ystauell a gorulvch eur yn y llav a'e loneit yndav o
win, ac y uelly dyuot hyt rac bron y brenhin. A gwedy adoli idav ar tal y
deu glin, kyuarch guell idav a heilyav arnav ual hyn, 'Lauart king, wasseil.'
A phan weles y brenhin pryt y uorvyn, anryuedu a wnaeth y theccet, ac yn
150   y lle ymlenwi o'e charyat a gouyn y'r yeithyd beth a dywedassei y vorwyn
a pheth a dylyei ynteu y dywedut yn vrtheb idi hitheu. Ac yna y dywavt yr
yeithyd vrthav, 'Arglvyd,' heb ef, 'hi a'th elwis di yn arglvyd ac yn urenhin
yn y hyeith hi, ac y uelly y'th anrydedvys. Yr hynn a dylyy ditheu y vrtheb
idi hi, hynn yw, sef yw hynny, 'Drincheil.' Ac yna y dywavt Gortheyrn
155   vrthi, 'Drincheil,' ac erchi y'r uorvyn yuet y gvin. Ac yr hynny hyt hediw
y mae y deuavt honno wedy yr adav ym plith y kyuedychwyr yn enys
Prydein.

Ac yna guedy medwi Gortheyrn, neidyav a wnaeth diawul yndav a
pheri idav gytsynhyav a'r paganes ysgymun heb uedyd arnei. A sef a
160   wnaeth Heingyst mal oed ystryvus, adnabot ysgavnder annvyt y brenhin,
ac ymgyghor a'e uravt ac a'e gedymdeithyon am rodi y uorvyn wrth
ewyllis y brenhin. Ac o gytgyghor y cavssant y rodi y'r brenhin, ac erchi
idav ynteu swyd Geint yn y hagwedi hi. Ac yn diannot y rodet y uorvyn
y'r brenhin, ac y rodes ynteu svyd Geint yn y hagwedi hi heb vybot y'r
165   gvr oed yarll yno, sef oed y henv Gvrgant. A'r nos honno y kysgvyt gan
y uorvyn, a mwy no messur y karvys Gortheyrn o hynny allan. A thri
meib yr uuassei y Ortheyrn kyn no hynny, sef oed eu henv, Kyndeyrn, a
Guertheuyr Uendigeit, a Phasken.

Gwrtheyrn and Myrddin

*After his marriage to Rhonwen, Gwrtheyrn is completely under the influence
of the Saxons. This angers the Britons so much that they depose him in favour
of Vortimer, his son by his first wife. Vortimer restores their territorries to the
Britons, but is poisoned by Rhonwen, thus enabling Gwrtheyrn to reclaim
power. Gwrtheyrn then invites Hengist to return with a select number of
retainers. Hengist accepts the invitation but his arrival with a larger number
of followers than had been expected alarms Gwrtheyrn and his nobles,
who plan to oppose them. Hengist, however, requests a peace conference.
Gwrtheryn readily agrees and organises a meeting at the village of Ambrius
but this proves abortive. Hengist gives a malicious order to his each of
followers to conceal a knife in his boot and, at a given signal, slit the throat of*

----

[12]   H1 *niuer kyuartal.*

the British nobleman who is seated next to him. The Britons put up a struggle and many on both sides are slain but Gwrtheyrn escapes to Wales.

A llawer a syrthvs yna o pob parth, ac eissyoes yr ysgymun uudugolyaeth honno a gauas y Saesson. Ac yr hynny eissyoes ny ladassant Gortheyrn, namyn y garcharu a chymell arnav rodi udunt y dinassoed a'r kestyll a chadarnleoed enys Prydein yr y ellvng. Ac yna y rodes Ortheyrn udunt pob peth o'r a uynnassant yr y ellvng. A guedy kymryt kedernyt ac aruoll y ganthav yd ellygvyt. Ac yna y kymerth y Saesson y ganthav Llundein a Chaer Euravc a Lincol a Chaer Wynt, gan lad eu kivdavtwyr megys y lledit deueit guedy ys¹³ adavhei eu bugeil. A guedy guelet o Ortheyrn y truan aerua honno ar y pryodoryon y gan yr ysgymun pobyl, sef a wnaeth ynteu kilyav parth ac emylyeu Kymry, cany vydat beth a wnaei yn erbyn yr ysgymun pobyl honno.

A galw attav holl doethyon a henuryeit y gyuoeth, a gouyn udunt beth a wnaei vrth hynny. Ac yna y kyghoret idav adeilat y castell cadarnhaf a allei yn y lle cadarnhaf a gaffei, megys y bei hvnnv yn amdiffyn idav, can collassei oll¹⁴ y lleoed cadarn o'e gyuoeth. A guedy crvydrav ohonav llawer o leoed y geissyav y ryv le hvnnv, o'r diwed y doeth hyt ym mynyded Eryri. A guedy caffael ohonav lle y bu adas ganthav y wneuthur y gastell, kynullav a wnaethput holl seiri mein o'r a allvt eu caffael, ac eu dvyn hyt yno. A guedy dechreu gossot y grvndwal onadunt, kymeint ac a wnelynt y dyd o'r gueith, trannoeth pan gyuotit neu daruydei y'r daear y lyngcu heb vybot dim y vrthav mvy no cheny ryffei eiryoet uch y dayar.

A guedy mynegi hynny y Ortheyrn, gouyn y'w dewinyon idav a wnaeth beth a wnaei hynny. Ac yna yd erchis y dewinyon idav keissyav mab heb tat idav, a llad hvnnv, a chymysgu guaet hvnnv a'r calch, ac irav y mein heuyt a'r calch a'r guaet hvnnv, a dineu y guaet yn y grvndwal hyt pan sauci y gucith y uelly. Ac yna yd anuonet [hyt] ym pob lle y geissyav kyuryv uab a hvnnv. A guedy dyuot deu o'r kennadeu hynny hyt y dinas a elwit guedy hynny Caer Uyrdin, nachaf y guelynt bvrn o weissyon yeueinc yn guare yn drvs porth y dinas. A sef a wnaeth y kennadeu dynessau ar y guare ac edrych arnadunt, ac eisted yn lludedic dyffygyavl, ac ymwrandav am y neges yd oedynt yn y cheissyav. A guedy bot y gueissyon yuelly yn guare yn hir, daruot a wnaeth [kynnennu]¹⁵ y rvng deu onadunt, a'r neill onadunt a elwit Dunavt a'r llall Myrdin. Ac yna y dywavt Dunavt vrth Uyrdin, 'Pa achavs,' heb ef, 'yd amryssony di a miui nac y kynnenny? Canys dyn tygheduenavl heb dat idav vyt ti, a mineu a hanvyf o vrenhinavl lin oblegyt mam a that.' A phan gigleu y kennadeu

170

175

180

185

190

195

200

---

¹³ H₁ *gwedy ass adawhei eu bugeil*
¹⁴ H₁ *y lleoed cadarn oll.*
¹⁵ Ll₁ *darvot a gwnaeth* **kynhennv** *er rvng dev or gweyssyon*

205 yr ymadrodyon hynny, dyrchauael eu hvyneb a wnaethant ac edrych ar
Vyrdyn, a gouyn y'r dynyon oed yn eu kylch pvy oed y guas. Ac vynteu
a dywedassant na wydynt pa dat yr ganassei ef. 'Y uam ynteu,' heb vynt,
'yssyd uerhc y urenhin Dyuet, ac yn y dref yma,' heb vynt, 'y mae yn
uanaches ym plith mynachesseu ereill yn eglvys Bedyr.'

210 Ac yn y lle, kychwyn a wnaeth y kennadeu ar gvnstabyl y gaer a'r dinas
ac erchi idav o bleit y brenhin anuon Myrdin a'e uam yn diannot hyt ar
y brenhin vrth wneuthur y ewyllis onadunt. A guedy eu dyuot rac bron
y brenhin, y haruoll yn anrydedus a wnaeth y brenhin (y uam Uyrdyn),
can gvydat y hanuot o urenhinavl anedigaeth. Ac odyna gouyn a wnaeth
215 idi pvy oed tat y mab. Ac yna y dywavt hitheu, 'Arglvyd,' heb hi, 'byv[16]
yv uy[17] eneit i nat adnabum i vr eiryoet ac na vybum pvy a grevys y mab
hvn y'm callon. Namyn hyn, un peth a wn. Pan yttoedvn ym plith uyg
kedymeithessei yn yr hundy, nachaf y guelvn yn dyuot attaf yn drech gvr
yeuanc teccaf yn y byt, ac yn dodi y dvylav amdanaf ac yn ymgaru a mi,
220 ac o'r diwed kydyav a mi a'm hadav yn ueichyavc. A gvybydet dy brudder
di a'th doethineb, arglvyd urenhin, na bu i mi eiryoet achavs a gvr namyn
hynny, megys y gvypvn i bot tat idav ef amgen no hvnnv.'

Ac anryuedu yn vavr hynny a oruc y brenhin, ac erchi dvyn Meugant
dewin attav y ouyn idav a allei hynny bot yn wir. A guedy dyuot Meugant
225 y'r lle a datcanu idav y gyuranc honno, ynteu a dywavt y keffyt yn llyureu y
doethon ac yn llawer o istoriaeu ereill bot llaver o dynyon a ryv anedigaeth
honno udunt. 'Apulenis,'[18] heb ef, 'a dyweit, pan draetha o Duv a'r seint, bot
ryv genedyl yn pressvylyav y rvng y lleuat a'r dayar, a rein hynny a alwnn
ni dieuyl gogwydedic, a rann yndunt o'r dayar ac o annyan dynavl, a rann
230 arall o annyan egylyon. A phan y mynnont y gallant gymryt dynavl figur
a drech arnadunt, a chydyav a'r guraged y uelly. Ac atuyd un o'r rei hynny
a doeth ar y wreigda hon ac a'e beichoges pan gaffat y guas yeuanc hvn.'

Ac yna guedy gurandav o Uyrdin yr ymadrodyon hynny, nessau
a wnaeth ar y brenhin ac adoli idav, a gouyn pa achavs yr dugessit ef a'e
235 uam hyt yno. Ac yna y dywavt Gortheyrn vrthav ynteu: 'Vy newinyon a
archassant ym keissyav mab heb tat idav, ac a guaet hvnnv irav y gueith,
ac y uelly y dywedynt y seuyll.' Ac yna y dywavt Myrdin: 'Arglvyd,' heb ef,
'arch di dvyn dy dewinyon di rac y mron i, a mi a brofaf arnadunt bot yn
gelwyd a dywedassant.' Ac anryuedu a wnaeth y brenhin y ymadravd, ac
240 erchi dvyn y devynyon rac y uron. A guedy eu heisted rac y uron, Myrdin
a ouynnvs vdunt beth oed yn llesteiryav y gueith. 'Canys y mae,' heb ef,

---

[16] MS *bvy.*
[17] MS *uy y.*
[18] RB *Apulenius,* H2 *apphlegyws,* Ll1 *Appvleyvs.*

'beth yn ymgelu ny at y'r gueith seuyll.' Ac ny allvs y dewinyon atteb idav. Ac yna y dywavt Myrdin: 'Arglvyd,' heb ef, 'arch di dvyn dy weithwyr [y gladu y dayar] yma, a thi a geffy llynn a dan y dayar, a hvnnv ny at y'r gueith seuyll.' A guedy guneuthur y clad a chaffael y llynn, yna y dywavt 245
Myrdin eilweith vrth y dewinyon: 'Dywedvch chui, dvyllwyr kelwydavc anhyedwyr, pa beth ysyd adan y llynn?' Ac yna tewi a wnaethant megys ket bydynt mut. Ac yna y dywavt Myrdin: 'Arglvyd,' heb ef, 'arch di disbydu y llynn drvy frydyeu, a thi a wely deu uaen geu yn y waelavt, ac y myvn y deu uaen dvy dreic yn kysgu.' A chredu a wnaeth y brenhin hynny 250
idav canys dywedassei wir am y lynn kyn no hynny. Ac erchi disbydu y lynn. Ac am bob peth o hynny anryuedu doethinab Myrdin a wnaei, a phavb o'r a oed y gyt ac ef yn credu bot dvwavl gyuoeth[19] a gvybot a doethineb yndav.

Myrddin's prophecies

Eman y dechreu Proffvydolyaeth Myrdin 255

Pan ytoed Gortheyrn Gortheneu yn eisted ar glan y lynn guehynedic y kyuodassant dvy dreic ohanav, o'r rei yd oed un guynn ac arall cohc. A guedy dynessau pob un y'v gilid onadunt, dechreu girat ymlad a wnaethant a chreu tan oc eu hanadyl. Ac yna gvrthlad y dreic coch a'e chymell hyt ar eithavoed y lynn. A doluryav a oruc hitheu a llidyav yn 260
uavr, a chymell y dreic wenn dracheuyn. Ac ual yd oed y dreigeu yn ymlad yn y wed honno yd erchis y brenhin y Uyrdin dywedut beth a arvydocaei hynny. Ac yn y lle sef a wnaeth yntau guehynnu y yspryt gan vylav a dywedut: 'Gwae hy y dreic coch, canys y haball ysyd yn bryssyav. E gogoueu a achub y dreic wenn, yr hon a arvydocaa y Saesson a ohodeist di. 265
E dreic coch a arvydocaa kenedyl y Brytannyeit, yr honn a gywersengir y gan y wenn. Vrth hynny y mynyded a westyteir val y glynneu, ac auonoed y glynneu a lithrant o wact. Diwyll y gristonogaeth a dileir, a chvymp yr eglvysseu a ymdywynnic. En y diwed y racrymhaa y gywarsangedic, ac y dywalder yr estronyon y gvrthvynepa. Canys baed Kernyv a ryd 270
canhorthwy, a mynygleu yr estronyon a sathyr dan y draet. Enyssed yr eigyavn a darystyngant idav a guladoed Freinc a uedhavt. Ty Ruuein a ouynhaa y dywalder ef, a'e diwed a uyd pedrus. Eg geneu y bobyl yd anrydedir, a'e weithredoed a uyd bvyt y'r a'e datcano.

ARTHUR

The section of Historia Regum Britanniae *which deals with Arthur is the longest in the entire work, even excluding the long introductory section*

[19] H2 *gwynnyeyth.*

about his wondrous conception. Paradoxically, although Arthur is heir to the kings who rescued Britain from the domination of the Saxons, and although he himself had some spectacular successes, he fails to re-establish British sovereignty on a permanent basis. Nevertheless, the ambiguous nature of his obituary offers hope of his return as the saviour of his people, provided they prove themselves worthy. Geoffrey's portrayal of Arthur is somewhat different from that of the native Welsh tradition, where he is a rough and ready military chieftain, who emerges as a deus ex machina *to accomplish seemingly insoluable feats, except when he is down on his luck, as in the poem* 'Pa Ŵr yw y Porthawr', *in the MS Peniarth I, known as* The Black Book of Carmarthen. *In HRB Arthur is depicted as an emperor, whose court is frequented by kings and noblemen from all over the known world. Removed from Celliwig in Cornwall to Caerlleon in South Wales, his court is depicted as the epitome of chivalry, a picture more appealing to a twelfth-century Norman audience, than the earlier less sophisticated portrayal in the Welsh texts.*

From Lewis, *Brut Dingestow,* VIII 19; IX 1, 9, 12–13; X 13-XI 1–2.

Uthr Pendragon's Celebration Feast

275 Ac ual yd oed gvylua y Pasc yn dynessau, anuon a wnaeth y brenhin
kennadeu y bob lle trvy enys Brydein y dyuynnu pavb o'r guyrda, yeirll, a
barvnyeit, a marchogyon urdavl hyt yn Llundein vrth anrydedu yr vylua
honno trvy lewenyd megys y dylyit, a guisgav coron y deyrnas am benn
y brenhin, a rodi y yavn y bavb a'e dylyet. Ac ymgynnullav a wnaeth
280 pavb vrth y guys hvnnv, a dyuot hyt yn Llundein o bob lle dros vyneb
enys Brydein. Ac anrydedu a wnaeth y brenhin yr vylua honno megys
y darparassei gan lewenyd, a diruavr lewenyd a gymyrth pavb yndunt o
welet y brenhin yn eu haruoll ac yn eu herbynneit mor llawen a hynny.
A chymeint o dylyedogyon a doethant yna, vynt ac eu guraged ac eu
285 meibyon ac eu merchet, ac yd oed deilvng y'r ryv wled honno.

Uthr and Eigyr

Ac ym plith y guyrda hynny y dothoed Gorlois yarll Kernyw, ac Eigyr
uerch Amlavd Wledic y wreic y gyt ac ef. Pryt y wreic honno hagen a'e
thegvch a orchyuygei holl wraged enys Brydein. A phan weles y brenhin
y wreic honno ym plith y guraged ereill, ymlenwi a wnaeth o'e charyat
290 yn gymeint ac na hanbvyllei o dim, namyn treiglav y holl uedvl a'e holl
enni a'e holl dihewyt yn y hanrydedu hi. Idi hi yd anuonyt y golvython a'r
anregyon, idi hi heuyt yd anuonyt y goruleheu eureit a'r guirodeu yndynt,
a'r heil mynych a'r geiryeu tiryon. A guedy cael gvybot hynny o'r yarll,
y gvr hitheu, llidyav a wnaeth ac adav y llys heb ganhiat y brenhin. A
295 chymeint uu y lit ac na allvt y ymchuelut tracheuyn na'e wahavd rac ouyn
colli y wreic, yr hon a garei ynteu y wuy no dim daearavl. Ac vrth hynny

llidyav a wnaeth y brenhin am ry adav y lys heb y ganhyat, ac anuon yn y
ol ac erchi idav dyuot y wneuthur yavn y'r brenhin. Canys un o sarhaedeu
brenhin yv adav y lys heb ganhyat. A guedy nat ymchuelei yr neb, tygu a
wnaeth y brenhin trvy y uar a'e lit yd anreithei holl gyuoeth Gorlois.   300

Ac yna heb un gohir, tra ydoed y llit hvnnv yn parhau y rygthunt,
kynnullav llu mavr a wnaeth y brenhin a chyrchu Kernyv, a dechreu llosgi
y dinassoed a'r kestyll a'r treui. Ac yr hynny eissyoes ny lauassvs Gorlois
ymerbynneit ac ef, canys llei oed y niuer noc un y brenhin. Ac vrth
hynny, sef y cauas ynteu yn y gyghor kadarnhau y gestyll, ac y uelly arhos   305
porth attav o Ywerdon. A chan oed mvy y oual am y wreic noc amdanav
ehun, sef a wnaeth y gossot hi yg castell Tintagol ar glan y traeth yn y
lle cadarnhaf oed yn y gyuoeth, ac ynteu a aeth yg castell Dymolt rac eu
caffael y gyt o dryc damwein ell deu.

A phan gigleu y brenhin hynny, sef a wnaeth ynteu mynet parth a'r   310
castell yd adoed Gorlois yndav, a guedy y gylchynu dechreu ymlad ac ef
a'e warchae, mal na chaffei neb na dyuot idav na mynet ohonav. A guedy
mynet yspeit vythnos heibyav, coffau a wnaeth Uthyr Bendragon caryat
Eigyr, a galv attav Vlffin o Ryt Garadavc, y gedymdeith a'e gytuarchavc, a
mynegi idav y uedvl yn y wed hon: 'Dyoer,' heb ef, 'mavr yv ynof ui caryat   315
Eigyr, ac nyt diheu genhyf na chollvyf uy eneit ony chahaf y wreic vrth
uyg kyghor. Ac vrth hynny,' heb ef, 'dyro ym gyghor drvy yr hvn y gallvyf
eilenwi uy ewyllis, canyt oes bedrusder genhyf uy aballu o'e charyat onys
caffaf.' Ac yna y dywavt Vlfin vrth y brenhin: 'Arglvyd,' heb ef, 'pvy a allei
rodi kyghor yti, pryt na bo ford yn y byt y ymgaffael a hi? Canys y castell y   320
mae hy yndav ysyd ar ben carrec yn y weilgi yn gaedic o'r mor o bob parth
idav. Ac nyt oes neb kyuryw ford yn y byt y galler mynet ohonav na dyuot
idav namyn ar hyt ethrykyg un garrec kyuyng ysyd o'r castell hyt y tir.
A'r garrec honno trywyr aruavc a'c catwei rac holl teyrnas ynys Brydein.
Ac eissyoes, arglvyd,' heb yr Vlfin, 'pei Myrdin uard a rodei y weithret   325
vrth dy uedvl di, mi a debygaf y gallut gaffael y wreic vrth dy gyghor.' Ac
yn y lle erchi a wnaeth y brenhin dyuynnu Myrdin attav, canys yn y llu
yd oed.

The Conception of Arthur

A guedy dyuot Myrdin, erchi a wnaethpvt idav rodi kyghor y'r brenhin,
trvy yr hvn y gallei gaffael Eigyr vrth y gyghor. A guedy gvybot o Uyrdin   330
meint oed garyat y wreic a'e serch yn y brenhin, doluryav yn uavr a wnaeth
a dywedut vrthav ual hyn: 'Arglvyd,' heb ef, 'o mynny di gaffael y wreic
vrth dy uynnu mal yd vyt yn y damunav, reit yv yt aruer o geluydodeu
newyd ny chlywyt eryoet y'th amser di. Canys mi a vnn geluydyt trvy
yr hon y gallaf ui rodi drech Gorlois arnat ti hyt na bo neb a adnapo nac   335

a wypo na bo Gorlois uych. Ac vrth hynny, os titheu a'e mynn minheu
a'th rithaf di yn rith Gorlois, ac a rithaf Vlfin yn rith Jurdan o Dindagol.'
Guas ystauell Gorlois oed hvnnv. 'A minheu a gymeraf drech arall arnaf
ac a deuaf yn drydyd y gyt a chui. Ac y uelly y gelly di yn ehouyn dibryder
340 mynet y gastell Tindagol a chaffael y wreic vrth dy gynghor.'

A gorchymyn a wnaeth y brenhin y'v annvylyeit warchadv y castell yn
da a chynnal yr ymlad, ac ymrodi a wnaeth ynteu y geluydodeu Myrdin.
Ac yna y gossodes Myrdin arnav yntev drech Gorlois, ac ar Vlfyn drech
Jurdan o Dindagol, ac ynteu Uyrdin ehun yn ryth Brythael arall, megys
345 na bei neb o'r a'e guelei a vypei na bei y guyr hynny uydynt yn eu guir
drech. Ac odyna kymryt eu hynt a wnaethant parth a chastell Tintagol,
a phan oed gyuliv gvr a llvyn y doethant yno. A guedy mynegi onadunt
y'r porthavr bot yr yarll yn dyuot, agori y pyrth a wnaeth yn diannot ac
eu hellwng y myvn, canyt oed neb o'r a'e guelei a vypei na bei yr yarll uei.
350 A'r nos hon hono kysgu a wnaeth y brenhin y gyt ac Eigyr gan ymrodi y'v
damunedic serch, canys y fals drech a dodassei Uyrdin arnav yr dvyllasei
y wreic, ac y gyt a hynny y geiryeu tvyllodrus dechymygedic a dywedei
ynteu. Canys dywedut vrthi a wnaeth ry dyuot ef yn lledrat o'r castell,
cany allei yr dim uot heb y guelet rac meint oed y ymgeled amdanei,
355 vrth vybot pa ansavd a pha lunyeith a uei arnei ac ar y gastell. A chredu
a wnaeth hythev yr ymadrodyon hynny, a guneuthur y uynnu ef. A'r nos
hon honno y cauas hitheu ueichogi, ac o'r beichogi hvnnv y ganet Arthur,
y gvr clotuorhaf ac arderchocaf a uu o'r genedyl wedy hynny, megys y
dangossant y weithredoed.

Arthur inherits the Kingdom

360 A guedy marv Vthyr Bendragon yd ymgynullassant holl wyrda enys
Brydein, yeirll a barvnyeit a marchogyon urdavl ac esgyb ac abadeu,
hyt yg Caer Uudei, ac o gytsynhyedigaeth pavb yd archassant y Dyuric
archesgob Caer Llion kyssegru Arthur uab Uthyr yn urenhin arnadunt.
Canys eu haghen ac eu kymellei, canys pan gigleu y Saesson marvolaeth
365 Uthyr Bendragon yd anuonassant vynteu ar eu kededyl hyt yn Germania y
geissyav porth, ac yr dothoet attadunt llyghes uavr, a Cholgrim y dywyssavc
arnadunt, y geissyav distryv kenedyl y Brytannyeit yn oreu ac y gellynt.
Ac yr daroed udunt goresgyn o'r parth drav y Humyr, sef oed hynny
tryderan yr enys. A guedi guelet o Dyuryc aghen y bobyl a'e thrueni,
370 kytdoluryav ac vynt a wnaeth, a chyssegru Arthur a gusigav coron y
deyrnas am y ben. A phymtheg mlvyd oed Arthur yna, ac ny chlywssyt ar
neb kynn noc ef y ryv deuodeu oed arnav o nerth a chedernyt a glevder
a daeoni. A chymeint o rat a rodassei Duv idav ac nat oed yn eithauoed
byt o'r a'e clyvei nys carei, ynoethach o'r a'e guelei, a hynny yn anedic
375 ganthav.

A guedy y hardhau o urenhinavl arvydon y deyrnas, ymrodi a wnaeth y haelder hyt nat oed havd idav caffael o da kymeint ac a oed reit idav y rody y'r savl uarchogyon a lithrei attav. Ac eissyoes pvy bynnac a uo ganthav haelder anyanavl y gyd a phrouedic uolyant, ket boet eissyeu arnav ar dalym, ny at Duw wastat achanoctit y argywedu idav. Ac vrth hynny, sef 380 a wnaeth Arthur, can oed yndav molyant yn kedymdeithocau haelder a daeoni, llunyeithu ryuel ar [y] Saesson, hyt pan uei oc eu da vynteu ac og eu svllt y gallei ynteu kyuoethogi y uarchogyon a'e deulu. A yavnder a dysgei y hynny, canys ef a dylyei holl urenhinaeth enys Brydein o wir dreftadavl dylyet. A chynullav a wnaeth holl yeuengtit enys Prydein, a 385 chychuyn parth a Chaer Euravc.

Arthur recovers lost territory and takes a wife

Ac yno yd oed tri broder a hanoydynt o urenhinavl uonhed a dylyet. Sef oed y rei hynny Lleu uab Kynuarch, ac Uryen uab Kynuarch, ac Araun uab Kynuarch. A rei hynny a dylyei tywyssogyaeth y guladoed hynny ac a oed eydynt kyn dyuot y Saesson y eu goresgyn. Ac yna y rodes Arthur 390 y Araun uab Kynuarch brenhinaeth Ysgothlont, ac y Leu uab Kynuarch y rodes yarllaeth Lodoneis ac a berthynei vrthi. Canys yr yn oes Emreis Wledic y rodessit Anna uerch Uthyr, chuaer y Arthur, yn wreic idav, yr hon oed uam Walchmei a Medravt. A guedy hynny y rodes y Uryen uab Kynuarch Reget adan y theruyn. A guedy daruot llunyeithu pob lle, a 395 dvyn yr enys ar y hen teilyngdavt, a rodi y bavb eu dylyet, y kymerth y brenhin wreic a hanoed o dylyedogyon Ruuein, a Guenhvyuar oed y henv ac yn llys Cadvr yarll Kernyv y magadoed. A phryt a thegvch y wreic honno a orchyuygei holl wraged enys Prydein.

Celebrations at Arthur's court in Caer Lleon

A guedy y dyuot enys Prydein, darparu a wnaeth trvy diruavr lewenyd 400 daly llys yn enys Prydein, a guisgav coron y priavt tcyrnas am y bcn, a galv pavb o'r brenhined a'r tywyssogyon a oresgynnassei hyt ar y wled honno. Sef amser oed hynny, y Sulgvyn. Ac aruaethu a wnaeth aruoll pavb trvy lewenyd y atnewydhau tagnheued y rygthunt trvy y teyrnassoed. A guedy menegi ohonav y uedvl y'v annvyleit, oc eu kytgyghor y cavssant darparu 405 y wled honno yg Caer Llion ar Vysg yg Gulat Uorgant. Canys teccaf lle oed hvnnv yn enys Prydein a chyuoethocaf o eur ac aryant a goludoed ereill, ac adassaf y anrydedu gvylua gymeint a honno. Canys o'r neill parth y'r dinas yd oed yr auon uonhedic honno yn arwein y llogheu hyt y dinas a'r brenhined yndunt o pedryuannoed byt, ac o'r parth arall y'r dinas yd 410 oed y gueirglodyeu a'r llvyneu a'r foresteu yn y theccau, ac o uyvn y gaer a'r dinas yd [oed] tei breinhavl goreureit. Ac euo oed eil dinas a gyffelybit y Ruuein o teccet y thei ac amlet y chyuoeth o eur ac aryant a meint y syberwyt. A dvy eglvys arbennic a oed heuyt yn y dinas yn anryded Iulius

415 uerthyr, a mynachloc guerydon yndi, a'r llall yn env Aron y gedymdeith, a
mynachloc canonwyr yndi, a honno oed trydyd archesgobty enys Prydein.
Ac yn yr amser hvnnv arderchavc oed dinas Caer Llion o deu can yscol
ac athraon yn canu yndun o amrauael geluydodeu. A chymeint a paratoet
yna o darmerth ac a oed teilvng y anrydedu y ryv wled honno. Ac yna yd
420 anuonet y bob gulat o'r a oresgynnassei Arthur y wahavd y brenhined a'r
tywyssogyon a'r yeirll a'r barvnyeit a'r marchogyon urdavl a'r guyrda y lys
Arthur y gymryt eu yavn ac eu dylyet ac eu breint.

A guedy ymgynnullav pavb y'r gaer a dyd yr wylua yn dyuot y gelwit
y tri archescob y'r llys vrth wisgav y teyrnwisc am y brenhin a choron y
425 teyrnas am y ben. Ac y Dyuric archescob y gorchymynnvt yr efferen, canys
yn y archescobty yd oedet yn daly y llys. A guedy guisgav am y brenhin,
kychvyn a wnaethpvt, ac ef yn urdasseid, parth ac eglvys yr archescobty,
a'r neill archescob o'r parth deheu idav yn kynnal y wisc, a'r llall o'r
parth assv, ac Araun uab Kynuarch urenhin yr Alban, a Chadwallavn
430 Llavhir urenhin Gvyned, a Meuryc urenhin Dyuet, a Chadvr urenhin
Kernyv yn herwyd eu breint ac eu dylyet yn arwein petwar cledyf eureit
yn noethon yn eu llav o ulaen y brenhin yn mynet y'r eglvys. Ac o bob
parth udunt y cvuenhoed o uynych a chanonwyr ac ysgolheigyon yn
amrauael urdassoed yn eu processio yn canu amrauael geinyadaeth ac
435 organ yn dvyn eu brenhin y'r uam eglwys vrth efferen. Ac o'r parth arall
yd oedet yn dvyn y urenhines yn wisgedic o urenhinavl wisc, a choron o
lavrwyd am y phen, ac esgyb ac athraon yn y chylch yn y dvyn y eglvys
y mynachesseu vrth efferen. Ac o'e blaen hitheu yn herwyd eu breint ac
eu dylyet pedeir guraged y brenhined a dywetpvt uchot yn arwein pedeir
440 colomen purwynnyon yn eu llav. Ac y gyt a hynny yr holl wraged gan
diruavr lewenyd yn y chanlhyn hitheu parth a'r eglvys vrth efferen.

A guedy daruot y processio ym pob un o'r dvy eglvys, kymeint oed yr
organ a'r geinnyadaeth a rac digriuet oed eu guarandav hyt na vydynt y
marchogyon yr dothoed yno pa un gyntaf o'r dvy eglvys a gyrchynt rac
445 dahet y kenit ym pob un onadunt, namyn kerdet yn doruoed o'r eglvys pvy
gilid. Ac ni magei ulinder udunt pei treulit yr holl dyd trvy wassanaeth
yr efferenneu. A guedy daruot kvplau dvywavl wassanaeth ym pob
un o'r dvy eglvys, guaret a wnaethpvt y am y brenhin a'r urenhines eu
brenhinolyon wisgoed, a guisgav amdanunt ysgavyn wisgoed.

450 Ac odyno yd aeth y brenhin y'r neuad, a'r guyr oll y gyt ac ef, a'r urenhines
y'r ystauell, a'r guraged oll y gyt a hitheu. A guedy gossot pavb y eisted yn
herwyd eu anryded, y kyuodes Kei pen svydwr yn adurnedic o ermynwisc,
a mil o dylyedogyon y gyt ac ef o un adurn a guisc ac ynteu, i wassanaethu
o'r gegin. Ac o'r parth arall y kyuodes Bedwyr pen trullyat, a mil y gyt

ac ynteu yn adurnedic o amrauael ac amliv wisgoed, y wassanaethu o'r 455
uedgell trvy amraualyon lestri, gorulycheu a phioleu eur ac aryant a chyrn
buelin goreureit y wallav amraualyon wirodeu y bavb herwyd y dirperei y
anryded. Ac o'r parth arall y hynny, yn neuad y urenhines yd oed aneiryf o
wassanaethwyr yn adurnedic o amrauaelyon ac amliv wisgoed yn rodi eu
gwassanaeth yn anrydedus yn herwyd kynneuavt. Ac yna yd oed amlvc ry 460
dyuot enys Prydein y'v hen ansavd a'e chyuoeth a'e drythyllvch yn gymeint
ac nat oed un teyrnas a ellit y chyffelybu idi. Ac a uei o uarchavc clotuavr,
o un rvysc ac arueu yd aruerynt. A'r gorderchwraged o un ryv dywygyat
yd aruerynt hvynteu, ac ny bydei teilvng gan un wreic kymryt un gvr
yn orderch idi yna namyn un a uei prouedic teir gueith y milvryaeth. 465
Ac y uelly diweirach yd ymwnaei y guraged, a chlotuorach yd ymwnaei y
marchogyon y milvryaeth.

Medrawd's Treachery

A phan ydoed yr haf yn dyuot, ac Arthur yn esgynnu mynyded Mynheu
vrth uynet y oresgyn Ruuein, nachaf kennadeu o enys Prydein yn menegi
idav bot Medravt y nei uab y chuaer wedy guisgav coron enys Prydein 470
trvy greulonder a brat, a ry gysgu gan Wenhvyuar urenhines, gan lygru
kyureith dvywavl neithoryeu.

Ac vrth hynny, ymchuelut a wnaeth ynteu tracheuyn, ac ellvng Howel
uab Emyr Llydav y tangneuedu y guladoed hynny a llu Freinc ganthav.
A chychuyn a oruc ynteu a guyr yr enyssed y gyt ac ef parth ac enys 475
Prydein. Ac yna yd anuonassei y bradvr tvyllvr ysgymun gan Uedravt
Selinx tywyssavc y Saesson hyt yn Germania y wahavd y niuer mvyhaf a
allei y gaffael hyt yn enys Prydein yn borth idav, gan rodi udunt o'r tu drav
y Hvmyr, ac yn ychwenec y hynny yr hyn a rodassei Gortheyrn Gortheneu
y Hors a Heingyst yn svyd Geint. A guedy cadarnhau yr amuot hvnnv y 480
rygthunt y doeth y tywyssavc ac vyth gan llong ganthav o Germania yn
llavn o paganyeit arvavc, a gvrhau y Vedravt megys y urenhin. Ac yn
achuanec y hynny ncur daroed idav duunav ac ef yr Yscotyeit a'r Fychteit
a'r Gvydyl yn erbyn Arthur y ewythyr. Sef oed eiryf y lu y gyt, y rvng
cristonogyon a phaganyeit, petwar vgein mil. Ac a hynny o niuer y gyt ac 485
ef y doeth yn erbyn Arthur hyt yg glan y mor y borth Northamtvn,[20] a
rodi brvydyr galet idav yn dyuot o'r llongeu y'r tir.

Ac yna y dygvydassant Araun uab Kynuarch urenhin Ysgothlont a
Gualchmei uab Guyar nei y brenhin, ac ar nyt oed havd eu rifav y gyt ac
vynt. Ac yn lle Araun uab Kynuarch y dodet Owein uab Vryen yn urenhin, 490
gvr a uu glotuavr wedy hynny yn llawer o uolyanheu. Ac eissyoes ket bei

---

[20] RB *hyt yn aber temys* 'as far as the Thames estuary'.

trvy lauur diruavr, Arthur a'e lu a gauas y tir, a guedy llad llawer onadunt kymell Medravt a'e lu ar fo. A chet bei mvy niuer Medravt, eissyoes trvy dysc guastat a pheunydyavl aruer ar ymlad, doethach a chymhennach
495   oed niuer Arthur. Ac vrth hynny y bu reit y Vedravt kymryt y fo. Ac yn y lle eissyoes ymgynnullav a wnaethant ar Vedravt y wasgaredicyon o bob man, a chyrchu hyt nos yny doethant y Gaer Wynt, a chadarnhau y dinas yn eu kylch. A phan doeth y chuedleu hynny ar Wenhvyuar urenhines, sef a wnaeth hitheu anobeithav yn uavr, a mynet o Gaer Euravc hyt yg Caer
500   Llion ar Vysc a guisgav amdanei yn uynaches y gyt a'r mynachesseu oed yno yn eglvys Julius Uerthyr, ac arwein eu habit odyna hyt agheu.

Ac ym pen y trydyd dyd, guedy daruot cladu y guyr lladedigyon, kychwyn a wnaeth Arthur am pen Caer Wynt yn flemychedic o lit am ry golli y savl ry gollassei o'e wyr gan Vedravt a'e lu. A guedy gvybot o Vedravt eu bot
505   yg kylch y dinas, bydinav a wnaeth ynteu, gan annoc y gedymdeithyon ac eu moli oc eu devred, a chyrchu allan y rodi cat ar uaes y'v ewythyr. A guedy dechreu y vrvydyr honno, diruavr aerua a wnaethpvt o bob parth, ac eissyoes mvhaf a las o barth Medravt, ac yn y diwed kymell arnav adav y maes a fo yn dybryt gewilyduus.

The Battle of Camlan

510   Ac ny handenvs Arthur,[21] hagen yna gohir vrth cladu y calaned, vrth ry dianc y bratwr y ganthav y mynychet hvnv, namyn gan diruavr urys kymryt y ford parth a Chernyv yny doeth hyt ar auon Camlan, y lle yd oed Uedravt a'e lu yn y arhos, gan uedylyav ohonav bot yn tegach idav y lad yno, neu ynteu a orffei, nogyt fo o le y le yn waradvydus a uei hvy no hynny.
515   Yd oed ganthav hagen etwa o'e lu chue guyr a chuech canwr a thriugein mil. Ac o hynny y gunaeth chue bydin, ac ym pob un onadunt chue guyr a thri ugeint a chuechant a chue mil, a thywyssogyon ar bob un onadunt. Ac o'r hyn nyt aeth yn y bydinoed y gunaeth lleng ordethol y gyt ac ef ehun. A guedy daruot idav lluneithu y uydinoed yn y wed hono, adav a wnaeth
520   y bavb onadunt, os ef a oruydei, medyant mavr eur ac aryant, meirch ac anryded, tir a daear a chyuoeth, ac erchi udunt o un uryt seuyll ac ymlad y gyt ac ef.

Ac o'r parth arall, gossot a wnaeth Arthur y lu ynteu trvy nav bydin, a thywyssogyon neilltuedic doeth y bob un onadunt. Ac annoc y pavb
525   a wnaeth ynteu llad y paganyeit ysgymunedic heb uedyd arnunt, y ry dugassei ynteu y bradvr tvyllvr ysgymun gan Vedravt attav y geissyav digyuoethi y ewythyr a'e dianrydedu. Ac achuanegu y ymadravd heuyt a oruc yn y wed hon vrth y lu: 'Y llu a welvch chui raccw yn avch erbyn,

---

[21]   H1 *ny handynwys arthur*, RB *ny hanbwyllwys Medrawt.*

o amrauael enyssed yd henynt, ac aghyurvys ynt ar ymlad. A chuitheu
kyneuyn gyurvys yvch o dysc peunydyavl ymlad. Ac vrth hynny ny   530
allant gvrthvynebu yvch na seuyll yn avch erbyn.' A guedy daruot udunt
annoc eu lluoed o bob parth, ar hynny ymgymysgu a wnaeth y bydinoed
a dechreu ymgymynu. A chymeint uu yr aerua yna o bob parth hyt pan
oed y rei byv yn ynuydu gan gvynuan y rei meirv, mal yd oed truan a
dolurus na'e datcanu na'e ysgriuennu. Canys o bob parth y brathei y guyr   535
ac y brethyt vynteu, y lladei ac y lledit vynteu.

A guedy treulyav llawer o'r dyd yn y wed honno, kyrchu a wnaeth
Arthur a'e uydin megys llew dywal newynavc y uydin y gvydyat bot y
bratvr tvyllvr anudonyl ysgymun gan Uedravt, ac agori fyrd a'r cledyueu
udunt, a guneuthur aerua antrugaravc onadunt. Ac ar y ruthyr hvnnv   540
y llas y bratvr gan Uedravt a llawer o uilyoed y gyt ac ef. Ac yr hynny
eissyoes ny foes y lleill, namyn kynnal eu hymlad yn vravl tra allassant
seuyll. Ac yna y bu y vrvydyr galetaf o'r a uu yn enys Prydein na chyn
no hynny na guedy, hyt pan dygvydassant yr holl tywyssogyon o bob
parth, ac vynt ac eu bydinoed. Ac o barth Medravt y llas Cheldeic ac   545
Elaes ac Ebrict a Himing, tywyssogyon Saesson, Gillamvri a Gillapatric
a Gillassor a Gillari o'r Gvydyl, yr Yscotyeit, a'r Fychteit, ac eu holl niuer
hayach a las.

Ac o parth Athur y llas Ebryct urenhin Llychlyn, ac Achel urenhin
Denmarc, a Chadvr Llymenic, a Chaswallavn, a llawer o uilyoed y gyt   550
ac vynt, y rvng Brytanyeit a chenedloed ereill. Ac y gyt a hynny yr
arderchavc urenhin Arthur a urathvt yn agheuavl, ac odyno a ducpvt hyt
yn enys Auallach y yachau y welioed. Ac ny dyweit y llyuyr amdanav a uo
diheuach na hyspyssach na hynny. Coron teyrnas enys Prydein hagen a
gymynnvs y Gustennyn uab Cadvr y gar ehun a'e gyfnessaf, ac ysef amser   555
oed hynny: dvy ulyned a deu ugeint a phymi cant guedy geni mab Duv o'r
Arglvydes Veir Wyry, y gvr a brynvs y cristonogyon da yr creu y gallon.

THE LOST SOVEREIGNTY OF BRITAIN

*Cadwaladr was the last king to hold sway over the whole British nation but
his success was short-lived. Britain was beset by plague and Cadwaladr fled
to Britanny. When the pestilence was over, Britain was once again a target for
invasion, but Cadwaladr was deterred from his intention of re-establishing
his rule by an angelic voice, which instructed him to go to Rome to do
penance and to be beatified by the Pope.*

*The three reports of Cadwaladr's death (A.D. 681) demonstrate clearly the
difference in style between Geoffrey and that of the unknown authors of the
Bruts which continue the History to the thirteenth century and beyond.*

From Lewis, *Brut Dingestow*, XII 18–19,

Ac yna yd ymedewis Catwaladyr Uendigeit ac yd ymvrthodes a phob
peth bydavl yr caryat tragywydavl teyrnas Duv, ac yd aeth hyt yn Ruuein.

560　Ac yna y cadarnhavs Sergius pap ef ym plith eiryf y seint gleinnyon, ac
yn y lle o deissyuyt heint y cleuychvs, ac yn y deudecuet dyd wedy Calan
Mei yd aeth o'r byt hvn ef y tragywydavl teyrnas wlat nef, yn yr vythuet
vlvydyn a phetwar ugeint a seith gant guedy geni mab Duv o'r Arglvydes
Ueir Wyry.

565　　Ac yna wedy kynnullav o'r Iuor uab Catwaladyr ac Ini y keuynderv yr
hyn a allassant o longeu vynt a doethant hyt yn enys Prydein, ac vyth
mlyned a thrugeint y buant yn ryuelu y dywal ac yn wastat ar y Saesson.
A nyt mavr dygrynoes udunt, canys y uarwavl tymestyl a uuassei o uall a
newyn yr daroed idi llad a distryv syberv genedyl y vrthunt. Ac o hynny

570　allan ny elwit vynt yn Urytanyeit, namyn yn Gymry. Ac o hynny allan
y gunaeth y Saesson yn gall ac yn doeth cadv tagnheued a duundeb y
rygthvnt ehunein, a diwyllyav y tired ac adeilat y dinassoed a'r kestyll. Ac
y uelly y bvryassant arglvydiaeth y Brytanyeit y arnadunt, ac vynt ehunein
yn medu holl Loegyr adan Edelstan yn tywyssavc arnadunt, y gvr kyntaf

575　o'r Saesson a wisgvs coron y teyrnas. Ac o hynny allan y colles priavt
genedyl yr enys eu henv ac eu dylyet, ac ny allassant y chaffael o hynny
allan, namyn yn uynych neu ynteu yn wastat godef keithiwet Saseson
arnadunt.

From Jones, *Brut y Tywysogyon Peniarth MS. 20 Version*, p.1.

Pedwar vgein mlyneδ a chwechant ac vn oyd oed Krist pan vu varwolaeth

580　vawr yn Ynys Brydein. Yn y vlwyδyn honno yδ aeth Kadwaladyr vab
Kadwallawn y brenhin dwaythaf a vv ar y Brytanyeid y Rufein ac yno y bu
varw y deuδecved dyδ o Galan Mei. Ac o hynny allan y kolles y Brytanyeid
goron teyrnas ac y kafas y Saesson hi, megys y proffwydassei Verδin wrth
Wrtheyrn Wrtheneu. Ac yn ol Kadwaladyr y dynessahawδ Iuor vab Alan

585　vrenhin Llydaw, nid megys brenin namyn megys tywyssawc. A hwnnw a
gynhelis pennaduryaeth ar y Brytanyeid wyth mlyneδ a deugeint ac yna
y bu varw.

From Jones, *Brenhinedd y Saesson*, p.2.

Gwedy daruot yr anodun vall dymhestylus a'r newyn girat, a dywetpwyt
vchot, yn oes Catwaladyr Vendigeit, y doeth y Saesson a goresgyn Lloegyr

590　o'r mor pwy gilid, a'y chynal a dan pymp brenhin, val y buassei gynt yn
oes Hors a Hengist, pan deholassant Gortheyrn Gortheneu o deruynev
Lloegyr, ac a'y rannassant yn pymp ran ryngthunt. Ac yna y symvdassant
henweu y dinessyd a'r trefi a'r randiroed a'r cantrefoed a'r sswidev a'r

ardaloed herwyd ev yeith wynt ehvn: London y galwassant Caer Llud;
Evirwic nev Jorck y galwassant Caer Effrauc; ac val hynny holl dinessyd   595
Lloegyr a symvdassant ev henweu, o'r rei yd aruerwyt yr hynny hyt
hediw onadunt. Hwndrwt y galweint cantref; ssire y galweint sswyd. Ac
y dwyn ar gof y'r neb a delei rac llaw yr arwyd dwillodrus ysgymvn a uu
ryngthunt pan ladassant holl deledogeon Ynys Brydeyn ar Vynyd Ambri,
sef oed hynny, 'Draweth howre sexes'; — ac am hynny y galwassant y   600
randiroed West ssex, Est Ssex, Sswth Ssex yr hynny hyt hediw.

NEST AND OWAIN

In Brut y Tywysogion *the events of the twelfth century are described in
greater detail than those recorded for earlier centuries, which are brief, terse
and annalistic. The episode of Nest and Owain has all the narrative qualities
of a good story. Nest was the daughter of Rhys ap Tewdwr, the last ruler of
Deheubarth. In 1100, she married Gerald of Windsor, who was appointed
Constable of Pembroke Castle by Henry I. She was renowned for her beauty
and has been called the 'Helen of Wales' because of her abduction by Owain
ap Cadwgan, possibly with her own connivance. She had many lovers,
including king Henry I, and is said to have had at least seventeen children.
One of her daughters, Angharad, was the mother of Gerald de Barry (Gerald
of Wales).*

From Jones, *Brut y Tywysogyon Peniarth MS. 20 Version*, pp. 41–47.

The Violation of Nest

[1106–1109] Blwy[dy]n wedy hynny y paratoes Kadgwawn vab Bledynt
brenhinyawl wled y wyrda y wlad, a gwahawd Ywein y vab o Bowys y'r
wled. A'r wled honno a wnaeth ef y Nodolic yr anryded y Yessu Grist.[22]
A gwedy daruod y wled klybot a wnaeth Ywein vod Nest verch yr   605
Arglwyd Rys ap Teudwr, gwreic Gerald swydwr,[23] yn y dywededic kastell.
A phan gigleu, mynd a oruc ac ychydic o niuer gyd ac ef y ymweled
a hi, megis a chyueilles; ac velly ydoeδ, kanys Kadwgawn ap Bledynt a
Gwladus verch Riwallawn, yr honn a oed vam y Nest a oedynt gefynderw
a chefnitherw, kanys Bledyn a Riwallawn a oedynt vrodyr, meibyon   610
Kynuyn o Angharad, verch Varedud vrenhin. A gwedy hynny drwy
anogedigaeth kythreul, kyffroi a wnaeth ef o serch a charyad y wreic, a
chyrchu y kastell ac ychydic o nifer gyd ac ef, megis yghylch pedwar gwyr
ar dec, o hyd nos; a heb wybod y'r gwylwyr, dros y mur a'r fos y doeth ef
y'r kastell a chylchynu y ty yn lle yd oed Gerald a Nest, y wreic, yn kysgu.   615

---

[22] BT (RB) *y Duw.*
[23] BT (RB) *ystiwart*, BS *gwassanaethwr.*

A dodi gawr ynghylch y ty a dodi tan yn y tei a'y ennynnu. A deffroi a oruc
Gerald o'y hun ac ofynhau, pan gigleu yr awr, a heb wybod beth a wnae.
A'y wreic a dyuod wrthaw, 'Na dos y'r drws, kanys yno y mae dy elynyon
yn y kylch, namyn dyred gyd a myuy.' Ac velly y gwnaeth ef. A hitheu a'y
620   duc ef y'r ysteuyll bychein a oed yghysswllt a'r ty, a thrwy dwll yr ysteuyll
bychein y diengis.

      A gwedy gwybod o Nest yn yspys y diang, gweidi o vewn a wnaeth
hi a dywedud, 'Pa beth a waedwch chwi yn ouer? Neur diengis y neb yd
oedoch yn y geissyaw.' Ac wynteu yna a doethant y mewn ac a'y keissasant
625   ymhob lle. A gwedy nas kawssant, daly Nest a wnaethant a'y deu vab, a'r
trydyd mab, a oed y Gerald o orderch, a merch. Ac yspeilyaw y kastell yn
gwbyl a wnaethant a'y losgi. A threissyaw Nest a wnaeth ef a bod genthi,
ac odyna ymchwelud adref. Kadwgan, y dad ef, nyd oed yn y lle, kanys ef a
athoed y Bowys y hedychu rei a oedynt yn erbyn Ywein, y vab, ac a athoed
630   ymeith y wrthaw.

      A phan gigleu Gadwgawn y chwedyl hwnnw, drwc vv ganthaw a brawhau
a wnaeth ef o dwy ford: o achaws treis yr arglwydes ac o achaws ofyn Henri
vrenhin am sarhaed y swydwr. A phan doeth ef dracheuyn, keissyaw
a wnaeth talu y wreic dracheuyn a'r anreith o bob ford, ac ny adpwyd
635   ydaw. Ac Ywein, o achaws y wreic a oed yn dywedud wrthaw yn wastad,
'O mynnu vynghael i yn gywir a'm kynnal ytt, gyllwg vy meibyon yw y
tad.' — ac o dra charyad y wreic, ef a yllyngawd y deu vab a'r verch.

The Consequences of Owain's Act of Violence

A phan gigleu Richyard, esgob Llundein, a oed swydwr yna y'r brenhin
yn Amwythic hynny, medylyaw a oruc ef dial sarhaed Gerald ar Ywein.
640   A galw attaw deu vab Riryd ap Bledyn, nyd amgen Madoc ac Ithael, a
dywedud wrthun val hynn, 'A vynnwch chw[i] ryngu bod y Henri vrenhin,
a haedu kyueillyach y ganthaw yn dragywydawl? Ac ef a'ch anrydeda
ac a'ch dyrcheif yn vwch no neb o'ch kydtirogyon ac a gyngoruynna
wrthywch ych holl genedyl.' 'Mynnwn', heb wynt. 'Ewch chwitheu,' heb
645   ef, 'a cheisswch Ywein vab Kadwgan a delywch ef, os gellwch. Ac onys
gellwch, gyrrwch ef a'y dad o'r kyfoeth ymeith, kanys gwnaeth gam yn
erbyn y brenhin, ac ef a wnaeth sarhaed a chywilyd y'r arglwyd vrenhin
a cholled vawr y Gerald y swydwr am y wreic a'y veibyon a'y gastell a'y
anreithyeu. A minneu a rodaf y chwi y kydmeithyon kywiraf a fydlonaf
650   nyd amgen, Llywarch vab Trahayarn, y gwr y lladawd Ywein y vrodyr, ac
Vchdryd ap Edwin.'

      Ac wynteu a gredassant hynny ac a gynnullassant luoed ac a doethant
ygyd ac a gyrchassant y wlad. Ac Vchdryd a anuones nifer y'r wlad ac

a orchymynnawd y bawb o'r a ffoei attaw ef kaffael onadunt amdiffyn. A llawer a gyrchassant attaw. A rei a gyrchawd Arwystli, ereill Vaelenyd, 655 ereill Ystrad Tywi, a'r rann vwyaf onadunt a gyrchawd Dyued, yn lle yd oed Gerald yn bennaf. Ac val ydoed ynteu yn mynnu ev diuetha wynt, ef a damweinnyawd y dyd hwnnw ry dyuod Gwallter, goruchaf ystus Kaer Loyw, y gwr y gorchymynnassei y brenhin lywodraeth teyrnas Loegyr ydaw, y Gaervyrdyn; a hwnnw a'y hamdiffynnawd rac eu diuetha. 660 Y rei a aeth Arwystli onadunt, y kyuarvv wyr Maelenyd ac wynt, ac y diuawyd. Y rei a gyrchassant ar Vchdryd onadunt, a diengis yn digoded. Y rei a gyrchawd Ystrad Tywi onadunt, a aruolles Maredud vab Ryderch yn hygar. Kadgwawn ac Ywein a gyrchassant llong a oed yn Aberdyfi, a dathoed kynn no hynny o Ywerdon a chyfnewid yndi. 665

Madoc ac Ithael y vrau[d] a Llywarch a doethant yn erbyn Vchdryd, a phebyllu a orugant yn y ryd a elwir Ryd Corruonet. Ac yn y diwed y doeth Vchdryd. Ac ef yn dyuod yno, y mynnassant wy gerded hyd nos yny gyuodei y dyd, y diffeithyaw y wlad. Ac ynteu a dyuod, 'Os da gennwch, nyd reid hynny', heb ef. 'Namyn ny dylyir tremygu Kadgwawn ac Ywein y 670 vab, kanys gwyr da kanmoledic ynt; a llawer o nerthoed agatuyd a gant ar nyd ydyw gyd ac wynt yr awr honn. Ac wrth hynny ny weda y ni vyned mor anhyspys a hynny, namyn kyweiryaw llu a lliw dyd goleu myned.' Ac o'r geiryeu hynny yr hedychwyd wynt ychydic, ac o hynny y gallawd y giwdawd diang. 675

Trannoeth y doethant wy y'r wlat. A gwedy y gweled yn diffeith, ymgerydu wynt ehun a wnaethant a chyhudaw Vchdryd a dywedud mae dichellyon Vchdryd oed hynny ac na wedei y neb ymgydmeithyaw ac ef. A gwibyaw a wnaethant a heb gaffael dim eithyr gre Gadwgan. A gwedy y chaffael, llosgi a orugant y tei a'r ysguboryeu a'r ydau ac ymchwelud y'r kcotyll drachcuyn. A diffeithyaw rei o'r a foaccei ar nawd y Lannbadern; ereill nys diuaassant. Ac yna y klywssant ry drigaw rei yn y lle y mae budygolyaeth a nawd y Dewi esgob, ac a elwir Llanndewivreui, gyd ac effeiryeid yr eglwys. Ac anuon a orugant y melldigedic drycysprydawl gyweithas hyd yno y lygru nawd yr eglwys ac y diua y giwdawd. A gwedy 685 hynny ymchwelud a orugant, wedy diffeithyaw ac anreithyaw y wlad oll, eithyr kyfleoed y seint e hunein — Dewi a Phadarn. A gwedy hynny mordwyaw a oruc Ywein ac ychydic o gydmeithyon, a vvessynt yn llosgi y kastell gyd ac ef, tu ac Ywerdon. A Murcard vrenhin, y pennaf o'r Gwydyl, a'y haruolles yn anrydedus, kanys gyd ac ef y buassei ef gynn no hynny, 690 pan vvassei y ryuel y Mon y gan y deu yeirll, wedy anuon o'y vrawd a rodyon y'r brenhin.

Kadwgawn a ymgelawd yngwlad Bowys ac anuon kennaadeu a wnaeth ar Richyard, swydwr y brenhin, a chaffael kyngreir y ganthaw, yny
695 hedychei a'r brenhin, pa ffuryf bynnac y gallei. A'r brenhin odyna a'y haruolles ac a'y gadawd mywn tref a gawssei ef gan y wreic, a oed Franges, merch y Pigod o Saesis. Yghyfrwg y petheu hynny, Madoc ac Ithael, meibyon Riryd, a achubassant rann Gadwgawn ac Ywein y vab o Bowys, a llywyassant yn anuolyannus ac yn aflwydyanus, kanys ny bu hedwch y
700 rygthunt ehunein.

A gwedy daruod hynny oll, ef a brynnawd Kadwgawn y gyfoeth ygHeredigyawn y gan y brenhin, drwy diruawryon wedieu, yr kanpunt. A phawb o'r a wasgaressit y bob lle a ymgynnullassant yno dracheuyn, kanys gorchymyn y brenhin a oed kynn no hynny, na thrigei neb
705 ygHeredigyawn, na chiwdawdwyr na gwyr dieithyr, ac na chynnhalyei neb wynt. A than yr amod hwnn y rodes y brenhin y dir y Gadwgawn: na bei gydmeithas yn y byd y ryngthaw ac Ywein, y vab, ac nas gadei y dyuod y'r tir ac nas kannorthwyei o neb ryw gyngor na nerth. A gwedy hynny yr ymchwelawd rei o'r a athoed y Werdon gyd ac Ywein ac ymgydyaw yn
710 geladwy gyd a chenedyl vdunt heb wneuthur dim ar gyhoed. A gwedy hynny yr ymchwelawd Ywein, ac nyd y Geredigyawn y trosses ef, namyn y Bowys a cheissyaw anuon kennadeu ar y brenhin; ac nyd oed neb a lauassei vyned ar y gennadwri.

GRUFFUDD AP CYNAN (c. 1055 — 1137)

Gruffudd ab Kenan was born in Dublin to a Welsh father and Irish-Scandinavian mother. He has the distinction of being the subject of the only extant biography to a lay person in medieval Wales written in Welsh. The following passages recount his struggle to claim his lost patrimony in Gwynedd, north Wales.

From Evans, *Historia Gruffud vab Kenan*, pp. 1, 17, 21, 6–7, 13–16.

Birth and Lineage

En dydyeu Edward, vrenhin Lloegyr a Therdelach, vrenhin Ywerdon
715 e ganet Gruffud vrenhin Gwyned en Ywerdon, en dinas Dulyn; ac yg kymvt Colomcell y magwyt, lle a elwir yg Gwydelec Svrth Colomcell. A tri milltir yv henne y urth y lle yd oed y vam a'e vamvaeth.

Y dat oed Kenan, vrenhin Gvyned, a'e vam oed Ragnell verch Avloed, vrenhin dinas Dulyn a phymet rann Ywerdon. Ac urth henne, bonhedicaf
720 gur oed y Gruffud hvnnv o vrenhinyaul genedel a llinyoed goruchel, megys y tysta ac[h] a bonhed y reeni.

Appearance and Character

Kedymdeitheon gvahanredaul Grufud a dywedynt y uot ef en wr
kymedraul y veint, a gvallt melyn arnav, ac emennyd guressauc, ac wynep
crwnn, da y liw, a llygeit maur guedus, ac aeleu tec, a baryf wedus, a
mvnugyl crwnn, a chnaut gvynn, ac aelodeu grymus, a byssed hiryon, ac   725
esgeiryeu vnyaun, a thraet tec. Kywreint oed a huaudel en amravaellyon
yeithyoed. Bonhedic oed enteu, a thrugarauc urth y givdaut, a chreulavn
urth y elynyon, a gwychraf em bruyder.

Marriage

Ac val yd oed Gruffud y velly, weithieu en rwyd, weithyeu en afruyd
racdav, ef a gymyrth gureic, Angharat y henv, merch y Ewein vab Edwin,   730
er honn a dywedynt doethyon y kyuoeth y bot en vonhedic, hyduf,
walltwenn, lygatvras, oskethloyu, a chorff gualcheid, ac aelodeu grymus,
ac esgeiryeu hyduf, a'r traet goreu, a byssed hiryon, ac ewined teneu;
hynavs, a huaudel, a da o uwyt a llynn, a doeth a chall, a chynghorwreic da,
trugarauc urth y chyuoeth, a chardodus urth achanogyon, a chyfreithus   735
ym pob peth. Ac o honno y bu idav meibeon a merchet. Enw y meibeon
vu Catwallavn, ac Ewein, a Chatwalader. A'e verchet oed Guenlliant, a
Maryret, a Rainillt a Sussanna, ac Annest. Ef a vu veibeon a merchet idav
heuyt o garyatwraged.

Gruffudd's youth

Pan ytoed Gruffud etwa en vab da y deuodeu a drythyll y vagyat, ac   740
yn esgynnv ar vlwydyned y yeuengtit en ty e vam, ac en troi ymplith y
chenedel, ymplith henne y managei y vamm idav beunyd pwy a pha ryv
wr oed y dat, a pha dref tat oed idav, a pha ryw vrenhinyaeth, a pha ryv
dreiswyr a oed en e phressvyllyav. A phan gigleu enteu henne, gorthrum
y kemyrth a thrist vu llawer o dydyeu. Ac urth henne y kerdus enteu y   745
lys Mvrchath vrenhin, a chvynav urthav ef en benhaf, ac urth vrenhined
Ywerdon y lleill, bot estravn genedloed en argluydi ar y dadaul deyrnas,
ac adolwyn udunt yn ysmalha rodi canorthuy idav y geissyav tref y dat.
A thruanu urthav a orugant, ac adav canorthuy idav pan delei amser.
A phan gigleu er atep, llawen vu, a dioluch henne y Duw ac udunt   750
wynteu.

Attempt to recover his lost patrimony

En y lle esgynnv llong a oruc, a dyrchavael hwyllyeu y'r gvynt, a cherdet
mor parth a Chemry, a chaffael porth Abermenei. Ac ena yd oedent
en argluydiau yn enwir ac en erbyn dylyet Trahaearn vab Caradauc a
Chenwric vab Riwallavn brenhinyn o Bowys, ar holl Wyned, a'e rannv y   755
rygthunt ry daroed udunt.

Ac ena yd anvones Gruffud gennadeu ar wyr Mon ac Arvon, a thri meib
Merwyd o Leyn, ac Asser a Meiryavn a Gugavn, a guyrda ereill, y erchi
udunt dyuot ar vrys y gyfruch ac ef. Ac hep ohir wynteu a doethant, a
760   chyvarch guell idav, a dywedut urthav: 'O damunet ry doethost.' Ena yd
adolygus enteu o'e holl enni udunt hwy y ganorthuyav y gaffael tref y dat,
canys ef oed eu hargluyd priodaur, a gurthlad y gyt ac ef yn wychyr o
arveu eu ampriodoryon argluydi dyuot o le arall.

Ac en e bei tervynedic y kyfruch, a gvahanedic y kyngor y kerdus
765   drachevyn y weilgi parth a chastell Rudlan hyt ar Robert Rudlan, barwn
enwavc, dewr o gedernyt, nei y Hu yarll Caer, a'e wediav a oruc am
ganorthuy en erbyn y elynyon a oedent ar dref y dat. A phan gigleu enteu
puy oed ef, ac y ba beth ry dothoed, a pha arch oed er eidav, ef a edewis
bot en ganorthuywr idav.

The Alliance between Gruffudd ap Cynan and Rhys ap Tewdwr

770   Ac en henne, wedy bot Gruffud bluydyned en Ywerdon, megys yn trwydet
y gyt a Diermit vrenhin ac y gyt a'r guyrda ereill, en y diwed ef a gynnvllus
llynges vrenhinyaul o Borthlarc a rodassei y brenhin idaw, en llavn o
Daenysseit a Gvydyl a Brytanyeit. A guedy lledu hwyllyeu ar e mor, a'r
gvynt en hyrwyd oc eu hol, a'r mor en dangneuedus, ef a doeth y Borth
775   Cleis ker llaw archescopty Mynyv.

Ac ene y kerdus Rys m. Teudur, brenhin deheubarth Kemry, a'r escop
a'e athraon a holl clas er argluyd Dewi ac vn eglvys Vynyv, hyt e borth.
A Rys gentaf a emadrodes val hynn a'r argluyd Gruffud: 'Hanbych well
Gruffud, brenhin brenhined Kemry! Atat ti yd wyf vi en fo. Rac dy
780   vronn y digvydaf ar dal vy glinyeu y erchi dy ganorthvy a'th nerth.' 'Pwy
wyt titheu,' hep y Gruffud, 'ac y ba beth ry doethost ema?' 'Rys wyf vi,'
hep enteu, 'm. Teudur, argluyd y kyuoeth hvnn ychydic kynn no hynn.
Ac er aur hon, en urthladedic ac en foedic ac en divlanedic haeach, yd
wyf en emdirgelu en e nodua honn.' 'Pwy a'th foes di?' hep y Gruffud.
785   'Argluyd,' hep enteu, 'tri brenhin o'r guladoed pennaf o Gemry ac eu
lluoed a disgynnassant y'm kyuoeth y diwed hvnn, a pheunyd e maent en
y hanreithyav.' 'Pwy,' hep e Gruffud, 'y brenhined a gerdant trwy dy wyr
di a'th gyuoeth mor vydinauc a henne?' 'Caradauc m. Grufud,' hep enteu,
'o Went Uch Coet ac Is Coet a'e Wenhvyssyon, a gvyr Morgannvc, a llawer
790   o albryswyr Nordmannyeit ganthav; Meilir m. Riwallaun a'e Bowyswyr
ganthav, Trahaearn vrenhin a gwyr Arwystli.'

A phan gigleu Gruffud enw y ormeswyr, froeni o gyndared a oruc,
a govyn idav pa beth a rodei er emlad drostav en erbyn y gvyr henne.
'Dyoer,' hep y Rys, 'hanner vyg kyuoeth a rodaf yt, ac y gyt a henne

guryogaeth a wnaf yt.' A chyvun a henne vu Gruffud. A guedy y kyfruch 795
hvnnv, wynt a gerdassant y gyt y egluys Dewi yn eu guedi. Ac eno yd
emwnaethant en geueillyon fydlavn trwy aruoll y greiryeu.

The Battle of Mynydd Carn

A guedy emdivnav onadunt en y lle honno a chemryt bendith er escop,
Gruffud a gerdus en er vn dyd hvnnv racdav, ef a'e Daenysseit a'e Wydyl
a llawer o Wyndit riuedi wyth ugeinwyr, a Chendelu m. Conus o Von oc 800
eu blaen. Rys enteu ac ychydic Deheuwyr a gerdus gyt ac wy, en llawen
ganthav y vryt o'e ganhorthvy.

A guedy kerdet dirvaur emdeith diwyrnaut, yg kylch gosper wynt a
doethant y venyd, en e lle yd oed lluesteu y dywededigyon vrenhined
uchof. Ac ene y dywaut Rys urth Ruffud vrenhin, 'Argluyd,' hep ef, 805
'annodun y vrvyder hyt avory, canys gosper yu er aur honn, a'r dyd ysyd
en trengi.' 'Annot di,' hep y Gruffud dan igyon, 'os mynny. Mivi a'm bydin
a ruthraf udunt hwy.' Ac y velly y bu. A dechrynv a orugant y brenhined
eissyoes, val y guelsant y torvoed budugaul amravael a bedinoed Gruffud
vrenhin a'e arwydyon yn eu herbyn, a gvyr Denmarc ac eu bwyeill 810
deuvinyauc, a'r Guydyl gaflachauc ac eu peleu haearnaul kyllellauc, a'r
Gwyndyt gleiuyauc tareanauc.

Gruffud gentaf emladwr a gyrchus y vrwyder en gyffelip y gaur ac y
lew, hep orfowys o danu y urthuynepwyr o gledyf lluchyadennaul. Gyrru
grymm en e wyr a oruc y emvrthlad ac eu gelynyon en wraul, a hyt na 815
rodynt udunt eu kefneu o nep ryw uod. Ac ena y bu vrwyder dirvavr y
chof y'r etiued wedy eu ryeni. Geuri er emladwyr a dyrchauwyt y'r awyr;
seinnyav a oruc y daear gan duryf y meirch a'r pedyt: y sein emladgar a
glywyt ympell; kynnvryf er arveu a seinnyei en venych: gvyr Gruffud en
dwyssav en wychyr, ac eu gelynyon en darystung udunt; chwys y llavur a'r 820
gvaet en gvneithur frydeu redegauc. Ac en henne, Trahaearn a drychut en
e gymperved, eny ytoed y'r llaur en varw, en pori a'r danhed y llyssyeu ir ac
en palualu ar warthaf er arveu; a Gucharki Wydel a wnaeth bacwn ohonav
ual o hwch. Ac en er vn lle hvnnv e digvydassant en e gylch o'e deulu e hun
pymp marchauc ar ugeint. Rei ereill onadunt a las en e vedin gentaf. Llawer 825
o uilyoed onadunt a las, a'r lleill a rodassant eu kefneu y wyr Gruffud ac
a emchuelassant ar fo. Gruffud enteu, o'e gnotaedic deuaut, en vudugaul
a'e hemlynvs wynteu, ef a'e niuer, trvy y llwyneu a'r glynnyeu a'r guerni
a'r mynyded en hyt e nos honno urth y lleuat, ac en hyt e dyd drannoeth.
A breit vu o diengis nep onadunt o'r vrwyder y eu gvlat e hunein. 830

A guedy darvot y vrwyder, ofynhav brat o barthet Gruffud a oruc Rys.
Ymdynnv a dan gel kyfliw gur a llwyn a oruc o gedymdeithas Gruffud

a'e wyr, ac nyt emdangosses y nep onadunt o henne allan. Ac am henne
y sorres Gruffud, ac am henne yd erchis Gruffud y'u wyr anreithyav
835   kyuoeth Rys. Ac y velly e darvu.

E menyd, hagen, y bu e vrwyder endav a eilw kiudaut e wlat Menyd
Carn. Sef yu henne menyd e garned; canys eno e mae diruaur garned o
vein, a dan er honn y cladwt rysswr yg kynnoessoed gynt.

Two reports of Gruffudd ap Cynan's death

From Jones, *Brut y Tywysogyon Peniarth MS. 20 Version*, p. 88. and MS
NLW Peniarth 267

Peniarth 20

[1136–1137] Yn y vlwydyn honno y teruynawd Gruffud ap Kyna[n],
840   tywyssawc Gwyned a phenn a brenhin ac amdiffynnwr a thagnefedwr
Kymru oll, y vvched amserawl yg Krist ac y bv varw wedy llaweryon
berygleu mor a thir a gwedy aneiryf vvdugolaetheu yn ryueloed ac ynnill
anreithyeu wedy diruawr verthed eur ac aryant wedy kynnullaw [gwyr]
Gwyned y gyt o'r amrauaelyon wladoed y gwasgarassei y Normannyeit
845   wynt, wedy edeilat llyaws o eglwysseu a'y kyssegru y Duw a'r seint drwy
gymrut olew ac ygen a chymun a chyffes ac ediuarwch o'y bechodeu a'y
wneuthur yn vanach a chael diwed da yn y berffeith heneint.

Peniarth 267

Wrth y diwed ynteu y doethant y gwyr muyaf a doethaf o'r holl gywoeth,
Dafyd eskob Bangor, Symeon archdiagon, gur adfet o oet a doethinap,
850   prior manachlog Kaer, a llawer o effeirieit ag ysgolheigyon yn irau y gorff
ef ag oleu kyssygredig, herwyd gorchymyn Yago ebostol. E feibeon hefyt
oed yno ymplith[24] hynny, ag ynteu yn eu bendigau wy, ag yn dywedut
pa ryu wyr vydunt ragllau, megis Yago padriarch yn bendigau y feibeon
gynt yn yr Eifft. A gorchymyn a orug udunt bot yn uraul a gurthwynebu
855   yn wychyr y eu gelynyon, ar y gyffelyprwyd ynteu yn y diwed dydyeu.
Eno hefyt yd oed Angharat vrenhines, y wreig briaut ynteu, ag idi y rodes
ynteu hanner y da, a duy randir, a phorthloed Abermenei. Eno yd oedynt
y ferchet a rei o'e neieint, ag y baub o'r rei hynny hefyt y rodes rann o'r
eidau yn ymborth udunt wedy y dyd ef.

860   Kymry a Gwydyl a gwyr Denmarc yntuy a drygyrfaethassant o
diguydedigaeth Gruffud vrenhin, fegis kuunfan yr Ideon am Iosue, fab
Nun. Duy vlyned a phetwar ugeint oed Ruffud, ag yna y bu farw; ag y

---

[24]   MS *yny y plith hynny*, Variant MSS *yno ymplith hynny*. (See further, *HGrK* p. 32 and *MPW*
     p. 51.)

Mangor y kladwyt y meun yskrin yn y parth assu y'r allaur fawr yn yr egluys. A gwediun ninheu hyt pan orffwysso y eneit ynteu yn yr un peth, nyt amgen yn Duw, y gyt ag eneidieu brenhined da ereill yn oes oessoed. Amen. 865

THE LORD RHYS

Rhys ap Gruffudd (1132-97), better known as the Lord Rhys, was the last powerful prince of Deheubarth. He was a grandson of Rhys ap Tewdwr and also of Gruffudd ap Cynan, through his mother Gwenllian. As a young man during the reign of Stephen, he struggled, with the aid of his brothers, to overthrow Norman rule in south east Wales, but his success was short-lived and on the succession of Henry II he was deprived of most of the lands he had gained. Later he took advantage of Henry's failure to subdue Gwynedd and regained his lost territories. This made him the most powerful leader in Wales, but after his death, his kingdom fell into disarray as a result of discord among his sons. He was a patron of the Church and of the arts, as is reported in the annals.

From Jones, *Brut y Tywysogyon Peniarth MS. 20 Version*, pp. 127, 137–39.

Patron of Poetry and Music

[1176] Y Nodolic yn y vlwydyn honno y kynnhelis yr Arglwyd Rys ap Gruffud llys yn arderchawc yn Aberteiui yn y kastell; ac y gossodes deuryw ymrysson yno, vn y rwng beird a phrydydyon, vn arall y rwng telynoryon a chrythoryon a phibydyon ac amrauaelyon genedloed gerd music. Ac ef a beris gossot dwy gadeir y'r gorchyvigwyr, ac ef a anrydedawd y rei hynny o rodyon ehelaeth. Ac o'r telynoryon gwas yeuang o lys Rys a gafas y vudygolyaeth. Y rwng y beird rei Gwyned a orvv. Pawb o'r eirchyeit a gauas y gan Rys yr hynn a geissyawd, hyt na wrthladwyt neb. A'r wled honno kynn y gwneuthur a vynegit vlwydyn drwy holl Gymry a Lloegyr a'r Alban ac Ywerdon a'r ynyssed ereill. 870 875

Obituary

[1197] Blwydyn wedy hynny y bu diruawr varwolaeth yn holl ynys Brydein a Freing ar bob ryw dyn. A'r dymestyl honno a ladawd aneiryf o'r bobyl a lluossogrwyd o'r bonhedigyon a llawer o'r tywyssogyon; ac nyt arbedawd honno y neb. Yn y vlwydyn honno, y pedweryd dyd [o] Galan Mei, y bu varw Rys vab Gruffud, tywyssawc Deheubarth ac anorchyuygedic ben holl Gymry. Ac y darystyngawd y anynat tyngetuen y vlwydyn honno, yr honn a oed datkanadwy drwy dagreuoed a choffadwy drwy dolur teilwng o gwynuan, kanys kolledus oed y bawb. Y dywededic Rys hwnnw, kanys hanoed o'r llin vonhedikaf a chanys oed eglur bennkenedyl 880 885

ef, a gyffelybawd y adwyndra wrth y genedyl; ac velly y dyblygawd ef
boned y vedwl val yr oed gynghorwr kenedyl a gorchuyugwr y kedyrn
ac amdiffynnwr y darystyngedigyon wyr, grymus ymladwr y kaeryd,
kyffrowr y toruoed a ruthrwr gelynolyon vydinoed.

890   Megys glewder baed koet yn chwyrnu neu ynteu y llew yn maedu y llawr
a'y lyw rac llit, velly y dywalhaei ef ymhlith y elynyon. Och am ogonyant
y ryueloed a tharyan y marchogyon, amdiffynnwr y wlat, tegwch arueu,
breich kedernyt, llaw haelyoni, llygat ac eglurder adwyndra, blaenwyd
mawrvryt, ymdywynnygrwyd dosparth, mawrvrydrwyd Herkwlff, eil
895   Achel herwyd garwder y dwyvronn, hynawster Nestor, glewder Tydeus,
kedernyt Samson, dewred Hector, llymder Curialius, tegwch a phryt
Paris, huolder Vlixes, doethineb Selyf, mawrvryt Ajax.

    Ac nyt ryued kwynaw yr angeu a wnelei y veint gollet honno. A'r
dymestawl Dynghetven greulonaf, chwaer y Antropos, heb wybot na
900   mynnu arbet y neb, yr honn a arueidyawd erchyruynu o gyngoruynnus
law personolaeth y kyfryw wr hwnnw, yr hwnn a gannorthwyawd kynn
no hynny y Dynghetuen, mam dynyadawl annyan, o hygar dechreu y
yeuengtit ef; ac odyna y diodefawd mynet dros gof goruchelder y rot, pan
vwryawd hwnn y'r llawr.

905   Och am diogel amdiffyn y tlodyon a'y nawd, dillat y noethyon, ymborth
yr essewydyon, diawt y sychedigyon; och am barawt helaethrwyd rodyon
y bawb o'r a'y keissyei. Digrif y ymadrawd, adurn y weithret, adwynder
moesseu, hynaws y ymadrawd, tec y wyneb, gwar a chyuyawn wrth
bawb.

A TALE OF TWO PRINCES

*After the death of the Lord Rhys, Llywelyn ap Iorwerth (1172–1240), known
as Llywelyn the Great, was the most powerful of the Welsh princes. In fact,
he and his grandson Llywelyn ap Gruffudd (c. 1225–82), known as Llywelyn
the Last, are the two princes who came closest to ruling the whole of Wales.
By taking advantage of the discord in the royal house of Gwynedd, Llywelyn
the Great succeeded in securing the kingdom of Gwynedd for himself. He
then expanded into Powys and Ceredigion. He formed an alliance with King
John of England by marrying his natural daughter, Joan, but subsequently
he supported the rebellious barons and challenged the king's supremacy in
Wales. In Aberdyfi in 1216, he presided over what was virtually a Welsh
parliament.*

From Jones, *Brut y Tywysogyon Peniarth MS. 20 Version*, pp. 154–56, 167,

172, 176–77, 180, 185, 189–90, 190–91, 196, 197–98, 201–02, 207, 208, 211, 215, 228.

Llywelyn ap Iorwerth's stuggle against King John

[1210] Dec mlyned a deucant a mil o oyd C[ri]st y duc Llywelyn vab 910
Jorr[werth] mynych gyrcheu am benn y Saesson drwy eu teruyscu yn
greulawn. Ac o achaws hynny y kynnullawd Jeuan vrenhin Lloegyr
diruawr lu ac y kyrchawd tu a Gwyned drwy aruaethu digyfoethi Llywelyn
a'y diuetha yn gwbyl. A gwyssyaw attaw gyt ac ef holl dywyssogyon
Kymry, nyt amgen Gwenwynwyn o Bowys a Hywel vab Grufud ap Kynan 915
a Madoc vab Gruffud Maelawr a Maredud vab Rotpert o Gedewein a
Maelgwn a Rys Vychan, meibyon yr Arglwyd Rys. A'r brenhin a doeth
hyt yg Kaer Lleon ac yna y perys Llywelyn ap Jorr[werth] mudaw y
Beruedwlat a Mon a'y holl da hyt ynyalwch Eryri. A'r brenhin a doeth yn
y aruaeth hyt gastell Dygannwy ac yno y doeth eissyeu bwyt ar y llu yn 920
gymeint ac y gwerthit wy yr keinyawc a dimei; ac yr oed gystal ganthunt
kic y meirch a'r anregyon goreu. Ac o achaws hynny yr ymchwelawd y
brenhin drwy waradwyd, wedy kolli llawer o'y wyr, amgylch y Sulgwynn
i Loegyr heb perffeithyaw dim o'y neges. A gwedy hynny am Galan
Awst yr ymchwelawd dracheuyn y Wyned a llu a oed vwy a chreulonach 925
ganthaw. Ac edeilat kestyll yndi a oruc a mynet drwy Gonwy auon tua
mynyded Eryri; ac anuon rei o'y wyr hyt Dinas Bangor yw y losgi a daly
Rotpert esgob Bangor yn y eglwys a'y brynnu a wnaethpwyt yr deukant
ehebawc.

Ac yna Llywelyn heb allu diodef kyndared y brenhin a anuones y 930
wreic, merch y brenhin, attaw drwy gyngor y wyrda y geissyaw hedychu
a'r brenhin, pa ffuryf bynnac y gallei. A gwedy kymrut o Lywelyn
diogelwch y vynet ar y brenhin ac y dyuot y wrthaw yn ryd, ef a aeth at y
brenhin ac a gymodes ac ef drwy rodi gwystlon o vonhedygyon y wlat y'r
brenhin; ac ymrwymaw ar rodi ohonaw y'r brenhin vgein mil o warthec 935
a deugeint emys. Ac ef a gennhadawd heuyt y'r brenhin y Beruedwlat
oll ac a berthynei wrthi yn dragywydawl. Ac yna yr hedychawd holl
dywyssogyon Kymry a'r brenhin, eithyr deu vab Gruffud ap yr Arglwyd
Rys mawr, nyt amgen Rys ac Ywein. A'r brenhin drwy diruawr lywenyd a
budygolyaeth a ymchwelawd y Loegyr. 940

Llywelyn ap Iorwerth and the de Breos/Braose family

*The fortunes of Llywelyn ap Iorwerth, Llywelyn the Great, were inextricably
bound up with the de Breos/Braose family, who had come over from
Normandy and had established themselves as powerful Marcher Lords.
Llywelyn supported Reginald de Breos/Braose in his conflict with King John
and reinforced the family ties through a dynastic marriage with his daughter,*

Gwaldys. His defection to the crown after the death of John in 1217 angered Llywelyn, who attacked his lands of Brecon and Gower and supported the claim of John de Breos/Braose the eldest of the four sons of Reginald's brother William, who had married Llywelyn's daughter, Margaret.

Reginald was succeeded in 1228 by his son, William, who was married to Eva Marshall, daughter of the first earl of Pembroke. He was captured by Llywelyn the Great in 1228 during the campaign in Kerry, but was released on payment of a ransom. Subsequently, he agreed to the marriage of his daughter, Isabella, with Dafydd, Llywelyn's only legitimate son. But it all ended in tragedy when on a visit to Llywelyn's court, William Breos/Breose was discovered in an adulterous relationship with Llywelyn's wife, Joan, and was hanged on 3 May 1230. With his death, the male line of the main branch of the family ceased, and the inheritance was divided between his four daughters. The family name, however, survived in the line of John de Breos, baron of Gower and Bramber.

[1215] Y vlwydyn honno y gwnaethpwyt Jorr[werth] abat Tal y Llychau yn esgob y Mynyw a Chadwgawn abat Llanndefit yn esgob ym Bangor. Ac yna yr hedychawd Gilys esgob Henford vab Gwiliam o Brewys a brenhin Lloegyr ac yr ymaruolles ac ef rac ouyn y Pab; ac yn ymchwelut
945   o lys y brenhin dracheuyn drwy orthrwm heint y bu varw yg Kaer Loyw am gylch Gwyl Marthin. Ac yn etiued ydaw ar dref y dat y doeth Reinallt y vrawt o Brewys ac y kymyrth yn wreic briawt ydaw merch Lywelyn ap Jorr[werth] tywyssawc Gwyned.

[1216] Ac Ieuan vrenhin ac amylder o wyr aruawc ganthaw a aeth y tu
950   a'r Ardal ac a doeth hyt yn Henford ac anuon kennadeu a oruc at Reinallt o Brewys ac ar dywyssogyon Kymry. Ac eruynnyeit vdunt gymodi ac ef o bob mod a oruc ef ac nys mynnassant. A chyrchu Maeshyueid a'r Hay a oruc ef ac ymlad ac wynt; a bwrw y kestyll y'r llawr a llosgi Kroes Oswallt a'y distryw oll.

955   [1217] Y rwng y damweinnyeu hynny y gwnaeth Reinallt o Brewys hedwch a'r brenhin. A phan weles Rys ac Ywein meibyon Gruffud eu hewythyr wedy adaw y ymaruoll a gwyrda y deyrnas, kyuodi yn y erbyn a orugant a dwyn kantref Buellt y arnaw a'y oresgyn oll eithyr y kastell. A Llywelyn vab Jor[werth] heuyt a lidyawd am y kymot hwnnw a chyffroi
960   llu a oruc yn erbyn Reinallt a chyrchu Brycheinnyawc ac ansodi toruoed a mynet wrth Aberhodni ac aruaethu distryw y dref yn gwbyl. A'r bwrdeissyeit heb allu ymderbynnyeit ac ef a doethant attaw a thrwy nerth Rys Jeuag vab Gruffud hedychu a wnaethant ac ef a rodi pump wystyl ydaw o'r rei bonhedikaf o'r dref o dalu kan morc ydaw dros hedwch y'r
965   dref.

Ac odyno y trosses y hynt y tu a Gwhyr drwy y Mynyd Du, ac yno llawer o'y swmerau a beryglawd. Ac yn Llangyuc y pebyllawd. A phan weles Reinallt hynny o distrywedigaeth yr oed yn y wneuthur, ef a doeth a chwe marchawc y gyt ac ef ac a ymrodes y Lywelyn. A thrannoeth Llywelyn a rodes ydaw kastell Seynenid; ac ynteu a'y gorchymynnawd y gatwedigaeth 970 Rys Gryg.

[1219] Blwydyn wedy hynny y kymyrth Rys Gryc merch yarll Caer yn wreic briawt ydaw, ac y kymyrth Jon o Brewys Marvret²⁵ merch yr Arglwyd Lywelyn yn briawt ydaw.

[1221] Yn y vlwydyn honno amgylch gwyl Nicolaws yr atkyweiryawd 975 Jon o Brewys drwy gannyat a chyngor yr Arglwyd Lywelyn kastell Abertawy.

Although Llywelyn seemed able to exercise control over some members of the de Breos/Braose family at that time, he was not so successful with other princes. In 1221, he was challenged by his own son Gruffudd for supremacy of Meirionydd and by Rhys Ieuanc, son of Gruffudd ap Rhys and Maud de Breos/Braose, who was disappointed at not being given the castle of Cardigan, but on the intervention of the king of England they became reconciled. However, Llywelyn's relationship with William Marshal, earl of Pembroke, was not so favourable. In 1223, Marshal mustered troops from Ireland and attacked the castles of Cardigan and Carmarthen. Llywelyn sent his son Gruffudd to oppose him but without success. Even the efforts of the King of England and the Archbishop of Canterbury to intercede were of no avail in settling the enmity between them. Finally his authority was challenged by the king himself.

[1228] Blwydyn wedy hynny y doeth Henri vrenhin Lloegyr a diruawr lu ganthaw o gedernyt holl Locgyr y Gymry drwy aruacthu darystwng yr arglwyd Lewelyn a'r holl Gymry ydaw. Ac yn y lle a elwir Keri y 980 pebyllawd. Ac yno yr ymgynnullawd yn gytduhun y gyt yr holl Gymry gyt ac eu tywyssawc; ac yna drwy greulonyon gyrcheu y eu gelynyon y gwnaethant diruawr deruysc arnadunt. Ac yno y delit Gwilym Jeuang vab Reinallt o Brewys, gwr arderchawc yn arueu, kyt bei jeuang ef. Yn vrathedic y karcharwyt ef; a thros y rydit y gorvv arnaw rodi kastell Buellt 985 a'r holl wlat a diruawr swm o aryant gyt a hynny y'r Arglwyd Lywelyn. A'r brenhin, wedy furyfhau tangneued y ryngthaw a Llywelyn, a gwneuthur o wyrda Kymry a oed yno wrogaeth ydaw, heb vrenhinawl anryded a ymchwelawd y Loegyr.

---

²⁵ RB *Maryret*; Mostyn 159 (a later MS) *Margret*.

990   [1230] Yn y vlwydyn honno y kroget Gwilyam Jeuang o Brewys, arglwyd Brycheinnyawc y gan yr Arglwyd Lywelyn yn Gwyned, wedy y dala yn ystauell Lywelyn gyt a merch brenhin Lloegyr, gwreic Lywelyn.

Burial of Joan and Llywelyn

[1237] Blwydyn wedy hynny y bu varw arglwydes Gymry, gwreic Lywelyn vab Jor[werth] a merch y vrenhin Lloegyr (Jon oed y henw) yn llys Lywelyn
995   yn Aber mis Chwefrawr; ac y kladpwyt y chorf mywn gard gyssegredic a oed yglan y traeth. Ac yno wedy hynny y kyssegrawd Hywel esgob manachloc y'r Brodyr Troednoeth yn anryded y'r Wynnuydic Veir; a'r tywyssawc a'y hedeilawd[26] oll ar y gost ef rac eneit yr arglwyes.

         [1240] Deugein mlyned a deukant a mil oed oet Krist pan vv varw yr
1000   Arglwyd Lywelyn vab Jor[werth] vab Ywein Gwyned, tywyssawc Kymry, eil Achel, wedy kymrut abit kreuyd yn Aber Ko[n]wy ohonaw a'y gladu yn anrydedus yno. Ac yn y ol y gwledychawd Dauyd, y vab o Jon verch Jeuan vrenhin Lloegyr. A'r Dauyd hwnnw y mis [Mei] rac wyneb a wnaeth wrogaeth y Henri, vrenhin Lloegyr, y ewythyr yng Kaer Loyw.
1005   A barwnyeit Kymry yr haf wedy hynny a wrhassant y'r brenhin; ac yna y koffaawd y Saseson eu hen deuawt ac yr anuonassant Wallter Maryscal a gallu mawr gyt ac ef y gadarnhau kastell Aberteiui.

The Accession of Llywelyn ap Gruffudd

Llywelyn the Great was succeeded in 1240 by Dafydd, his only legitimate son by Joan, daughter of King John. Nevertheless, although his uncle, Henry III of England, was prepared to acknowlege him as heir to Gwynedd, he was reluctant to concede to him the right to rule his father's conquests outside Gwynedd. Under Welsh law, however, his older half-brother Gruffudd also had the right to inherit a share of his father's territories. Henry upheld this Welsh custom, known as gavelkind, clearly because it was to his advantage to divide the lands of his subject princes and, by diminishing their resources, weaken their power. Ironically, in spite of a favourable outcome to his quest to inherit his rightful share of his patrimony, Gruffudd was released from incarceration by Dafydd, only to be imprisoned by King Henry III in the Tower of London. In trying to escape from his cell at the top of the building by means of a knotted sheet, he fell to his death in 1244. Two years later, Dafydd died and was succeeded by Gruffudd's two eldest sons, Owain and Llywelyn.

[1246] Blwydyn wedy hynny blwydyn glawawc oed. Y mis Mawrth y bu varw taryan Kymry Dauid vab Llywelyn yn y lys yn Aber a'y gorff a

---

[26] MS *hedeileilawd.*

gladpwyt yn Aber Conwy y gyt a chorf y dat. A gwedy nat oed etiued 1010
ydaw o'y gorff, ef a wledychawd yn y ol deu neieint ydaw nyt amgen
deu vab Gruffud vab Llywelyn, Ywein Goch a Llywelyn. A'r rei hynny,
o gyngor doethyon y wlat, a rannhassant y kyfoeth yn deu hanner y
ryngthunt.

[1255] Yn y dydyeu hynny y kyuodes teruysc y rwng meibyon Gruffud 1015
vab Llywelyn, Ywein Goch a Dauyd y vrawt o'r neill parth, a Llywelyn o'r
parth arall. A Llywelyn drwy ymdiret y Duw yn diergrynnedic a arhoes
dyuodyat y vrodyr yn y erbyn a diruaur lu ganthunt. Ac yn digyffro yn
yr ymlad yn ennyt awr ef a delis y vrodyr ac a'y karcharawd wedy llad
llawer o'y gwyr a ffo ereill. Ac ef a oresgynnawd eu holl dired heb dim 1020
gwrthwynebed ydaw.

*Llywelyn adopted his grandfather's policies of expansion, and was eventually
acknowledged as the most powerful prince in Wales. The other Welsh
princes accepted him as their overlord and paid homage to him, while he
in turn paid homage on their behalf to the king of England. In early 1274,
there was a plot to kill Llywelyn by his brother, Dafydd, and Gruffudd ap
Gwenwynwyn of Powys. The plot failed and Dafydd and Gruffudd fled to
England, where they were supported by the king and carried out raids on
Llywelyn's lands. This increased Llywelyn's emnity to the English crown and
in 1275 he refused to pay homage.*

[1256] Blwydyn wedy hynny y doeth Edward vab Henri vrenhin, ac ef
yn yarll Kaer, y edrych y dired a'y gestyll ynGwyned val amgylch Awst.
A gwedy y ymchwelut ef y Loegyr y doeth bonedigyon Kymry wedy eu
hyspeilyaw o'e rydit ac eu dylyet at Lywelyn vab Grufud, a dangos ydaw 1025
drwy dagreu eu trallodus gethiwet y gan y Saesson a mynegi ydaw vot
yn well ganthunt eu llad yn ryuel dros eu rydit nogyt diodef eu sathru
yn andylyedus y gan estronyon. A'r dywededic Lywelyn, o'e hannoc hwy
a'e kyngor a'y harch, a gyrchawd y Beruedwlat a chyt ac ef Maredud vab
Rys Gryc; ac erbynn penn yr wythnos ef a'y gorysgynnawd oll. A gwedy 1030
hynny ef a gymerth gantref Meironnyd yn y law. A'r tir a oed eidaw
Edward yng Keredigyawn, a rodes ef y Varedud vab Ywein, a Buellt a
rodes y Vared[ud] vab Rys gan ysbeilyaw a gyrru ymeith Rys, y nei, o'e
gyuoeth a'y rodi y Varedud a hep attal dim ydaw ehun eithyr clot ac
anryded 1035

[1258] Blwydyn wedy hynny yr ymaruolles holl Gymry y gyt ac
y rodassant lw ar gadw kywirdeb a duhundeb y gyt dan sentens
ysgymundawt ar y neb onadunt a'y torrei. Ac yn erbyn y llw hwnnw yr
aeth Mared[ud] vab Rys heb gadw y lw.

1040   [1264] Blwydyn wedy hynny — heb vynet dros kof y teruysc a oed
        y rwng Henri ac Edward, y vab, a'y kymorthyeit o'r neill parth yr y
        vlwydyn kynn no hynny a'r yeirll a'r barwnyeit o'r parth arall — yr
        ymgynnullawd brenhin yr Almaen a brenhin Lloeger a'y meibyon a'y
        hymaruollwyr Duw Merchyrgweith hyt y maes Leaws[27] y ymlad yn
1045   erbyn yr yeirll a'r barwnyeit a oedynt yn keissyaw kyfreithyeu a dylyet
        y deyrnas ac ar vedyr eu daly. A gwedy diruawr ymlad yn y maes
        hwnnw yr ymchwelawd yr ewyllys dracheuyn ac y delis yr yeirll a'r
        barwnyeit y brenhined a deu uab Henri vrenhin, nyt amgen, Edward
        ac Edmwnt, a phump barwn ereill ar hugein y gyt ac wynt, wedy llad
1050   llawer o varchogyon a bonedigyon ereill val amgylch deng mil o wyr y
        brenhined. A gwedy hynny y gyllyngawd yr jeirll a'r barwnyeit vrenhin
        y[r] Almaen wedy kymrut kyngor onadunt ac adaw y gwyr ereill oll yn
        y karchar. Yn y vlwydyn hono y kauas Kymry hedwch rac y Saesson ac
        y bu Lywelyn vab Gruffud yn dywyssawc ar Gymry oll.

The Last Stand of Llywelyn ap Gruffudd

*In 1276, Edward declared Llywelyn a rebel and in 1277, gathered an
enormous army to march against him. He was supported by Dafydd ap
Gruffudd (Llywelyn's brother) and Gruffudd ap Gwenwynwyn (lord of
part of Powys), but by early 1282, however, Dafydd seceded and on Palm
Sunday, he attacked the English at Hawarden Castle and then laid siege
to Rhuddlan. In spite of the previous differences between them, Llywelyn
supported his brother and the revolt spread to other parts of Wales. Leaving
Dafydd behind to safeguard Gwynedd, Llywelyn led a campaign in the
south and was killed at Cilmeri, near Builth.*

1055   [1282] Dyw Sul y Blodeu y torres rwg Llewelyn ap Gruffud ac Edward
        brenhin Lloigyr. A'r kanhaiaf gwedy henne y doeth y brenhyn a'y lu
        hyt en Rudla[n] ac er anvones llynges hyt en Mon a Howel ap Grufud
        ap Edneved en dywisauc en ev blaen ac wynt a goresgynassant Von ac
        a vanassant goresgin Arvon. Ac ena y gwnaethpwyd y bont ar Venei ac
1060   y torres y bont o tra llwith ac y bodes aneirif o'r Saesson ac ereill a las.
        Ac ena y gwnaethpwyd brat Lliwelyn en e clochte en Mangor y gan y
        wyr ef ehvn.

        Ac ena er edewys Lliwelyn ap Gruf[ud] David y vraud en gwarchadw
        Gwyned, ac entev ef a haeth a'e lu y goresgyn Powys a Buellt, ac ef
1065   a goresgynaud hyt en Llanngaenten ac odena ef a anvones y wyr a'y
        distein y gymmryd gwrogaeth gwyr Brecheinyauc ac adaw y tywissauc
        a bychydic o wyr gyd ac ef. Ac ena y doeth Rosser Mortymyr a Grufud

---

[27]   *kyfranc lews* is inserted in the margin.

ap Gwennwynwyn a llu er brenhyn gantwynt en direbud am ev penn.
Ac ena y llas Llywelyn a'y orevgwyr. Dyw Damasius Pap pethewnos o'r
vn dyd kyn dyw Nodolic a dyw Gwener oed y dyd hvnnw.   1070

NOTES

1   *Eneas Yscvydwyn ... a foes* 'Aeneas White-shield ... fled': subj. + *a* + vb. is a common sentence pattern in MW and one realization of the so-called 'abnormal order'; for discussions, see *GMW* § 199, Borsley et al., 286–96; Willis, 'Old and Middle Welsh' in Ball and Müller, *The Celtic Languages*, 144–48.

1   *gvedy daruot ymladeu Tro* 'after the Trojan wars were over': the meaning of *daruot* here is 'to finish'; see *GMW* §154 N. The reference is to the legendary war between Greece and Troy, from which Aeneas escaped with his father Anchises and son Ascanius to found a new city on the site of Rome in Italy. The most likely source for this story in the Middle Ages would have been, not Homer's *Iliad*, but Dares Phrygius's *De Excidio Troiae Historia*,'History of the Destruction of Troy'. For the Welsh text, see Owens, *Fersiynau*. An English translation is to be found on line: http://www.theoi.com/Text/DaresPhrygius.html.

2   *yg gvlad* (yng ngwlad): for ways of expressing nasalisation in MW, see the Introduction, xliv.

3   *yr hon* 'the one who': the demonstratives *yr hvn, yr hon, y gvr* are often used as the antecedent of a non-defining relative clause, particularly in translated works, see *GMW* §74.

5   *gvedi gveled o Turn ... hynny* 'and after Turnus ... saw that': the preposition *o* marks the agent (*Turn*) of the verbal noun (*gveled*), see *GMW* § 181(a). For the rules of marking semantic roles (agent and patient) on verbal nouns, see Willis, 'Old and Middle Welsh' in Ball and Müller, *The Celtic Languages*, 151–52.

5   *Tvrn vrenhyn Rutyl* 'Turnus king of the Rutuli': lenition occurs because the noun *brenhyn* is in apposition to Tvrn, see *GMW* §19.

5–6   *kyghoruynnu a llydyav a oruc* 'he became jealous and grew angry': in MW narrative the construction: vn. + *a* + *goruc / gwnaeth* + subj. (stated or understood) is very common, see *GMW* § 180 (3) and Thomas, *'(GWNAETH). Newidyn'*, 252–80.

7   *Lauynya merch Latinus*: cf. note 5 where the noun in apposition is lenited, but here lenition is either not realized or not shown orthographically.

8   *dyewed* (diewedd): double pl. of *dyd* 'day', formed by adding a pl. ending to the already pl. *dieu*, 'days', a form normally used with numerals, see *GMW* §33.

9   *A gvedy dyrchauael Ascanius ar vrenhynavl gyvoeth* 'And after
         Ascanius had been raised to royal power': cf. *Ascanius, regia potestate
         sublimatus* (GM § 6.52–53) 'having been exalted by royal power'.

10–11   *ac y dodet arnav Syluyus*: lit. 'and "Silvius" was placed upon him', i.e.
         he was named Silvius.

13   *o'e dewynyon* 'to his magicians': for *o'e*, see *GMW* § 56. N2.

13–14   *pvy a'r veychogassey y vorvwyn* 'who had impregnated the maiden':
         a'r = *a* (relative pronoun) + *'r* (perfect particle < **yr**, a variant of **ry**), see
         GMW §§ 79, 187.

14   *gvedy dewynav onadunt* 'after they had prophesied': for *onadunt,* see
         Glossary *o*¹ and for the syntax, see note 5 above.

16   *A gvedy darfey ydav treyglav* 'After he had traversed': *daruod* is
         used here as an auxiliary verb with a verbal noun as subject, lit. 'after
         traversing [had] happened to him'; for 'i-clauses', see Willis, 'Old and
         Middle Welsh' in Ball and Müller, *The Celtic Languages,* 152–53 (48,
         49).

16–17   *y dav ar* 'he will come to': in MW there were originally two prepositions
         ar, the first, from an older *ad,* meaning 'to' and with the conjugated
         forms *attaf* etc. (found frequently with verbs of motion) and the
         second meaning 'on' with the conjugated forms *arnaf* etc.; *ar* 'to' was
         superseded by *at*; see *GMW* §§205, 220.

19   *ar y theuydle y bu varv*: the Latin original is *in natiuitate eius mortua
         est* (GM § 6.60–61), lit. 'she died at his birth'. The components of
         the word *teuydle* are *(e)tifedd* 'heir' + *lle* 'place' giving the phrase
         the meaning 'she died on her heir (-producing) place'; cf. *GPC s.v.
         etifeddwely* 'childbed'.

20   *ar uaeth*: according to Celtic custom, a noble youth would be placed
         in the care of foster parents rather than be reared in his father's court,
         the rationale of the practice being to strengthen alliances against
         a common enemy. Usually the child would be placed with a lower
         ranking family who would see fosterage of a noble youth as a means of
         increasing their own power and status. See Lloyd, *History,* i, 310 and ii,
         549–50 and Anderson, *'Urth Noe e Tat'*, 1–11.

23   *y kerdet* (yn cerdded) 'walking': *y* is a variant of the particle *yn* used
         before a vn. It is thought to have been used originally before the 1ˢᵗ and
         2ⁿᵈ inf. pronouns in the combinations *y'm* and *y'th* but later before other
         pronouns and possibly on its own before a vn. (without a mutation) as
         here, although these examples may be simply textual errors: see *GPC*
         (s.v. *i*⁵) and *GMW* § 222.

23   *Sef a oruc Brutus anelu bva* 'This Brutus did, he aimed a bow': for the
         syntax of *sef,* see *GMW* § 55 f; this is the substantival use here, often
         realized as *sef* + *a* + *goruc/gwnaeth* + subj. + vn. Its cataphoric emphasis

on the verbal noun is difficult to convey in English. See also Borsley et al., 317–18.

28   *hyd y Groec* (hyd yng Ngroeg) 'as far as Greece': for the notation of the nasal mutation, see the Introduction, xliv and cf. *yg gvlad* note 2 above.

29   *yg keythywet* 'in bondage': in MW (unlike Mod W) the prep. *yn* 'in' is sometimes used with an indef. noun, *GMW* § 244.

30   *y genedyl honno* i.e. the Trojan race: the Latin text is more specific: *Pirrus etenim filius Achilles post euersionem Troiae predictum Helenum compluresque alios secum in uinclis abduxerat* (*GM* § 7.68–69), 'Pyrrhus son of Achilles after the sack of Troy took away with him the aforementioned Helenus and several others in chains'.

35   *o'e bryd* 'in respect of his appearance': for *o* on this sense, *GPC s.v. o*[1].

36   *sef achavs oet hynny* 'the reason was this': for adjectival *sef* + noun, see *GMW* § 55 f 2.

38   *pa beth bynnac a damweyney ydav nac eur nac aryant* 'whatever gold or silver came to him by chance': lit. 'whatever happened to him (by chance), whether gold or silver'; cf. Lat. *et quicquid auri uel argenti . . . adquirebat* (*GM* §7.74–75) 'whatever gold or silver he acquired'. See *GPC s.v. damweiniaf* and *GMW* § 90 for *pa beth bynnac*.

39–40   *y bavb o'r a'e mynhey y gantav* 'to all (of those) who desired it from him': for the combination of prep. *o* + dem. pron. *ar* + rel. part. *a* often found after *pawb* or the superlative degree, see *GMW* § 75.

42–3   *ac eu rydhau* 'and release them': *ac eu* becomes *a'u* in later texts; see *GMW* §§ 56 N3, 231 N1.

44   *y Wenn Ynys* 'the Blessed Isle': only in the Welsh translations is Britain so named; cf. *Erat tunc nomen insulae Albion* (*GM* § 21.453), 'at that time the name of the island was Albion'. *Albion* is the name used for Britain by Ptolemy and one can see that it would have appealed to Geoffrey, because of its similarity to *Alba* or *Alba Longa,* the mother city of Rome built by Ascanius, the son of Aeneas.

45   *yn y kyuanhedu* (yn ei chyfaneddu): the aspirate mutation, normally found after the poss. pron. 3 sg. f. *y*, is not shown here orthographically.

46–7   *bodlavn uuant y'r lle vrth bressvylav yndav* 'they were pleased with the place for the purpose of living in it': the Welsh translator's attempt to convey the Latin *affectum habitandi Bruto sociisque inferebat* (*GM* § 21.455–56), 'it brought to Brutus and his companions a desire to live [there]'. For *wrth* meaning 'for the purpose of', see *GMW* § 243. In MW *bodlavn* can be followed by the prep. *y, ar* or *gan*; *GPC s.v. bodlon.*

50–1   *guneuthur dyruawr gyuanhed arnei* 'they made a huge habitation on it': i.e they populated it densely; cf. *ut in breui tempore terram ab aeuo inhabitatem censeres* (*GM* § 21.458–59), 'so that in a short space of time, you would think the land had been occupied from eternity'.

53   **Kam Roec**: lit. 'crooked Greek', a spurious explanation of the origin of *Cymraeg*, the Welsh name for the Welsh language. Cf. *Vnde postmodum loquela gentis, quae prius Troiana siue* **curuum Graecum** *nuncupabatur, dicta fuit Britannica*, 'For this reason the language of his people, previously known as Trojan or 'crooked Greek', was henceforth called British' (*GM* § 21.461–62). It also shows that Geoffrey was familiar with the Welsh name of the language.

55   **y gaer a'r dinas**: this appears to be a doublet; cf. *GM* § 22.490 *ciuitatem* which in post-augustan Latin means 'city': see L&S, *s.v. civitas*.

55   **a thri meyb**: *meyb/meib* is the pl. form of *mab* found with numerals, see *GMW* §51(b). *Meibion* is the more generally used pl. form.

58   **y cladwyt** (y'i claddwyd): *y* is a fusion of *y* (the pre-verbal particle) + *y* (the inf. pron. 3 sg.); see *GMW* § 58.

59   **y rannvt** (y rhannwd): -*vt* is a variant of the more common impers. pret. ending –*vyt*: see *GMW* § 135.

64   **Humyr urenhyn Dunavt**: Lat. *Humber rex Hunorum* 'Humber king of the Huns' (*GM* § 23.12). *Dunavt* is a personal name (see ll. 201, 202 text), used here in error for *Hunavt*.

65   **hyt ar Locrinus**: see note 16–17.

80   **ac mal yd oed engirolaeth Corineus y that**: lit. 'and as was the cruelty of her father', which could mean (i) 'with the same cruelty as that of her father' or (ii) 'as she was [of] the cruelty of C. her father'; cf. *paterna insana furens* (*GM* § 25.58) 'inflamed with paternal frenzy'.

83   **Beli Mawr** (Beli Fawr): lenition of the adj. after a personal name is not shown orthographically here, see *GMW* § 22. In Geoffrey's *Historia* the form is *Heli* (*GM* § 53.367) but in MW prose his name is Beli. See Bromwich, *Trioedd*, 281–83, 425, B. F. Roberts, *Cyfranc*, xii–xiv, Jankulak, *Geoffrey*, 35–36 and also http://rhyddiaithganoloesol.caerdydd.ac.uk.

89–90   **y gelwit, y cladvyt**: see note l. 58 above.

92–3   **nyt oed oet arnunt**: lit. 'there was not [sufficient] age on them', i.e. they were not of an age, they were minors.

101–3   **a uynnynt … a uynnei … a uynnynt** 'some wanted … others wanted … others wanted': technically concord between subject and verb indicates the abnormal order, while lack of concord indicates the mixed order: see *GMW* §146 and §199, Borsley et al., 306–07 and Willis, 'Old and Middle Welsh' in Ball and Müller, *The Celtic Languages*, 145–51. In the above quoted instance, however, there appears to be no semantic difference in the employment and non-employment of agreement.

103   **un oc eu kenedyl**: for *oc eu* which later became *o'u*, see *GMW* §231, N1., and cf. note 42–3 above.

104 *Gortheyrn Gortheneu*: more commonly known as *Gwrtheyrn Gwrtheneu*, (see l. 584). Henry Lewis points out (*BrD* 235) that the earliest recorded example of the name *Guorthigirn Guortheneu* occurs in *Historia Brittonum* (ed. John Morris), 74, § 49. In the Vatican Recension of the *Historia Brittonum* (ed. Dumville), 82 § 19, 83 § 20 the name is recorded as *Gurthegirunus/Gurthegirnus*. The prefix *guor-* gives the variant forms *gor-* and *gwr-*. In Latin he is called *Vortigernus*. The meaning of *Gortheyrn* is 'chief lord' and that of *gortheneu* is 'very thin'. See Nora K. Chadwick, 'Bretwalda ...', *BBCS* XIX iii (1961), 225–30 and 'A Note on the Name Vortigern' in H. M. Chadwick et al., *Studies*, 34–46; also Bartrum, *Dictionary*, 338–42 and *Celtic Culture* (ed. Koch), Vol III. *s.v. Gwrtheyrn*.

104–5 *yarll oed hvnnv ar Went ac Ergyng a Yeuas*: in the Latin he is simply described as *consul Gewisseorum* 'earl of the Gewissei' (*GM* § 94. 151). It seems that the translator is adding an explanation of his own about the identity and status of Gwrtheyrn. As the Welsh name for the Gewissei was Iwys (see Williams, *Armes Prydein*, 8.108, 14.181), one can see how it may have become confused with Yeuas (Ewias or Ewyas), an ancient Welsh kingdom on the border between Wales and England, and this may have led to the additional association with Gwent and Ergyng (Archenfield in English).

108 *dy tat ti y syd uarv, a'th urodyr y syd ry yeueinc* 'your father is dead, and your brothers are too young': this seems to be an example of *y syd*, the relative form of the 3. sg. of the pres. indic. of *bot,* in a non-relative context. The sentence follows the so-called abnormal order, in which there is no emphasis, contrastive or otherwise, on the constituent preceding the preverbal particle. For arguably similar instances in MW, cf. *Dy geuynderw yssyd urenhin yn Ynys y Kedyrn* 'Your cousin is king in the Island of the Mighty' and *Riannon uy mam yssyd yno* 'Rhiannon my mother is there' (*PKM* 49.10, 18–19). See note 1 above.

108–9 *ry yeueinc vrth wneuthur brenhin onadunt*: lit. 'too young for making a king of them', i.e. 'to be made king'; cf. *et fratres tui propter aetatem sublimari nequeunt* (*GM* § 94.154–55), 'your brothers on account of their age cannot be elevated'. For the use of the verbal noun corresponding to a passive meaning in English, see *GMW* § 182.

109–10 *Ac ny welaf innheu o'th lin ditheu a allo bot yn urenhin* 'And I do not see from your lineage/family [one] who may be able to be king': the rel. part. *a* 'who' may be used without an expressed antecedent: *GMW* § 77(c).

111–12 *minheu a ymchuelaf vyneb y bobyl a'r kyuoeth parth ac attat titheu*: lit. 'I will turn (or change) the face of the people and the land towards you too'. The use of *ymchuelaf vyneb* is hard to explain; it could be understood figuratively in the sense of 'status, respect', *GPC s.v. wyneb*

3.(b). Gortheyrn's proposal is that he would: (i) cause the people to support Constans, (ii) see to it that he was divested of his monk's habit and (iii) make him king. In return he expected Constans to increase his wealth and eventual claim on the kingship.

112–13   *ac a baraf dy dynnu o'r abit hvnnv* 'and I will cause you to be removed form that habit': i.e. Gwrtheyrn will see to it that Constans is released from the monastic order. For the use of the verbal noun corresponding to a passive meaning in English, see note 108–9 above.

119   *marv uuassei*: 'he had died'.

121   *wrth ry tynnu o'r creuyd* 'because of (his) having been removed from monastic life': the pref. pronoun genitival object of the vn. is not expressed. For the perf. part. *ry,* see *GMW* §§ 185, 186.

131   *ry daroed*: the perf. part. seems to have lost its force here, see *GMW* § 185 N.2.

131   *yr uarw* 'had died': var. on *ry uarw/farw*. In these selections *yr* for *ry* occurs only in BD. According to Henry Lewis (*BrD* xlix) the particle became increasingly rare after the thirteenth century. See also *GMW* § 187.

131   *a'e chyghorwyr*: the aspiration in *kyghorwyr* shows that *y teyrnas*, to which the inf. pronoun *'e* refers, is regarded as a f. noun despite the fact that no soft mutation is shown after the def. art.

142   *yr adeilat deissyuyt yr wnathoedyt* 'the building that had been newly constructed': *deissyuyt* functions as an adverb within the relative clause it precedes, see *GMW* §2 51(d); for *yr*, see note 131 above, and *GMW* § 65, N.2 for its use in relative clauses.

142–3   *y marchogyon newyd dyuot* (y marchogion newydd ddyfod) 'the newly arrived knights': on this adverbial use of *newydd* before a vn. to denote the immediate past, see *GMW* §251 N.

143   *niuer bychan* 'a small retinue': H1 has *niuer kyuartal*. See *PKM* 135 where Williams suggests 'modest, moderate' as the meaning of *kyuartal*.

148   'Lauart king, wasseil!': the interpreter explains in the following passage that the Saxon girl has honoured Gortheyrn by addressing him as 'Lord king' and drinking to his health. *Wasseil* is Old English *wæs hæil* 'be healthy' and the correct reply is *drincheil* (cf. l. 155 text).

158   *diawul* (diafwl): < *diawl*, a borrowing from Latin **diablus*. *Diafwl* is a re-formation of *diawl* under the influence of the pl. form *diefyl*; see *GPC s.v. diafol, diafwl*.

159–60   *sef a wnaeth H . . . adnabot ysgavder annvyt y brenhin* 'H understood the fickleness of the king's disposition': cf. *comperta leuitate animi regis* (GM § 100.360), lit. 'the king's fickleness having been understood'. Wright translates, 'H. recognised the king's lack of judgement.'

160   *mal oed ystryvus*: the meaning seems to be, 'since/because he was
        scheming', cf. Lat. *ut erat prudens* (*GM* § 100.360) 'as he was experienced';
        ut can be causal, L&S, *s.v.* B4.

162   *y cavssant*: 'they decided'; see *GPC* s.v. *caf*.

163   *yn y hagwedi* 'as her dowry': for a discussion on the predicative particle
        yn, see *GMW* §244.N. In the Welsh laws, *agwedi* is the term used for
        the gift which is given to a girl on her marriage by her family. In this
        instance, her husband gives a gift to the girl's family in return for
        her hand in marriage. This is closer to *cowyll*, the term used for the
        gift given to the girl by the husband the day after the marriage in
        recognition of her virginity. The difference is that both *agweddi* and
        cowyll were the possession of the girl, not of her family. See Jenkins and
        Owen, *Welsh Law of Women*, 187–88, 196.

165   *sef oed y henv Gvrgant* 'this was his name, Gwrgant': for the construction
        with substantival *sef*, see note 23 above. Since no sandhi-h is expected
        after poss. pron. 3 sg. m. (*GMW* § 26), *henw* is best understood as a
        variant of *enw*, see *GPC*, s.v. *enw*, *henw*.

165–6   *A'r nos honno y kysgvyt gan y uorvyn*: for the imprs. form *kysgvyt* in
        the phrase *kysgu gan* 'to cohabit, to marry', cf. *Kyn daruot y wled honno
        y kyscwyt genti* (*PKM* 50), lit. 'Before the end of the feast there was a
        sleeping with her'.

176   *guedy ys adavhei*: since the conj. *gwedy* is found with and without the
        particle *y(d)* (*GMW* § 266), *ys* here could be either particle *y* + inf. pron
        −*s*, as suggested by Henry Lewis (*BrD*, 240) or the syllabic form *ys* of
        the inf. pron. (*GMW* § 59). H1 gives the reading *gwedy ass adawhei eu
        bugeil*.

180   *A galw*: the vn. is often used instead of a finite verb; see *GMW* § 180
        (4).

181–2   *kyghoret idav adeilat y castell cadarnhaf a allei yn y lle cadarnhaf a
        gaffei* 'he was advised to build a very strong castle in the strongest place
        he could get': for the superlative *cadarnhaf*, see *GMW* § 41 (c). In the
        Latin text he was told to build a *turrim fortissimam* (*GM* § 106.500) 'a
        very strong castle'; for *turris* with this meaning, see L&S *s.v* II A.

182   *megys y bei hvnnv yn amdiffyn idav* 'so that that might be a protection
        for him': the Lat. suggests that *amdiffyn* is a noun here, *quae sibi
        tutamen foret* (*GM* § 106 500) 'which would be a refuge for him'.

182–3   *can collassei oll y lleoed cadarn o'e gyuoeth*: *oll* 'entirely' is used as an
        adverb qualifying *collassei*, see *GPC s.v.* *oll* 2(a).

183–4   *A guedy crvydrav ohonav llawer o leoed*: the insertion of a phrase
        between the vn. (*crvydrav*) and its so-called 'genitival object' (*llawer o
        leoed*), as here, could cause lenition of the latter, and this became the
        rule in later Welsh (Morgan, *Treigladau*, §161d), but here the initial
        consonant of *llawer* remains in its radical form.

184   *y ryv le hvnnv* 'such a place as that': see *GMW* § 99 (b).

186   *holl seiri mein o'r a allvt eu caffael* 'all the stone masons that one could find': lit. 'of those whose finding was possible': for the syntax of the genitival relative clause, see *GMW* § 69. The poss. pron. 3 pl. *eu* refers back to the demonstrative (*a*)*r* which can be sg. or pl.; see *GMW* § 75 and note 39–40 above.

187–8   *kymeint ac a wnelynt y dyd o'r gueith*: lit. 'as much as they would do by day of the work '. *O'r gueith* is dependent on *kymeint*; *y dyd* is adverbial.

188   *neu daruydei y'r daear y lyngcu* 'it happened that the earth swallowed it': for *neu*, affirmative particle, see *GMW* §188; for *daruot* as auxiliary verb, see note 16 above. The poss. '*y*' refers back to *kymeint … o'r gueith*.

188–9   *heb vybot dim y vrthav mvy no cheny ryffei eiryoet uch y dayar* ' without any more knowledge of it than if it had never been above the earth': the 3 sg. m. prep. *y vrthav* refers to *kymeint … o'r gueith*. For the use of the spirant mutation in *ryffei* < *ry* (perf. part.) + *pei* (impf. sub. of *bod*), 'had been', see *GMW* § 24 (e). Cf. Lat. *Sed quicquid una die operabantur, absorbebat tellus illud in altera, ita ut nesciret quorsum opus suum euanesceret* (*GM* 106.504–06), 'But whatever they completed in one day, the ground swallowed it the next (day) so that they did not know where the work had disappeared to'.

190   *gouyn y'w dewinyon idav a wnaeth* 'he asked his soothsayers': cf. Lat. *consuluit iterum magos suos* (*GM* § 106.506–07) 'he consulted again his soothsayers'. The Welsh seems to be a mixture of two constructions: (i) **gouyn y'w dewinyon a wnaeth* 'he asked [to] his soothsayers' and (ii) **gouyn dewinyon idav a wnaeth*, lit 'he asked soothsayers to him (i.e. of his)'. For a similar construction in MW, cf. *a phenneu eu dwy goes y'r meirch* (*BR* 9 16–17) 'and the tops of the horses' legs', lit. 'and the tops of their two legs to the horses'.

193–4   *hyt pan sauei y gueith* 'so that the work would stand': cf. *ut fundamentum constaret* (*GM* § 106.509) 'so that the foundation would stand'. For *hyt pan* to express purpose and result, see *GMW* § 269 (b) and *GPC, s.v. hyd*.

197   *yn drvs* 'in front of the gate' (not 'door'): cf. Lat. *ante portam* (*GM* §106.512).

199   *ymwrandav am y neges yd oedynt yn y cheissyav* 'listening out for the mission they were seeking': cf. Lat. *exploraturi quod quaerebant* 'looking for what they sought' (*GM* §106.513). For the syntax of the genitival relative clause, see *GMW* § 69, the poss. pron *y* within the periphrastic construction *bot* + *yn* + vn. refers back to the antecedent *neges*.

200–1   *daruot a wnaeth [kynnennu] y rvng deu onadunt* 'quarreling broke out
        between two of them': cf. *subita* **lis orta est** *inter duos iuuenes* 'a quarrel
        suddenly broke out between two youths' (*GM* §106.514).

202–3   *Pa achavs ... yd amryssony di a miui nac y kynnenny* 'Why ... do you
        contend with me and quarrel?': for *na(c)* 'or, and', see *GPC*, s.v. *na*[4]
        1(a).

207–8   *Y uam ... yssyd uerhc y urenhin*: on this use of *yssyd*, see above note
        108.

212   *vrth wneuthur y ewyllis onadunt* 'in order that they might do his will':
        for a similar construction, cf. *vrth gadv eu gvlat onadunt* (*BrD* 83) 'in
        order that they might guard their country' and see *GMW* § 243. For
        onadunt, see Glossary o[1] (xi) and note 5 above.

213   *y haruoll yn anrydedus a wnaeth y brenhin (y uam Uyrdyn)*: the
        Latin reads *excepit rex diligenter matrem* 'the king received the mother
        graciously' (*GM* §107.528). The pref. pron. *y* preceding *haruoll* (arfoll)
        could be either the 3 sg. f. or 3 pl. poss. pron. + the verbal noun *aruoll*
        'he received her/them'. In this example, however, it would appear that
        the scribe, realising the ambiguity, added *y uam Uyrdyn* as a gloss, so
        to speak, to ensure that the audience/reader would realise that it was to
        Myrddin's mother that the welcome was extended

215–16 *byv yv uy eneit i nat adnabum* 'my soul is alive that I do not know':
        Henry Lewis's emendation of *bvy* to *byv* is confirmed by the Latin,
        Vivit anima tua et uiuit anima mea ... quia neminem agnoui (*GM*
        139. §107.531), lit. 'your soul lives and my soul lives ... because I knew
        no-one'. Wright translates, 'Upon your soul and mine', an expletive
        which could also be applied to the Welsh text.

218–19 *nachaf y guelvn yn dyuot attaf yn drech gvr yeuanc teccaf yn y byt*:
        the sentence seems incomplete without an object of *guelvn*; one would
        expect *nachaf y guelvn yn dyuot attaf [rywun] yn drech gvr yeuanc
        teccaf yn y byt* 'lo I saw coming towards me **someone** in the form of
        (the) fairest young man, in the world'; cf. *apparebat michi* **quidam** *in
        specie pulcherrimi iuuenis* (*GM* 139 §107.533–34) 'there appeared to me
        someone in the guise of a very handsome young man'. For another
        example of a superlative adj. not preceded by the def. art., see *GMW* §
        47; cf. *Ac vn uerch a oed idaw deckaf yn y byt* (T. Jones, *Ystoryaeu*, 133),
        'and he had one daughter, (the) most beautiful in the world'.

222   *megys y gvypvn i bot tat idav ef amgen no hvnnv*: lit. 'as I would know
        that he has a father other than this one': this is ambivalent and the
        syntax seems corrupt. The impf. sub. *gvypvn* suggests that it should
        be followed by a conditonal clause: **megys y gvypvn i* **pe bei** *tat idav
        ef amgen no hvnnv* 'as I would know, **if** he had a father other than
        this one'; cf. *Sciat prudentia tua ... quod aliter uirum non agnoui qui
        iuuenem istum genuerit* (*GM* § 107.539–40) 'Your wisdom would know

… that in no other way have I known a man who would have begotten this young man'.

226–7 *bot llaver o dynyon a ryv anedigaeth honno udunt* lit. 'that there were many people with that kind of birth to them': the expected def. art. before *ryw* (see *GMW* § 99) is not visible here and has merged with its initial <r>, **a'r ryv anedigaeth honno*.

227 *Apulenis … a dyweit, pan draetha o Duv a'r seint* 'Apulenis … says, when he speaks about God and the saints': cf. *Nam ut Apulegius de deo Socratis perhibet* 'For as Apuleius records in *De deo Socratis*'(*GM* 139 § 107.545–46). There is confusion about the form of the author's name but the reference is to the Latin work by the second century African born philosopher Lucius Apuleius. See also Index of Personal Names below.

228 *rein hynny*: *rein* 'these' is a contracted form of (*y*) *rhai* + the dem. pron. *hyn* (see *GPC s.v. rhain*[1]); the addition of *hynny* is redundant, but occurs elswhere in this text (*BrD* 90.12, 117.21).

230 *A phan y mynnont*: *pan* is usually followed directly by the verb. Here, therefore, it could be preceded by the pref. obj. pron. 'and when they wanted **it**.'

232 *pan gaffat y guas yeuanc hvn* 'when this young man was conceived': cf. *unus ex eis huic mulieri apparuit et iuuenem istum in ipsa generauit*, 'one of them appeared to this woman and fathered this youth.' (*GM* § 107.549–50).

237 *ac y uelly y dywedynt y seuyll*: there appears to be an omission in the transcription of this sentence; a comparison with the Latin: *et quasi ilico opus constaret* (*GM* § 108.562), 'and the work would almost immediately stand firm' suggests that the periphrastic construction *y bydai yn seuyll* 'it would stand' was intended here.

239–40 *ac erchi dvyn y devynyon rac y uron* 'and he ordered the soothsayers to be brought before him': lit. 'and bade the bringing of the soothsayers before him'. For the use of the verbal noun corresponding to a passive meaning in English, *GMW* §182; cf. note 108–9 above.

242 *ny at y'r gueith seuyll* 'which will not allow the [building] work to stand': lit 'which will not allow to the building work a standing'; *at* is the mutated form (after neg. *ny*) of *gat*, 3 sg. pres. of *gadaw*, 'to allow, to permit'; for neg. rel. clause, see *GMW* § 65. *Gadaw* is both trans. and intrans. and is regularly followed by *y* 'i': see *GPC*, *s.v. gadaf*.

249 *a thi a wely* 'you will see': for future reference of the present tense, see *GMW* § 119 (e).

251–2 *Ac erchi disbydu y lynn* 'And he ordered the emptying of the lake': for passive meainng of vn., see note 108–9 above. Initial /λ/ of *llynn* is indicated by <l>, see *GMW* §9. and Introduction, xl.

257 *dvy dreic … o'r rei yd oed un guynn ac arall cohc* 'two dragons … of which, one was white and the other red': for the syntax of the relative

clause, see *GMW* § 70 N.2; for the use of *y rei* as antecedent, see *GMW* § 74

259   *y dreic coch*: cf. *y dreic wenn* (261) where the feminine form of the adj. is used. According to *GPC*, *dreic* (*draig*) can be both a masculine and feminine noun but the spirant mutation in *a'e chymell*, which follows, shows that it is regarded as feminine here, although the mutation is not shown in the qualifying adj. *coch*.

270   *baed Kernyv* 'The Boar of Cornwall': a metaphorical reference to King Arthur.

271–2   *Enyssed yr eigyavn* 'the islands of the ocean': in MS Pen. 16 these islands are identified as *ywerdon ac orc ac islond. a godlond. a llychlyn. [a] denmarc. ar enysseu ereill tanyas a mon a manau ac enys weith* (*BrD* 242) 'Ireland, and the Orkneys and Iceland and Gotland and Scandinavia [and] Denmark and the other islands, Thanet? and Anglesey and the Isle of Man and the Isle of Wight'.

272   *guladoed Freinc* 'the countries of France': cf. Lat. *Gallicanos saltus* (*GM* §112.41) 'Gallic forests/woodland pastures'. As Henry Lewis (*BrD* 242) has shown, MS H2 has *ac a ued ar vessyd freinc* 'and what he possessed of the open countryside of France', which is closer to the Latin. Pen. 16, however, has *A thrausseu fr[e]inc* 'the districts of France'.

274   *y'r a'e datcano*: see *GMW* §75; 'to those who proclaim it'.

275   *y brenhin*: Uthr Pendragon; see Index of Personal Names below.

279   *a rodi y yavn y bavb a'e dylyet* 'and gave everyone his right and entitlement': for the legal significance of these terms, see Jenkins, *The Law*, 339–40.

280   *y guys hvnnv*: *guys* can be m. or f. but it is f. elsewhere in the texts from which these extracts are taken.

284–5   *A chymeint o dylyedogyon a doethant yna … ac yd oed deilvng y'r ryv wled honno* 'And as many of the noblemen came there … as were worthy of that kind of feast': for the construction *cymeint … ac yd oed*, see *GMW* § 44. *Teilwng* is normally followed by the prep. *o*, but the translator may have been influenced by the Latin *laeto conuiuio digni* (*GM* §137.454) 'worthy of a joyous feast'. In Latin the adj. *dignus* is normally followed by the ablative, but the translator may have interpreted it as a dative, which is identical in morphological shape, and consequently employed the prep. *y* in Welsh.

289   *o'e charyat* 'from love for her': objective genitive.

290–1   *treiglav y holl uedvl … yn y hanrydedu hi*: *treiglaw* can be both trans. and intrans. but the Latin *rex … totam intentionem suam circa eam uerteret* (*GM* § 137.457–58) 'the king … turned all his attention towards her', suggests that *y brenhin* (288) is the subject and *y holl uedvl* is the object; see *GPC s.v treiglaf*.

293–4   *A guedy cael gvybot hynny o'r yarll, y gvr hitheu* 'And when the earl,
        her husband, got to know this': for the use of the vn. depending on *cael*
        'get, receive', see *GMW* § 182(d).

298–9   *Canys un o sarhaedeu … heb ganhyat*: Henry Lewis (*BrD* 267) points
        out that this is a later interpolation since it is not included in *Brut y
        Brenhined* from RB, H 1, H 2, Ll 1 manuscripts nor in the Latin, but
        a similar assertion is made in the Cotton Cleopatra version of *Brut y
        Brenhined*: *canys sarhaet vaur oed idaw adaw y llys heb ganhyat* 'for it
        was a huge insult for him to leave the court without his consent'. There
        is a reference to the three insults to a king in S. E. Roberts, *Legal Triads*,
        40, but this one is not included.

309   *dryc damwein*: loose compound. The meaning seems to be 'bad luck,
        disaster'; cf. Lat. *infortunium* (*GM* §137.473).

323   *ethrykyg un garrec kyuyng* 'a headland of a single stone('s breadth)': cf.
        Lat. *angusta rupes*, 'a narrow cliff' (*GM* § 137.484).

324   *trywyr aruavc a'e catwei* 'three armed men could protect it': *catwei*
        is impf. tense, probably expressing possibility; see *GMW* § 120(g). Cf.
        Lat. *Ipsum tres armati milites prohibere* **queunt**, 'Three armed knights
        could hold it against you', (*GM* § 137.485).

325–6   *pei Myrdin uard a rodei y weithret vrth dy uedvl di* 'if Myrddin
        Fardd added his action to your intent': in *GM* §137.486, *Myrdin uard* is
        referred to as *merlinus vates*, 'Merlin the seer/poet'. Geoffrey seems to
        have been confused about the identity of Myrddin, whom he named
        Merlinus. In pre-Galfridian literature, Myrddin is portrayed as a
        poet and vaticinator associated with the Old North, but in Geoffrey's
        Historia he is relocated in Caerfyrddin (Carmarthen) and identified
        with Ambrosius, the wonder boy of the *Historia Brittonum*: *Merlinus
        qui et Ambrosius dicebatur* (*GM* 141 § 108.565–66) 'Merlin, who was
        also called Ambrosius'. By the time he composed his later work, *Vita
        Merlini*, Geoffrey had acquainted himself with the original legend and
        portrays Myrddin as the wild poet of the woods who had lost his reason
        as a result of battle trauma, and in his madness had received the gift
        of prophecy. For further reading, see Padel 'Geoffrey of Monmouth
        and the development of the Merlin legend', *CMCS* 51 (2006), 37–65,
        Jankulak, *Geoffrey*, 78–93.

334   *ny chlywyt eryoet* 'that were never heard of': cf. Lat. *Inauditis*, 'unheard
        of', (*GM* §137.494).

344–5   *megys na bei neb o'r a'e guelei a vypei na bei y guyr hynny uydynt yn
        eu guir drech*: lit. 'so that nobody of those who saw them would know
        that it was not those men who were in their true appearance' (i.e., that
        those men were not in their true appearance). The impf. subj. (*g*)*vypei*
        is probably under the influence of the Latin *ita ut nemini quod fuerant*

compararent (*GM* § 137.502) 'in such a way that they would reveal to no-one what they had been'.

347   *a phan oed gyuliv gvr a llvyn* 'when man and bush were the same colour': i.e. at dusk, cf. Lat. *in crepusculo* (*GM* §137.503).

349   *canyt oed neb o'r a'e guelhei a vypei na bei yr yarll uei*: lit. 'since there was no one of those who saw him who knew that it was not the earl that he was', cf. 344–5 above.

350   *a'r nos hon hono*: *nos hon* has become *noson*, synonomous with *nos*, 'night'. When the original meaning of *noson* 'this night' was forgotten, *honno* was added for the sake of clarity, cf. *y dwthwn* (< *y dydd hwn*) *hwnnw*; see Morris-Jones, *Welsh Grammar*, 29.

364   *ac eu*: *ac* is a form of the rel. part. *a*, doubtless by analogy with the conj. and prep. *a*(*c*). Here it is used with 3 pl. pref. pron.; see *GMW* §65 N. 3.

366   *y dywyssavc*: *yn dywyssavc*; see above note 23.

368   *Ac yr daroed udunt goresgyn o'r parth drav y Humyr* 'And they rose to supremacy from the far side of the Humber': the Latin adds, *usque Katanesium ad mare* (*GM* §143.7) 'as far as the sea at Caithness'. For *yr daroed*, see notes 16 and 131 above.

371–2 *ac ny chlywssyt ar neb ... y ryv deuodeu* 'and such marks of character had not been reported about anyone': for *clywed ar* 'to be reported about' see *GPC s.v. clywaf*.

373–4 *A chymeint o rat a rodassei Duv idav ac nat oed yn eithauoed byt o'r a'e clyvei nys carei, ynoethach o'r a'e guelei* 'And God had bestowed such goodness upon him that there was not in the extremities of the world amongst those who heard of him, any who would not love him, much less amongst those who saw him': the Latin is much more concise: *in quo tantam gratiam innata bonitas praestiterat ut a cunctis fere populis amaretur* (*GM* §143.10–11), 'in whom his innate goodness ensured so much esteem that he was loved by almost everyone'. For *o'r a'e clyvei/ guelei*, see note 39–40 above.

374–5 *a hynny yn anedic ganthav* 'and that innate with him': i.e. he had that naturally — a general reference to his goodness; see 373–4 above. See also Glossary *s.v. gan* (v).

377   *hyt nat oed havd idav caffael o da kymeint ac a oed reit idav y rody* 'so that it was not easy for him to obtain (of) goods as many as it was necessary for him to give': the Latin is very concise: *ut ei quod dispensaret deficeret* (*GM* § 143.12–13) 'so that what he should dispense was lacking to him'. The meaning is that he ran out of gifts.

378   *y'r savl uarchogyon a lithrei attav* 'to all those knights who flocked (lit. flowed) to him': for adjectival use of *sawl* 'as many, so many, all' followed by a relative clause, see *GMW* § 103 (b).

380   *ny at Duw wastat achanochtit y argywedu idav* 'God will not allow continual need to harm him': *at* is the mutated form (after neg. *ny*) of

gat, 3 sg. pres. (here with future reference) of *gadaw*, 'to allow, to permit'; one would expect a construction like that of 242 *ny at y'r gueith seuyll*, but the prep. *y* immediately precedes the vn. which makes the phrase akin to the rare constructions mentioned in *GMW* § 181 N). *Argywedu* is often followed by the prepositions *ar* or *i*: see *GPC s.v. argyweddaf*.

383–4   **a yavnder a dysgei y hynny**: there seems to be a missing element in this sentence. The usual pattern is *dysgu* X *y* Y 'to teach s.th **to** s.o', which would lead one to expect **a yavnder a dysgei y Arthur hynny* or **a yavnder a dysgei* y[*daw*] *hynny*. The Latin *Commonebat etiam id rectitudo* (*GM* 193 §143.16–17), 'Right reminded [him] of that', suggests that the meaning of the Welsh is 'and right taught (him, i.e. Arthur) that', namely that he was the rightful ruler of Britain.

387   **yno**: refers to *Caer Efrawg* 'York', which Arthur visited after defeating the Saxons and making peace with the Scots.

387   **tri broder** 'three brothers': *broder* (variation of *brodyr*) is the pl. of *brawt* 'brother'. In ModW numerals are generally followed by sg. forms, but in MW many examples of a pl. noun occur, see *GMW* §51 (b).

389–90   **A rei hynny a dylyei tywyssogyaeth y guladoed hynny ac a oed eydynt kyn dyuot y Saesson**: *ac a oed eydynt* can either be interpretated as a relative clause with the rare by-form *ac a* of the relative pronoun (see *GMW* §65 N. 3), 'And these had a right to the sovereignty of those lands *which* (i.e. the sovereignty) *was theirs before the coming of the Saxons*', or, following Henry Lewis' interpretation (*BrD* 234), as the second of two coordinated abnormal sentences linked by *ac*, 'And these had a right to the sovereignty of those lands *and it* (i.e. the sovereignty) *was theirs before the coming of the Saxons*'. For the syntax of coordination under the latter reading and *tywyssogyaeth* as the subject of the second clause cf. Borsley et al., 300. The Latin text has *qui antequam saxones preualuissent principatum illarum partium habuerant* (*GM* §152.202–03), 'who, before the Saxons had taken control, had held the sovereignty of those parts'.

390   **y eu goresgyn**: for *y eu*, see *GMW* §56 N3.

392   **yarllaeth Lodoneis ac a berthynei vrthi** 'the earldom of Londonesia and [all] that which belonged to it': the relative clause is here used without expressed antecedent (*GMW* § 77), and *ac* (conj.) + *a* (rel. pron.) is thus different from *ac a* (either relative pron. or conj. + pre-verbal part.) in 389–90 above.

396   **ar y hen teilyngdavt** 'to its former dignity': cf. *in pristinam dignitatem* (*GM* §152.208–09).

400   **dyuot enys Prydein**: note the absence of the prep. *i* 'to' to denote destination. Whether this is a scribal error or what Ifor Williams (*Canu Aneirin*, 84–85) explains as an 'Accusative of Motion To without a preposition' is impossible to tell.

412-13　*euo oed eil dinas … o teccet y thei ac amlet y chyuoeth*: there is much uncertainty about the gender of *dinas*. From the earlier occurrences of *dinas* in this text it is impossible to tell whether it is a masculine or feminine noun, as lenition of initial <d> is not visible. In this example, however, the 3 sg. m. pron. *euo* indicates that it is masculine, whereas the spirant mut. after the pref. pron. (*y thei*) suggests that it is feminine. Similarly in 415, the 3 sg f. form *yndi* referring to *dinas* suggests that it is a feminine noun. Some nouns which vacillate in gender are old neuters, see Morris-Jones, *Welsh Grammar*, 228–29.

417　*arderchavc … o deu can yscol* 'famed for two hundred schools': for *arderchavc*, see GPC^2, s.v. 431. It is a mistranslation of the Lat. *gymnasium ducentorum phylosophorum*, 'a school of 200 scholars' (*GM* §156.322).

418　*yn canu yndun o amrauael geluydodeu* 'speaking in them of various arts': *canu* normally means 'to sing/to chant', but it can also mean to 'state / to say', *GPC*, s.v. (1c), which is the most likely meaning here. There is no mention of singing or chanting or of speaking in the Latin, merely a statement of the fact that the scholars were 'skilled in astronomy and other sciences', *qui astronomia atque ceteris artibus eruditi* (*GM* § 156.323).

418-19　*A chymeint a paratoet yna o darmerth ac a oed teilvng*: lit 'And as much (of) provision was then prepared as was fitting': *o darmerth* is dependent on *cymeint* in spite of the interpolation of *a paratoet yna*. The meaning is 'and as much provision as was fitting was then prepared'.

422　*eu yavn ac eu dylyet ac eu breint*: for the legal significance of *yavn* and *dylyet*, see note 279 above and for *breint*, see Jenkins, *The Law*, 319. This triplet does not appear in the Latin and has been inserted into the Welsh text as a narrative device. The meaning is that he invited all those wo had a right to be there.

427　*ac ef yn urdasseid* 'and he ordinate': *a(c)* is sometimes placed before an independent phrase, forming an absolute construction, which is nevertheless subordinate to the main clause in meaning: see *GMW* § 252. It corresponds to the Latin ablative absolute construction, which represents a subordinate clause: *rege … insignito* (*GM* § 157.359), 'lit. the king … distinguished (here by a crown)', i.e. 'after he had been crowned.'

431　*yn herwyd eu breint ac eu dylyet* 'according to their privilege and right': cf. *quorum ius id fuerat* (*GM* § 157.362–63), 'whose right this was'. This illustrates again the Welsh tendency to employ doublets. For *breint* and *dylyet*, see notes 279 and 422 above.

439-40　*pedeir guraged … yn arwein pedeir colomen purwynnyon*: note the inconsistency here in the use of sg. (*colomen*) and pl. (*guraged*, *purwynnyon*) respectively of nouns and adjectives following the numeral, see *GMW* § 51.

443   **rac digriuet oed eu guarandav** 'because it was pleasant to listen to them': for *rac* with causal meaning preceding the eqv. degree of the adj., see *GMW* § 45. Cf. Lat. *prae nimia dulcedine* (*GM* §157.370) 'because of the exceeding sweetness (i.e. of the music)'.

445–6   **o'r eglvys pvy gilid** 'from one church to the other': i.e. from church to church: see *GMW* § 105 N. 1.

452   **Kei pen svydwr** (Cai ben swyddwr) 'Cai the chief steward': in the Welsh laws, the *swyddwr* was the court officer responsible for serving food and drink, see *GPC s.v.* Nouns in apposition usually lenite, see note 5 and 7 above.

462   **Ac a uei o uarchavc clotuavr**: lit. 'and what there was of a famous knight' i.e. all the celebrated knights, cf. *a oed o of* (Thomson, *Branwen*, 29), 'and all the blacksmiths', lit. 'and [that] which was of a blacksmith'; see note by Parry-Williams in *BBCS* i (1921), 104–06.

463   **o un rvysc ac arueu yd aruerynt**: it is difficult to decide which of the many meanings of *rwysg* and *aruerynt* are applicable here. *GPC s.v. rhwysg* (b) gives 'majesty, dignity, glory, splendour, pomp, ostentation'; for *aruer o* the first edition of *GPC s.v. arferaf* 1(c) gives 'to wear habitually' but this meaning is omitted from the updated edition. Cf. Lat. *unius coloris uestibus atque armis utebatur*, which is loosely translated 'he wore clothes and arms of a single colour' (*GM* § 157.387), since the basic meanings of *utor* are 'to use, employ, enjoy, adopt' (L&S *s.v.*). The concept the translator is trying to convey is that they enjoyed the same glory and wore the same armour.

463   **gorderchwraged**: these mistresses were objects of courtly love within the chivalric order. Lines 463–7 present an epitome of the chivalry topos on which the plots of many later romances were based.

464   **ac ny bydei teilvng gan un wreic** 'and it would not be fitting in the opinion of any woman': *gan* can be used with an adj. to denote feeling, state of mind, judgement or opinion, see *GPC s.v* (3) and *GMW* § 208.

465   **y milvryaeth**: i.e. *ym milvryaeth*, 'in battle'.

470   **y nei uab y chuaer**: the special relationship between a man and his sister's son was known as the avunculate. In some early societies a man's heir was his nephew rather than his own son, cf. the relationship between Bendigeidfran and Gwern in the tale of *Branwen ferch Llŷr* (Davies, *Mabinogion*, 22–34) and see also Ó Cathasaigh, 'The sister's son'. The nature of Medrawd's relationship to Arthur therefore exacerbates his treachery. In the Latin version Geoffrey says he will not remain silent on the *infamia praenuntiati sceleris* (*GM* § 177 5) 'the disgrace of the reported crime', perpetrated by *sceleratissimus proditor*

ille Modredus 'that most foul traitor Modred. (GM § 177.10). This is omitted from BD.

473–4   *Howel uab Emyr Llydav*: the Bretons invariably come to the aid of the beleaguered Britons; see Introd. xvi.

476   *y bradvr tvyllvr ysgymun gan Uedravt* 'the accursed traitor [and] deceiver, namely Medrawd': *gan* is sometimes used before a personal noun in apposition with the sense 'namely', see *GMW* § 208.

478–9   *gan rodi udunt o'r tu drav y Hvmyr*: 'giving them [lands] from the far side of the Humber': the Humber seems to have been regarded as a natural boundary between the Britons and the Saxons. At a later stage in the *Historia*, after the so-called *Edefflet* (Ethelfrid, King of the Northumbrians) was defeated by the Britons under the leadership of Cadfan, he was banished to the other side of the Humber *a Chaduan yn urenhin ar enys Prydein oll wedy hynny ac yn eidav coron Lundein* (*BrD* 192), 'and Cadfan king over the whole of the isle of Britain after that and in possession of the crown of London'.

479   *yr hyn a rodassei Gortheyrn*: in return for their help in battle, Gwrtheyrn rewarded the immigrant Saxons with various gifts and lands. Later he gave Kent to Hengist in return for his daughter's hand in marriage, and finally he conceded his cities and castles to redeem his life. See text ll. 158–79.

483   *neur daroed*: this is a combination of the affirmative pre-verbal particle *neu*, and the perfect particle *ry* (*GMW* §188) with a form of the aux. verb *daruot*.

486   *y borth Northamtvn* 'to the port of Northampton': as Northampton is landlocked, this cannot be a reference to that particular town; cf. *Ac y peris guneuthur fyrd … o Penryn Kernyv hyt yn Cathneis ym Prydein … ; a ford arall … o Uynyv hyt yn Northamtvn* (*BrD* 275). Henry Lewis thought this was a reference to Southampton, but it is unlikely to be that port in this context. There is much variation concerning the location of this battle; cf. Lat. *in Rutupi portu* (GM § 177.20), namely Richborough; in the RB version *hyt yn aber temys,* 'as far as the Thames estuary'.

489   *ar nyt oed havd eu rifav* 'those who were not easily counted': lit. 'those whose counting was not easy'. For *ar* as a dem. pron., see *GMW* § 75 and for genitival rel. clause *GMW* § 69.

500   *a guisgav amdanei yn uynaches* 'and dressed as a nun': *yn* is predicative.

501   *arwein eu habit* 'wearing their habit': i.e. led a monastic life.

503–4   *y savl ry gollassei* 'those whom he had lost': for substantival use of *sawl* as antecedent to rel. pron., see *GMW* § 103 (a).

510   *ny handenws Arthur hagen yna gohir vrth cladu y calaned*: RB has *ny hanbwyllwys Medrawt yna gohir wrth gladu y ladedigyon*, 'Medrawd did not bother to wait there to bury his slain', which Henry Lewis

regarded as the correct version (*BrD* 275). The Latin text has: *Qui deinde, non multum curans quae sepelitio peremptis fireret, cito … iter arripuit* (*GM* § 178. 43–44), lit. 'He then, scarcely caring what burial would be given to his dead, hurriedly … fled'. Perhaps the confusion in transmission arose from the fact that Medrawd is not mentioned by name in the Latin text, but by the rel. pron. *qui* 'who', which the translator or scribe thought referred to Arthur. The meanings given for *handdenu, hamddenu* in *GPC* which could apply to this context are 'to spend time over (sth.), concern oneself with'. The text in BD, therefore could be translated, 'A., however, did not concern himself then with the delay in burying the dead'.

511   *y mynychet hwnnw* '(with) that frequency': in this adverbial phase, the equative degree of the adj. *mynych* 'often' is used as a noun: see *GMW* § 44. The reading in H1 is *y sawl weith hynny* 'so many times'. The meaning is that Medrawd escapes with such frequency; cf. Lat. *quoniam tociens euassisset*, 'because he had escaped so often' (*GM* § 178.45).

512   *hyt ar auon Camlan*: for theories about the possible location of Camlan, see Jackson, 'Once again', 56; Padel, 'Geoffrey of Monmouth and Cornwall', 13–14; Bartrum, *Dictionary*, 97–99; *Celtic Culture* (ed. Koch), Vol. I, *s.v. Camlan*.

515–16   *chue guyr a chuech canwr a thriugein mil*: for pl. noun with numeral, see note 387 above. Ancient and medieval historians were not precise in their recording of numbers. They would exaggerate the strength of their armies and the numbers of those slain to suit their own purpose, which was the glorification of the protagonists and the vilification of the enemy. This would have been Geoffrey's view of history too and, to a clergyman like him, these particular numbers would have sprung readily to mind, as they have a biblical significance. God created the world in six days, (Genesis 2.2) and commanded that one should work on six days of the week only (Exodus. 20.8–9). The serahpim that appeared to Isaiah had six wings (Isaiah. 6.1–3). Six hundred and sixty six is a significant number too: in the Old Testament it is the number of gold talents Solomon received annually (1 Kings 10.14) and in the New Testament it represents the anti-christ (Revelations 13.18).

526   *gan Vedravt*: see note 476 above.

529   *aghyurvys ynt ar ymlad*: cf. *belli usus ignaros* (*GM* §178.61) 'unskilled in the exercise of war'. The translator has rendered the Lat. dependent genitive by the prep. *ar*. This passage is in reported speech in the Latin.

530   *kyneuyn gyurvys yvch o dysc peunydyavl ymlad* 'you are habitually skillful by daily training in fighting': the adj. *kyneuyn* (cynefin) is used

adverbially here to form a loose compound with the following adj. *cyurvys* (cyfrwys). For *o* see Glossary o¹ (iii).

534   *gan gvynuan y rei meirv* 'with lamenting the dead': although the Latin has *morientium gemitus*, 'groans of the dying' (*GM* §178.65–66), *cwynfan* in the Welsh context has to be interpreted as 'lamentation', as the *meirw* 'dead' cannot groan!

535–6   *Canys o bob parth y brathei y guyr ac y brethyt vynteu, y lladei ac y lledit vynteu*: this formula is found in early Welsh praise poetry, the best known example being *A chet lledesynt, wy lladasan* 'although they were killed, they killed' (Williams, *Canu Aneirin*, 14). The understood subject of *lladei* is *guyr*.

553   *y llyuyr*: this is the book of ancient British history which Geoffrey had allegedly received from his friend Walter, Archdeacon of Oxford. (see Introduction xvii-xix). There is no reference to it at this point in the Latin text, however, nor in RB or H2, although it is mentioned in the dedication and in the body of the text. This addition by the author of *Brut Dingestow* suggests that he is aware of the ambiguous nature of Geoffrey's statement, that Arthur is mortally wounded but has been taken to the isle of Avalon to recover. This contradictory report of Arthur's fatal wound, but possible recovery, seems to symbolise Geoffrey's ambivalent loyalty, both to the indigenous inhabitants of Britain and to the conquerors. The loss of British sovereignty would please the Normans; the possibility of its recovery would hearten the Welsh: see Jarman, *Sieffre/Geoffrey*, 83 and Jankulak, *Geoffrey*, 74–76.

558   *yd ymedwis*: Cadwaladr departed from Brittany where he had gone to seek help to re-establish himself in his homeland, which had been the victim of civil unrest, plague and attack.

561–2   *y deudecuet dyd wedy Calan Mei*: cf. *duodecima ... die kalendarum Maiarum* (*GM* 281 §206.585) 'the twelfth day of the Calends of May'. The fact that the Welsh translator writes *wedy* 'after' shows clearly that he was ignorant of the Roman system of calculating dates. The Roman system had 3 distinct references of time in every month: the Calends fell on the 1st of the month, the Nones on the 5th, the Ides on the 13th, but in March, May, July and October the Nones and Ides fell on the 7th and 15th of the month respectively. Any dates which fell between these three distinct points were calculated inclusively by the number of days which fell short of the next fixed point. Therefore, counting backwards from the point of reference, the 12th day of the Calends of May is the 20th of April.

562   *yd aeth o'r byt hvn ef y tragywydavl teyrnas wlat nef* 'he went from this world to the eternal kingdom of the land of heaven': for the delayed subject (*ef*) of the verb (*aeth*), see Borsley et al., 316.

563   ***seith gant***: in the Dingestow manuscript, this is emended to *chwe chant* in a later hand above the line. There is disagreement among the manuscripts about this date. The Welsh version in the Jesus MS gives the date of his death as 12 December 688, the Latin version as 20 April 689 (*GM* §206.586). As Lloyd points out in *History* ii 230, n.9, 'The plague in the reign of Oswy which, according to the *Saxon Genealogies*, carried off Cadwaladr, can hardly be any other than the famous pestilence of 664'. He explains the confusion by Geoffrey's identification of Cadwaladr as Caedualla of Wessex.

565   ***o'r Iuor***: the def. art. is sometimes found with a proper noun: see *GMW* §29a. Iuor and Ini set sail from Brittany where Cadwaladr had taken refuge.

568   ***A nyt mavr dygrynoes udunt*** 'And it did not avail them much': cf. *Sed non multum profuit* (*GM* § 207.589), 'It did not benefit them much'. According to Henry Lewis (*BrD* 280) *nyt mavr dygrynoes* could be an error for *ny mavr dygrynoes* as *mavr* forms a loose compound with the verb, or *nyt mavr* could be the main clause followed by an oblique relative clause without a particle preceding the verb. For an adj. used adverbially placed at the beginning of the sentence, see *GMW* § 251 (a).

579   ***Pedwar ugein mlyneδ a chwechant ac vn***: Thomas Jones points out (*BT* (*Pen. 20 trans.*) 129) that the opening entries of the *Chronicle of the Princes* are based partly on the *Annales Cambriae* (the earliest surviving Latin version of the Annals of Wales which is found in Harleian MS 3859) and partly on the concluding sections of Geoffrey's *Historia* (*GM* §§ 205–08). The date of Cadwaladr's death in the Pen. 20 version of the Chronicle is 681: see above note 563.

579–80 ***pan vv varwolaeth vawr*** : this is recorded briefly in AC: *Mortalitas magna fuit in Britannia*, 'there was a huge fatality in Britain', but substantially elaborated by Geoffrey of Monmounth (*GM* 277–79 § 203). The translator of BD attributes the plague, which caused severe deprivation and loss of life, to the wrath of God: *BrD* 204–05.

582   ***y deuδecuet dyδ o Galan Mei*** 'the twelfth day from the Calends of May': on the Roman system of calculating dates, see note 561–2 above.

583–4   ***y proffwydassei Verδin vrth Wrtheyrn Wrtheneu***: initial lenition of the subject (*Verdin*) following the finite verb frequently ocurs in MW, particularly after 3 sg. impf. and plpft.; see *GMW* § 21(a). For the alternative form of the name Gwrtheyrn Gwrtheneu, see text ll. 104 and 591. Myrddin's prophecy to Gwrtheyrn predicts that survivors of the fatal plague, mentioned above in note 579–80, will be forced to leave their native land, which will succumb to Saxon domination (*BrD* 105).

588   ***yr anodun vall dymhestylus a'r newyn girat*** 'the abysmal tempestuous pestilence and dire famine'; see note 579–80 above.

590   *o'r mor pwy gilid* 'from one end of the sea to the other'; see note 445–6 above.

590–1   *val y buassei gynt yn oes Hors a Hengist*: see ll. 138–68 of these selections.

593   *dinessyd a'r trefi*: in MW *dinas* could be either a city or town (fortified or unfortified) or a stronghold (*GPC* s.v.), whereas *tref* is more of a territorial division: see *BS* 279.

593   *randiroed*: from *rhan* 'share, portion' + *tir* 'land', therefore 'share-lands' or 'land portions', according to Thomas Jones (*BS* 279). It is used in three ways according to *GPC* s.v. *rhandir*: (1) part of a country, area, region, district; (2) territorial unit in Welsh laws 'share land'; (3) share/portion (of land, especially as inheritance), patrimony. There is inconsistency in the Welsh laws as to what constitutes a *rhandir* in sense (2). According to *The Book of Iorwerth*, the text of the Vendotion or northern code of law, it consists of 16 acres (Wiliam, *Iorwerth*, 60.20–21), whereas according to *The Book of Blegywryd*, the text of the Demetian or southern code of law, there are 312 acres in a *randir* (Williams and Powell, *Blegywryd*, 71.9). See also Jenkins, *The Law*, 257 (92.22*n*) and 269 (122.23*n*), *BS* 279 and *The Book of Colan*, a 'revised edition' of The Book of Iorwerth (Jenkins, *Colan*, 161).

593   *cantrefoed*: from *cant* 'hundred' and *tref* 'town', literally 'a hundred towns'. A division of land which contains two or more commotes and approximately a hundred homesteads or large farms: see Davies, *Conquest*, 12, 20–21.

593   *sswidev*: in ModW one of the meanings of *swydd* is, 'county, shire', but Thomas Jones (*BS* 280) points out that it would be anachronistic to translate it as such in this context and suggests 'province' as a more suitable rendering. Another meaning is 'a unit of land or territory, often denoting a lordship': see *GPC* s.v. (b).

594   *ardaloed*: Thomas Jones (*BS* 280) suggests that *ardal* is used here for a division which is larger than a *swydd*. It is possible that *sswideu* and *ardaloed* correspond to the Latin *provinciae* and *regiones*: see Stenton, *Anglo Saxon England*, 290–94, 496–97.

596–7   *symvdassant ev henweu o'r rei yd aruerwyt yr hynny hyt hediw onadunt*: lit . 'they changed their names from those which one used for them from then until today'. Semantically one would expect 'to those names' rather than 'from those names'. For a*ruerwyt … onadunt*, see *GPC*[2] s.v. *arferaf*.

598   *yr arwyd dwillodrus* 'the treacherous sign': the reference is to the abortive peace conference arranged by Gwrtheyrn between the Britons and Saxons, when Heingyst (Hengist) ordered each of his men to conceal a dagger in his hose and at the given signal kill the Briton nearest to him: see *GM* §104, *BrD* 99.

599   *Mynyd Ambri* 'The Mount of Ambrius': the Latin genitive form *Ambri*
      has been retained here. This name corresponds to Geoffrey's *in pago
      Ambrii* (*GM* 135 §103.458) 'in the village of Ambrius', which is recorded
      in Griscom's edition of HRB as *in pago (c)ambrii* 'in the village of the
      Cambrians'. The translation of this name in BD is *Maes Kymry* (*BrD*
      99).

600   *draweth howre sexes* 'draw your knives': in *BrD* 99 the form of this
      ancient Anglo-Saxon signal is *Nimet oure saxes*, and translated as
      Kympervch avch kyllyll 'take your knives', cf. *Nymyd ovyr sexes* (*GM* 135
      §104.462). Other variants are, *Nemet ovre saxas* (MS Harlech), *Draweth
      hwr sexes* (Cleopatra B v *Brut*): see BS 280. There is a play on the word
      Saxon here: see Ross, 'Hengist's watchword', 81–101.

602   *Blwy[dy]n wedy hynny*: the events referred to the previous year are:
      (i) the victims of land erosion in Flanders settling in Dyfed with the
      permission of King Henry I, (ii) the building of Cenarth Castle, as a
      safe-haven for his wife, children and possessions, by Gerald, the officer
      of Pembroke castle.

604   *A'r wled honno a wnaeth ef y Nodolic* 'And he held that feast at (the)
      Christmas': *y Nodolic* (variant of *Nadolig*) is used adverbially here. For
      the use of the article preceding names of feasts, see GMW § 29(c).

606   *y dywededic kastell* 'the aforementioned castle': i.e. Cenarth Castle; see
      note 602 above.

607   *ychydic o niuer* 'a small force': lit. 'a little of a force'. (B)*ychydig* is often
      follwed by '*o*', see *GMW* §112(b).

611–12 *drwy anogedigaeth kythreul* 'at the instigation of the devil': cf. *BS*
      104 *a gwedy y gyflenwi o gythreulaeth*, 'after he had been filled with
      devilment'. The Red Book version (*BT (RB)* 54), on the other hand reads,
      o annoc Duw 'at the instigation God'. This anomaly is clearly the result
      of a Latin phrase such as *instigatione* (or *suggestione*) *diaboli/diabolica*
      being misunderstood or miscopied as *instigatione* (or *suggestione*) *divi/
      dei/domini/divina*: see Introduction, xxxi.

612   *o serch a chariad y wreic* 'by passion and love for his wife': objective
      genitive.

614   *dros y mur a'r fos y doeth ef* 'he came over the rampart and ditch': cf.
      BT (RB) 54 *wedy [g]wneuthur clawd dan y trotheu*, 'after having secretly
      made a hole under the threshold'. *BS* omits mention of the mode of
      access.

616   *a dodi tan yn y tei*: *tai* here probably means 'buildings' or 'outhouses':
      see *BT* (*Pen. 20 trans.*) 28.

619   *yn y kylch* 'around it': the reference is to *drws*, which is masculine. One
      would expect lenition after the 3. sg. pers. pron. *y* but the mutation is
      not shown here.

623   *Neur diengis y neb yd oedoch yn y geissyaw* 'The one whom you
        were seeking has escaped': the poss. pron *y* within the periphrastic
        construction *bot* + *yn* + vn. refers back to the antecedent *y neb*, cf. 199
        above and *GMW* § 69.

625   *A gwedy nas kawssant* 'And after/when they didn't find him': for *gwedy
        na*, see *GMW* § 266. *–s* is 3 sg. inf. pron.

629–30 *ac a athoed ymeith y wrthaw* 'and had gone away from him': i.e. had
        deserted him.

631   *A phan gigleu Gadwgawn*: note the lenition of the subject after the
        finite verb *cigleu*: see *GMW* § 21 (a) and cf. 583–4 above.

631   *y chwedyl hwnnw* 'that news': the phrasing here is more neutral than in
        the other versions: *BT (RB)* 56 *y gweithret hwnnw*, 'that deed'; *BS* 106 *yr
        anghyfreith* 'the unlawful act'.

632   *o dwy ford*: lit. 'of two ways'. Thomas Jones translates 'for two reasons'
        (*BT (Pen. 20 trans.)* 29). For 'o' used in this sense, see *GPC s.v.* 14 (a).

632   *treis yr arlwydes*: objective genitive, 'the assault on the lady'; cf. 612.
        The reading in the Red Book version (*BT (RB)* 56) is more explicit, *y
        treis gyt a wnathoedit* 'the common assault that had been made'. In that
        context, *gyt* is an adj. qualifying *treis*. The lenition to *kyt* suggests that
        treis is a f. noun even though lenition after the article is not shown. The
        meaning is 'common assault' or possibly an assault in which the victim
        co-operated: see *GPC s.v trais.*

633   *sarhaet y swydwr*: objective genitive, 'the injury [done] to the steward'.
        cf. 612.

636   *vynghael i*: for marking of nasal mutation, see Introduction, xliv-v.

636   *yw y tad* 'to their father': this combination of *yw* (a form of the prep. *y*
        'to' with the 3 sg. or 3 pl. pref. pron.) occurs in the selections from Pen.
        20. Thomas Jones (*BT (Pen. 20)* xviii) suggests it may be dialectal. The
        usual forms are simply *y*, a contraction of *y + y*, or *yw*: see also *GMW*
        §56 N3.

637   *o dra charyat y wreic* 'because of great infatuation for the woman': cf.
        612 above.

637   *ef a yllygawd y deu vab a'r verch*: in *BS* 17 there is an additional
        comment: *ac attal ev mam ganthaw yntev*, 'and kept their mother with
        himself'.

639   *medylyaw a oruc ef dial sarhaed Gerald ar Ywein* 'he thought to
        avenge upon Owain the injury done to Gerald': lit. 'to avenge the insult
        of Gerald upon Owain'. The recipient of the *dial* 'revenge' is freqently
        preceded by the prep. *ar*: see *GPC s.v.*

642–4   *ef a'ch anrydeda ac a'ch dyrcheif ... ac a gyngoruynna wrthywch ych
        holl genedyl* 'he (i.e. the king) will honour and exalt you ... and all your
        kinsmen will be envious of you': for this abrupt change of subject in
        co-ordinating clauses, see Borsley et al. 299–301 (ex. 40 in particular).

650   *y gwr y lladawd Ywein y vrodyr* 'the man whose brothers Y. killed':
      for the genitival construction see *GMW* § 69. The RB version likewise
      records the death of 'brothers' (*BT* (*RB*) 58); cf. BS which has one
      brother only: *canys Oweyn a ladassei y vraut ef*, 'for Owain had killed
      his brother' (*BS* 106). Thomas Jones is of the opinion that the plural is
      the correct reading here, as it is recorded in all three texts that Owain
      had slain Meurig and Griffri, sons of Trahaearn: see *BT* (*Pen. 20 trans.*)
      163, *BS* 102, *BT* (*RB*) 52.

658   *ef a damweinnyawd* '*there/it happened*': *ef a* can be employed as a pre-
      verbal particle or 'expletive subject', see *GMW* § 191 and Borsley et al.,
      297–98.

661   *Y rei a aeth Arwystli onadunt*: *onadunt* is dependent on *y rei*, i.e. *y rei*
      onadunt a aeth Arwystli 'those of them who went to Arwystli'. Note the
      absence of a prep. before *Arwystli* to indicate goal of motion: cf. 400
      above.

661   *y kyuarvv wyr Maelenyd ac wynt*: the ending *–bu*, *–fu* sometimes
      causes lenition of the subject: see *GMW* § 21(a) and cf. 583–4 and 631
      above.

667   **Ryd Corruonet** (Rhyd Corfonedd): MS *Cozruonet*; *BT* (*RB*) 58 *Ryt*
      Cornuec and *BS* 108 *Ryt Coruonec*. It is difficult, if not impossible, to
      give the correct reading until the site has been definitively identified.
      On the grounds that there is a place called *Moel Cerneu* in the vicinity,
      George Owen in his *The Description of Penbrokeshire*, 434–35, suggested
      that it is the same ford as that which was later called *Rhyd Meirionydd*
      on the road between Borth, near Aberystwyth, and Llanbadarn Fawr.

668   *Ac ef yn dyuod yno*: lit 'And he coming there', i.e. as he was coming: see
      note 427 above.

671–2 *a llawer o nerthoed agatuyd a gant ar nyd ydyw gyd ac wynt yr awr honn*
       'and perhaps they will have much support/plenty of reinforcements that
       they do not have (lit. is not with them) now': for *ar ny(d)* 'that which …
       not', see *GMW* § 75 and for uses of *(yd)yw* in negative and subordinate
       contexts, *GMW* § 148.

672–3 *ny weda y ni vyned mor anhyspys a hynny*: Thomas Jones (*BT* (*Pen. 20*
       trans.) 30) translates, 'it is not proper for us to go so unawares as that'
       but *GPC²* s.v. *anhysbys* prefers the meaning 'secret, clandestine', which
       seems more accurate in this context: 'it is not proper for us to go as
       secretly as that'.

679   *gre Gadwgan* 'Cadwgan's stud': lenition of the proper noun *Cadwgan*
      occurs because it is in a genitival relationship after a f. sg. noun; see
      GMW § 19.

679–80 *A gwedy y chaffael* 'And after obtaining it': this could be a reference to
        y wlat 'the land' or more likely to *gre Gadwgan* 'Cadwgan's stud'; both
        nouns are feminine.

680–1   *y'r kestyll*: *BS* 108 also has *kestyll*, cf. *BT* (*RB*) 60 *y pebylleu* 'to their tents'.

681   *ar nawd* 'for sanctuary': see *GPC s.v. nawdd* 9 (a). In the Welsh laws *nawdd* was originally connected with the right of individuals to afford protection within certain temporal and geographical limits. This concept extended to the right of the church to offer sanctuary: see Jones and Owen, 'Twelfth-century Welsh Hagiography', 55–56.

682   *ereill nys diuaassant*: lit. 'others, they did not destroy them'. The inf. 3 pl. pron. *-s* is used anaphorically to emphasise *ereill*; see *GMW* § 194.

687   *eithyr kyfleoed y seint e hunein* 'except the precincts of the saints themselves': this contradicts the other texts of BT: cf. *RB* 60 *yn orwac hayach yd ymhoelassant eithyr cael anuolyanus anreith o gyulyeoed y seint*, 'they returned well-nigh empty-handed save for having taken infamous spoil from the precincts of the saints', and *BS* 108 *ac anreithiaw yr eglwissev yn llwyr* 'and plundered the churches completely'.

691   *y deu yeirll*: this is a reference to Robert, Earl of Shrewsbury and his brother Arnulf, who sought the help of King Muirchertach of Ireland (1086–1119) in their conflict with King Henry I of England: see *BT* (*Pen. 20 trans.*) 22–3 and *BT* (*RB*) 41–43.

691   *wedy anuon o'y vrawd* 'after being sent by his brother': the 3 sg. poss. pron. is invisible in **wedy'i anuon,* lit. 'after his sending'. The meaning is confirmed by the corresponding passage in *BT* (*RB*) 60, 61 *ac yd anuonyssit ef y gann y urawt* 'he was sent by his brother'.

697–8   *Madoc ac Ithael … a achubassant rann Gadwgawn ac Ywein y vab* o **Bowys**: this is a clumsy construction: *rann* is qualified by two phrases, a genitival phrase, *G. ac Y. y vab*, and by a prepositional phrase *o Bowys*. Thomas Jones translates 'Madog and Ithel … seized Cadwgan's and his son Owain's portion of Powys' *BT* (*Pen. 20 trans.*) 31.

706–7   *na bei gydmeithas yn y byd y ryngthaw ac Ywein*: Thomas Jones translates 'that there was to be no comradeship at all between him and Owain' (*BT* (*Pen. 20 trans.*) 31). *na* introduces a noun-clause ultimately dependent on *yr amod hwnn* 'this condition', *GMW* § 194 (b).

709–10   *ac ymgydyaw yn geladwy gyda chenedyl vdunt*: there seems to be a tautology here: *ymgydyaw* < *ym* (reflexive) + *cuddiaw* (ModW. *cuddio*), 'hid themselves'; *celadwy* also bears the meaning 'concealed'. Thomas Jones translates, 'and they lurked concealed with kinsmen of theirs' (*BT* (*Pen. 20 trans.*) 31). For the prep. *y* denoting possession, see *GMW* § 221(d).

711–12   *ac nyd y Geredigyawn y trosses ef namyn y Bowys* 'and it was not to Ceredigion that he made his way but to Powys': an example of the mixed order, *GMW* § 199, producing contrast between Ceredigyawn and Powys.

714–15   *En dydyeu Edward, vrenhin Lloegyr a Therdelach, vrenhin Ywerdon e ganet Gruffud vrenhin Gwyned en Ywerdon* 'In the days of Edward, king of England and Terdelach, king of Ireland, was born Gruffudd, king of Gwynedd, in Ireland': this is an echo of Matthew 2.1. The English and Irish kings are Edward the Confessor (1042–66) and Toirdelbach Ua Briain (d.1086), grandson of Brian Boru (d. 1014), king of Munster and the most powerful king in Ireland following the death of Diarmut mac Mail na mBó of Leinster in 1072: see O Cróinín, *Early Medieval Ireland*, 277–79 and Duffy, 'Ostmen', 378–96. For *Ywerdon*, see G.R. Isaac, 'A note on the name of Ireland in Irish and Welsh' *Ériu* 59, 2009, 49–55. For lenition of nouns in apposition, see note 5 above.

716   *kymvt Colomcell … svrth Colomcell*: Columcille was a sixth century Irish saint. A *cwmwd* or commote is a unit of land in medieval Wales, within which the court for administering the law was held; two would constitute a *cantref* 'hundred': see Jenkins, *The Law* 121. It is unlikely that there was an area of Dublin bearing the name *kymvt Colomcell*, but *Svrth Colomcell* corresponds to *Sord Coluimcille*, anglicized as Swords, where there was a Columbian monastic foundation seven miles north of Dublin (*MPW* 86). Flanagan has identified the place where Gruffudd ap Cynan was brought up as Cloghran, a few miles south of Swords ('*Historia Gruffud vab Kenan*', 78). There is evidence from Welsh and Irish sources of a connection between Gruffudd's descendants and the area: see also Duffy, 'The 1169 invasion', 104–05.

716   *y magwyt*: lit. 'one brought him up'. The inf. pron. *y* has been absorbed into the pre-verbal particle; *y (y) magwyt* was later written *y'i magwyd*.

717   *tri milltir*: *milltir* is regarded as a m. noun here, but *tri* has been changed to *tair* in later manuscripts: see *HGrK* 1.

717   *a'e vamvaeth*: the meaning is *wet-nurse* here rather than *foster-mother* (see *GPC s.v. mamaeth*), as it is unlikely that his mother and foster-mother would have lived together three miles away from *Svrth Colomcell*, where, according to the *Historia*, Gruffudd was reared.

718   *Kenan, vrenhin Gvyned*: that Cynan had never been king of Gwynedd is suggested by BT and other sources for this period, where Gruffudd is regularly referred to as the grandson of Iago: see *BT (Pen. 20 trans.)* 16; *BT (RB)* 28; *BS*, 28. The appellation 'G., grandson of Iago', however, would have been more normal in Ireland than in Wales: see *VCG* 127 and Charles-Edwards, *Early Irish and Welsh Kinship* 220–24, Maund, 'Gruffudd, grandson of Iago' 109–16 and Duffy, 'Ostmen' 385–87. For the lenition of *brenin*, see note 5 above and cf. *verch* 718 below.

718–19   *Ragnell verch Avloed, vrenhin dinas Dulyn* 'Rhagnell daughter of Afloedd, King of Dublin': in the Irish text, *Banshenchus*, 'History of Women', *Ragnailt ingen Amlaib* is named as one of the most notable women of the world but there is no record of her in any source, other than the *Historia*, as wife of Cynan and mother of Gruffudd (*MPW* 86). However, as Gruffudd called one of his daughters Ranillt, a variant of Ragnell, it is possible that Ragnailt was indeed his mother. For Gruffudd's ancestry see Thornton, 'Genealogy' and Maund, *Ireland* 175–77. The form *Avloed* is an oral borrowing of some Irish form of the Norse *Áleifr, Ólafr*, such as *Amlaib/Amhlaeibh* (*HGK* cxiii and *MPW* 87). He has been identified as either Amlaib Arnaid (Olaf Arnaid) or as Amlaib son of Sitriuc, called *nGall* in the Annals in 1029, and who had links with Wales. The first was killed as a young man in 1012 and never became king of Dublin and the second also died before his father in 1034 and never became king: see further Duffy, 'Ostmen', 378–96 and cf. *Amlavd Wledic*, Eigyr's father (*BrD* 136.15). It is not surprising to find a name of Norse origin, as Dublin was originally a Scandinavian settlement.

719 *a phymet rann Ywerdon* 'a fifth part of Ireland': i.e. 'a province', in this case Leinster. *Pymhe*t corresponds to the Irish term *coiced* 'fifth'; an explanation of the term's origin is given in the tale of *Branwen ferch Llŷr* (Thomson, *Branwen* 18).

720 *o vrenhinyaul genedel* 'of royal descent': cf. *Prosapia … quam nobilis ac regia oriundus erat*, 'From how noble and regal a lineage he stemmed' (*VGC* 52 § 2).

721 *megys y tysta ac[h] a boned y reeni*: there is obviously an omision in the MS. Paul Russell (*VGC* 127) suggests reading *ac a* as *ach a*, giving the meaning 'as the lineage and the pedigree of his parents testifies', echoing the doublets *Prosapia … quam nobilis ac regia* of the Latin text. This seems more likely than D. Simon Evans's emendation: *megys y tysta ac [y traeth]a boned y reeni* 'as the pedigree of his parents testifies and relates' (*MPW* 23, 53). *Tystia* is the expected form, but loss of <-i-> is rare in this text: see *HGrK* 38. The meaning of *reeni* here could be 'ancestors', rather than 'parents'.

722–3 *gwr kymedraul y veint*: lit. 'a man, moderate [with respect to] his size', cf. *llog diruawr y meint* 'a ship, enormous [with respect to] its size' (*YBH* 5). The noun *gwr* is qualified by a complex adjectival phrase consisting of an adjective, a possessive pronoun referring back to *gwr* and a noun which pertains to a characteristic of the man denoted by *gwr*. For a discussion of the construction, see Mac Cana 'An Old Nominal Relative Sentence ' and *GMW* § 40.

723 *ac emennyd guressauc*: the Latin text has *capite calido* (*VGC* 72 § 20), translated by Russell as 'a clever head'. Acccording to *GPC* s.v. (c) *gwresog* covers a wide range of nuances, and here probably means 'keen'.

726–7   *amravaellyon yeithyoed*: these languages were probably Irish, Norse, Welsh, French, English and Latin, see *MPW* 114. For <-ll-> = /-l-/, see Introduction, xl.

727   *kivdaut*: the appropriate meaning here is 'armed band, troop, army' (*GPC* s.v. *ciwdod*); cf. Lat. *in milites clementem* 'merciful towards his soldiers' (*VGC* 72 §20).

728   *em bruyder* 'in battle': for *yn* before an indef. noun, see note 29 above.

729–30   *Ac val yd oed Gruffud y velly, weithieu en rwyd, weithyeu yn afruyd racdav* lit. 'And as G. was thus, sometimes [it was] easy, sometimes difficult for him': cf. Lat. *Dum variis fortunae fluctibus iactaretur Griffinus, modo prosperis, modo adversis* 'While G. was being tossed about by the variable waves of fortune, sometimes favourable, sometimes unfavourable' (*VGC* 76, 77 §24), where the adjs. *prosperis* and *adversis* qualify *fluctibus* 'waves'. For *rwyd rac* compare *ual y bei rwydach racdaw gaffel y neges* 'so that it was easier for him to accomplish his mission' (Williams, *Kedymdeithyas* 6).

732   *goskethloyu*: compound adj. 'of bright appearance', from *gosget/gosgedd* 'appearance, form' + *gloyw* 'bright, stunning'. Brightness of appearance in a woman is a quality especially praised in medieval Welsh love poetry.

740   *mab da y deuodeu*: lit. 'a boy good [with respect to] his manners'. i.e. good-mannered, courteous. For the syntax, see note 722–3.

741   *esgynnv ar vlwydyned y yeuengtit en ty e vam* 'reaching (lit. ascending upon) the years of his youth in his mother's house': there is an inconsistency here, as in 716–17 he is said to have been reared three miles away from his mother and wet-nurse. That mention is made of his mother alone, rather than his parents, has suggested to Duffy ('Ostmen' 391) that he may have been a posthumous child.

742   *ymhlith henne* 'during that [period]': it is difficult to tell which precise stage of his youth this was. For *henne* denoting an unspecified point or period in time, see *GMW* § 92(d).

742   *managei*: *manag-* is the stem of the vn. *menegi* which has affection extending over two syllables. Later *myneg-* was adopted as the stem. The imperfect tense indicates the repetitive nature of Ragnall's reminders.

743   *a pha dref tat oed idav* 'and what patrimony he had': for the legal implications of the collocation *tref tad*, see Jenkins, *The Law* 136.

744–5   *gorthrum y kemyrth* 'he felt sad': cf. Lat. *Quibus … vocibus anxius* 'Upset by these words' (*VGC* 58, 59 § 9); *gorthrum* can be both a noun 'sadness' and an adj. 'troubled' (see *GPC* s.v *gorthrwm*) but, in view of the use of the particle *y*, the most likely interpretation here is to regard *gorthrwm* as an adj. used adverbially at the beginning of a sentence in the abnormal order.

746-7   *Mvrchath vrenhin a chvynav urthav ef en benhaf, ac urth vrenhined*
         Ywerdon y lleill: *Mvrchath vrenhin* could be Muirchertach Ua Briain:
         see Duffy, 'Ostmen', 394–95. For *lleill* used adjectivally after a definite
         noun instead of *arall* or *eraill* 'other, others', see *GMW* § 96 (b).

750   *dioluch henne y Duw*: lit. 'he acknowledged that to God', i.e. he
         thanked God for that: *GPC s.v. diolchaf*.

754   *yn enwir ac en erbyn dylyet*: Evans translates 'unjustly and contrary
         to right' (*MPW* 59). The Latin text has *iniuste ac indebite* 'unjustly and
         undeservedly' (*VGC* 60, 61 § 10.).

755   *brenhinyn* 'petty king': in the Latin text he is a full blown *rex* 'king'
         (*VGC* 60 § 10).

755-6   *a'e rannv y rygthunt ry daroed udunt* 'and they divided it between
         them': lit. 'and its dividing between them happened for them'. For
         daroed udunt, see note 16 above.

760   *o damunet ry doethost*: lit. 'being eagerly awaited you have come':
         for this use of o see *GPC s.v. o*[1] (14a); Evans translates 'Your coming
         is welcome' (*MPW* 59). The Latin text is less partial and merely states
         adventus causas querunt 'they asked the reasons for his arrival' (*VGC*
         60 § 10).

763   *ampriodoryon argluydi dyuot o le arall* 'unrightful lords who had
         come from elsewhere': in *ampriodoryon* (amhriodorion), the negative
         prefix *an-* causes nasal mutation, not shown fully here. In *argluydi
         dyuot*, the vn. *dyuot* is used adjectivally: lit. 'having arrived lords', see
         GMW § 180 (7).

764   *en e* (yn y) 'when' (see *GMW* § 76), not to be confused with *yny* 'until'
         (see *GMW*, 244–45).

765-6   *hyt ar Robert Rudlan ... nei y Hu yarll Caer* 'as far as Robert of
         Rhuddlan ... nephew of Hugh Earl of Chester': this relationship is
         not corroborated elsewhere: cf. Lat. *vel versus castrum Rudlan versus
         Robertum ... vel ad Hugonem comitem Cestriae* '**either** to the castle of
         Rhuddlan to Robert ... **or** to Hugh, Count of Chester' (*VGC* 60 § 10).
         Russell (*VGC* 137) suggests that there may have been a textual error
         of transmission here, with *neu* 'or' being misunderstood by a later
         amanuensis as *nei* 'nephew'.

767   *a oedent ar dref y dat* 'who were [ruling] over his patrimony': for *ar* in
         this sense, see *GPC*[2] *s.v.* 4(d).

767   *enteu*: the reference is to Robert of Rhuddlan.

770   *wedy bot Gruffud bluydyned en Ywerdon* 'after G. had been for years
         in Ireland': after two unsuccessful attempts at establishing himself as
         permanent ruler of Gwynedd, Gruffudd returned to Ireland where he
         remained for several years.

775   *archescopty Mynyv* 'the archbishop's house of St David's': the claim of St
         David's to be recognised as a metropolitan see was a major issue during

the bishopric of Bernard, who died in 1148. His successors, however, were required to swear on oath not to pursue this goal. Nevertheless, Gruffudd's son, Owain Gwynedd, was in favour of the campaign to promote St David's to metropolitan status. See *MPW*, 107–08, *VGC*, 46–47 and Jones, '*Historia Gruffud*', 154.

776   **brenhin deheubarth Kemry**: *Deheubarth* often stands on its own as the name of the southern kingdom of Wales, but here it means 'southern part'.

776   **escop**: this is Sulien, who spent two terms as Bishop of St David's: 1073–78 and 1080–85 (*MPW* 109). He spent much of his life in Llanbadarn and in Ireland. His son, Rhigyfarch was the author of a Latin Life of St David.

777   **holl clas er argluyd Dewi** 'the whole community of the lord David': Lat. *chorus universus Sancti Davidis* 'the whole choir of St David' (*VGC*, 68, 69 § 17). For the title *arglwydd* when addressing a bishop, cf. *Arglwyd escop, … dy uendith* (*PKM* 63), 'Lord Bishop, … your blessing'.

777   **ac vn eglvys Vynyw** 'and the one (i.e *clas*) of the church of Menevia': for *un* used instead of a noun with a dependent noun or adjective to avoid repetition, see *GMW* § 97 (a, 3). For *Mynyw,* see note 775 above.

778   **Hanbych well**: the usual greeting of an inferior to a superior. The reply would be *Graessaw Duw* or *Dyw a ro da it*: see Charles-Edwards, 'Honour and Status', 125–26. By choosing this mode of address for Rhys ap Tewdwr the author of HGK was implying that Rhys acknowleged Gruffudd as his superior.

779   **brenhin brenhined Kemry**: in reality it is highly unlikely that the ruling prince of Deheubarth, in spite of his straitened circumstances and his need for allies, would have greeted the exiled claimant to the throne of Gwynedd as 'king of the kings of Wales', but as with the greeeting above, the author of the text wants to make a point here and uses the title to indicate rank. Rhys also addresses Gruffudd first and by the title *arglwyd*.

780–1   **Pwy wyt titheu**: in answer to this question, not only does Rhys ap Tewdwr give his name, but also his rank, as it was an important social convention that the interlocutor should know both the name and the status of the person who was addressing him, before any form of relationship could take place. Cf. the exchange between Pwyll and Arawn in the First Branch: see Thomson, *Pwyll* 2 , Davies, *Mabinogion* 3–4 and also Charles-Edwards, 'Honour and Status' 126–29.

784   **Pwy a'th foes di?** 'Who has put you to flight/caused you to flee?': *ffoi* is usually intransitive but here it is used transitively with the meaning 'put to flight'.

786   **disgynnassant y'm kyuoeth**: although *disgyn* can mean 'attack' (see *GPC* 1047 (2)), the corresponding Latin phrase *in hunc principatum*

delati, 'who come into this realm', lit. 'having been brought down to this realm' (*VGC* 68, 69 § 17), suggests that the meaning here is 'descended upon my country'.

788–93 **Caradauc m. Grufud ... henne**: for a detailed discussion of the transmission of this section, see *VGC* 25–27.

789 **Gwenhvyssyon** 'men of Gwent': double plural form: *Gwenhvys* (< *Gwent* + *-wys* plural ending borrowed from Lat. plur. ending *-enses*) + *-yon* plural ending.

790 **albryswyr** 'crossbow men': < *albras* (< Middle Eng. *arblast, alblast* < OFr. *arbaleste* 'cross-bow') + *-wyr* 'men': see *GPC²* s.v. *albrasiwr*.

795 **guryogaeth a wnaf yt**: there is no evidence that Rhys ever paid homage to Gruffudd, although he did pay homage to William the Conqueror on the latter's visit to St David's shortly after the battle of Mynydd Carn. Nerys Ann Jones ('Mynydd Carn', 77–79) presents an interesting theory that the author of HGK, in his attempt to portray Gruffudd as being superior to the other princes of Wales, has distorted the facts and has based the report of Rhys's proclaimed intention of accepting Gruffudd as his overlord on his actual performance of the act of homage to the King of England.

797 **trwy aruoll y greiryeu** 'by swearing on his (i.e. David's) relics': for *arfoll creiriau* 'to swear on holy relics by taking hold of them', see *GPC²* s.v. *arfollaf*. Affirming an assertion on oath was an important part of medieval society; the more public the act, the greater the incentive to abide by the conditions and the greater the loss of honour which would ensue the failure to do so: see Charles-Edwards, 'Honour', 135–41. Cf. *Ac yna yd aethant y gadarnhau eu kedymdeithyas a duundeb y ryngthunt drwy lw ac aruoll, ym Manachloc Seint Iermin, uchben yr allawr vawr a'r creiryeu gwynnyaeithyat a oedynt yno* (Williams, *Kedymdeithyas*, 7), 'And then they went to affirm their friendship and concord between them **through oath and pledge** in the Monastery of Saint Germain above the high altar and the holy relics that were there'.

798 **emdivnav** 'to reach an agreement': < *ym-* (reciprocal prefix) + *dyunaw* 'to join, agree' 'to unite, unify, combine, join, agree, be reconciled': see *GPC*, s.v. *dyunaf* (a) 75.

798 **y lle honno**: *lle* is sometimes f. in MW; cf. *y lle hon*, 'in this place' (Thomson, *Pwyll* 3.58).

800 **riuedi wyth ugeinwyr**: lit. 'the numbers of eight score men', i.e. 160 men.

801–2 **en llawen ganthav y vryt o'e ganhorthvy**: lit. 'joyful with him his mind because of his help', i.e. he had a joyful mind, because of the help he was receiving.

803 **A guedy kerdet dirvaur emdeith diwyrnaut**: Evans translates, 'And after they had marched a full day's journey' (*MPW* 67). There is a

biblical ring about *ymdaith diwrnod*, see 1 Kings 19.4, which is absent from the Latin: *Longo itinere dimenso ad vesperem* (*VGC* 68 § 18), lit. 'after a long journey measured out towards evening'.

804–5   *dywededigyon vrenhined uchof* 'the above mentioned kings': *uchof* (prep. *uch* 'above' with 1 sg.) is used here as an adverb. The 2 sg. *uchot* later developed as the adverbial form, see *GMW* § 63(d)N.

807   *dan igyon*: Evans translates 'with a sigh', but it could be one of the other meaings of *igyon* 'to sob, weep convulsively, gasp': see *GPC s.v. igiaf*. This does not occur in the Latin, which is less emotive, see *VGC* 68 § 18 and note p. 147.

810–11 *bwyeill deuvinyauc*: cf. the double edged axe was commonly used by the Scandinavians: see *MPW* 111.

811   *gaflachauc* 'equipped/armed with javelins/spears': < *gaflach* (borrowing from Middle Ir. *gablach* 'spear, forked branch') + *-auc* adj. ending. Jenny Day ('Ongyr gwŷr', 32) thinks it may have been a forked implement but quotes Swanton, *Spearheads*, 35, where it is called a small barbed javelin. See also Breeze, 'Celtic etymologies', on line www.accessmylibrary.com/…/celtic-etymologies-old-english.html.

811   *peleu*: this could be (i) pl. of *pêl*, 'bullet', referring to the Irish war-flail, from which hung iron balls attached to chains or (ii) an attempt to Cymricise the Latin *pila*, pl. of *pilum*, 'javelin': see *MPW* 111. It does not occur in the Latin text (*VGC* 68 § 18), which has *Hybernos iacula ferreis cuspidibus ferentes* 'the Irish carrying spears with iron-tips'.

812   *Gwyndyt gleiuyauc tareanauc*: lit. 'spear- and shield-bearing men of Gwynedd'. Both adjectives contain a noun + *-auc* adj. ending (cf. *gaflachauc* above). *Gleiuyauc* 'bearing a lance' < *glaif* from ME/OFr *glaive* 'spear, sword'. Again this is absent from the Latin, which is more restrained in describing the warriors and their weapons.

813   *Gruffud gentaf emladwr* 'Gruffudd [as] the first fighter': the mutation of *cyntaf* suggests that it is in apposition to *Gruffudd*, cf. the corresponding Latin *Griffinus proelium primus irruit*, 'G. was the first to rush into battle' (*VGC* 68, 71 §18).

813–14 *en gyffelip y gaur ac y lew* 'like a giant and a lion': cf *non secus ac gigas vel leo* 'just like a giant or a lion' (*VGC*, 68, 71 §18). A similar comparison occurs after the description of the Battle of Bron yr Erw (*MPW* 33 and *VGC* 64 §14; see 1 Maccabees 3.3–4.

815–16 *a hyt na rodynt udunt eu kefneu* 'and so that they would not retreat': lit. 'and so that they would not give (to) them their backs'. For *hyt na*, see *GMW* § 269 (b). The Latin text has *et ne terga adversariis darent exhortans* 'and urging them not to turn their backs to the enemy' (*VGC* 70, 71 §18). The Welsh translator or scribe has omitted the participle *exhortans* here.

816–17 **brwyder dirvavr y chof** 'a very memorable battle': lit. 'a battle great [with respect to] its memory'. For the syntax, see note 722–3 above.

821 **Trahaearn a drychut** (a drychwd): see Glossary *s.v. trychut*; for the verbal ending see *GMW* § 135.

829 **urth y lleuat** 'with the aid of the moon': for the meaning 'through, with (the aid of)' see *GPC s.v. wrth* 6 (a).

830 **y eu**: See note 390 above.

832 **kyfliw gur a llwyn** 'at dusk': for this native idiom, see note 347 above.

836–7 **Menyd Carn**: the location has not been precisely identified, but is thought to be in Pembrokeshire, about 20 miles from St David's; see *MPW* 111–12, Moore, 'Gruffudd ap Cynan', 45 and Jones, 'Mynydd Carn', 78–81. The reports of the Battle of Mynydd Carn in the Chronicles are very different from that of the *Historia*. In BS and RB Trahaearn ab Caradog and Caradog ap Gruffudd and Meilyr ap Rhiwllawn are slain in the battle of Mount Carn by Rhys ap Tewdwr with the assistance of Gruffudd ap Cynan, whereas in the Peniarth 20 version, Rhys perishes with the above mentioned three princes, and it is then that Gruffudd ap Cynan arrives at the scene of the battle. The author of HGK on the other hand makes Gruffudd the chief protagonist (see note 813 above).

839 **y vlwydyn honno**: if Gruffudd ap Cynan died in 1137 aged 82, the year of his birth would be 1055.

844–5 **o'r amrauaelyon wladoed y gwasgarassei y Normannyeit wynt** 'from the various lands to which the Normans had scattered them': this is an awkward construction. One would expect the relative clause to contain a conjugated form of the prep. *y* which refers back to the antecedent, **o'r amrauaelyon wladoed y gwasgarassei y Normannyeit wynt* **udunt**; cf. *y coedyd y foassant* **udunt** 'the woods to which they fled': *GMW* §70. The RB version is much clearer, *wedy kynullaw [gwyr] Gwyned y priawt wlat, y rei a daroed y gwasgaru kyn no hynny y ymrauaelon wladoed y gan y Normanyeit* 'after gathering to their own land [the men of] Gwynedd, who had before that been dispersed to various lands by the Normans' (*BT* (*RB*) 116). For the use of the independent personal pronoun as object of the verb *gwasgarassei*, see *GMW* § 55 (a).

846 **olew ac ygen** (yngen): the combination *olew* 'oil' and *ygen* (a variant of *angen* from Lat. *unguen* 'a fatty substance, ointment, unguent' (L&S, *s.v.*), used as a doublet means 'sacrament of the sick (extreme unction), anointing of the sick': see *GPC*[2] *s.v. angen*[2].

850 **prior manachlog Kaer**: the prior of this institution is not named by the author of the *Historia*. In *HGrK* 107 Evans identifies this institution as the monastic church dedicated to St Werburgh. Hugh Earl of Chester founded a monastery in Chester in 1093. See *MPW* 130 and *VGC* 168.

851 **herwydd gorchymyn Yago ebostol**: see Letter of James 5.14, 'Is one of you ill? He should send for the elders of the congregation to pray over

him and anoint him with oil in the name of the Lord'. Russell points out that the reference is not entirely appropriate, in as much as James is referring to annointing as a means of healing, whereas here it is used at the time of Gruffudd's death (*VGC* 169).

851–2 *E feibeon hefyt oed yno*: cf. Lat. *Erant una eius filii* 'his sons were with him' (*VGC* 88, 89 § 35). The plural subject followed by the verb in the singular makes this a mixed sentence: see *GMW* § 146.

853 *Yago padriarch yn bendigaw y feibeon*: his words are to be found in Genesis 49.2–27.

855 *ar y gyffelyprwyd ynteu*: lit. 'on his likeness', an attempt to render the Lat. *ad similitudinem Iacobi*, 'in imitation of Jacob'. For *similitudo* in this sense, see L&S, *s.v* IIA.

855 *yn y diwed dydyeu* 'in his last days': Evans suggests reading *yny ddyddyeu* 'in his days' (*MPW*, 132); Russell, on the other hand, thinks that it is an attempt, however cumbersome, to translate the Lat. *postremis suis temporibus* 'in his latter years', lit. 'in his last times' (*VGC* 169).

856 *y wreig briaut ynteu*: lit. 'his lawful wife', i.e. his wedded wife.

857 *randir*: see note 593 above.

858 *neieint*: Lat. *filiorum nonnulli* 'some of their (i.e. Gruffudd's daughters') sons'. Since *nai* < Lat. *nepos* which in post-Augustan Latin can be a nephew as well as as grandson (L&S, *s.v.* B1), the translator probably mistakenly wrote *neieint* 'nephews' instead of *wyrion* 'grandsons'. Russell thinks that this is a more likely explanation than to consider it as an archaism, preserving the original use of *nai* in the sense of 'grandson'. For their identity see *VGC* 169; see also Maund, *Ireland.* 91 (fig. 51).

858–9 *rann o'r eidau* 'part of his possessions': *eidau* (eiddaw) is a stressed poss. pron. 3 sg. 'one's own', here used as a substantive with the article: see *GMW* § 57.

861–2 *fegys kuunfan yr Ideon am Iosue, fab Nun* 'like the lamentation of the Jews for Joshua son of Nun': Joshua led the Hebrews after the death of Moses and brought them to Canaan. Although his death and his final words are recorded in detail, there is no mention of the lamentation of the people: see Book of Joshua, Chapters 23 and 24. There seems to be a greater similarity to the reaction of the people to the death of Judas Maccabaeus: 'Great was the grief in Israel, and they mourned him for many days': 1 Maccabees 9.20.

864–5 *A gwediun ninheu hyt pan orffwysso y eneit ynteu yn yr un peth, nyt amgen yn Duw*: Evans translates, 'And let us pray that his soul may rest in the same, namely God' (*MPW* 83). For *hyt pan,* see 193–4. It is difficult to understand what is meant by *peth* in this context. In any case, it is a very cumbersome translation of the Latin *Praecemurque ut*

eius anima ... in Domino conquiescat 'And let us pray that his soul may
rest in peace in the Lord' (*VGC* 90, 91 § 35).

865   *yn oes oessoed*: this is not in the Latin text, but it is an expression
which the translator employs earlier, in the section where Gruffudd
distributes his wealth *a'e gyfyawnder ynteu a bara yn oes oessoedd* 'and
his justice will continue **for ever**' (*MPW* 50). In the above-mentioned
passage it translates the Latin *in aeternum* (*VGC* 88 § 34) but in the
concluding paragraph of this work, it seems to be a direct translation
of the biblical Latin *in saecula saeculorum*, 'for ever and ever', which
concludes the Lord's Prayer.

869   *ymrysson*: this is the earliest record of a competitive meeting in which,
according to Welsh Law, a chair was awarded as a prize to the winning
poet, who then acquired the status of *pencerdd* (chief poet): see Davies
et al., (eds.) *Encyclopaedia, s.v. Eisteddfod*. In the contest described here,
musicians were likewise rewarded with a chair.

869   *beird a phrydydyon*: it is difficult to decide whether this is a doublet or a
reference to different types of poets. According to the Welsh laws, there
were three types of poets: the *cerddor*, who was under instruction to the
pencerdd (chief bard), the *bardd-teulu*, poet of the household(-troops)
and the *pencerdd* himself; see J. E. Caerwyn Williams, *The Court
Poet*, 51–58; Jenkins, *The Law*, 371. Caerwyn Williams also discusses
the terms *pencerdd* and *prydydd*, which seem to be interchangeable
in the contexts he quotes (ibid. 102). In the minds of later generations,
however, there appears to be a hierarchical difference, because in the
fourteenth-century compilation *Pum Llyfr Kerddwriaeth* (lit. 'Five
Books of Poetry'), which set down the rules for poetic compositions, it
states clearly that a *prydydd* may not be a *pencerdd* until he has mastered
all the possible errors of prosody, (Williams and Jones, *Gramadegau'r
Penceirddiaid*, 124).

870   *kerd music* 'the craft of music': as well as 'song, poem, the art of poetry,
music', *cerdd* can also mean 'craft, art; occupation': see *GPC s.v. cerdd*[1]
(b). In *BT* (*RB*) 166 this class of competition is referred to as *kerd arwest*
'string music' (see *GPC*[2] *s.v arwest* (b)); in *BS* 182 as *cerd tant neu gerd
tavot* 'vocal or instrumental music or poetic art, poetry' (*GPC s.v. cerdd*[1]
(*Cfn.*)).

871   *dwy gadeir*: the winning poet or musician would be given a chair as
a prize. According to the Welsh Laws, the *pencerdd* 'chief bard' was
one of the fourteen court officials who had a chair in the court of the
king or prince (Jenkins, *The Law* 7–8). Later in the bardic system, a
miniature silver chair worn on the left shoulder signified that the bard
was either a *pencerdd* or a teacher of *cerdd dafod* or *cerdd dant* (*GPC
s.v. cadair* 2(a)). The custom of awarding a chair to the winning poet

is still observed in modern competitive festivals of the arts, known as *Eisteddfod(au)*: see *Celtic Culture*, (ed. Koch), Vol II. *s.v. Eisteddfod.*

872   *gwas jeuang*: in *BS* 182 he is named as *mab i Eilon grythor* 'son of Eilon the fiddler'.

879–80 *ac nyt arbedawd honno y neb* 'and that (the pestilence) spared no-one': according to *GPC arbed* is sometimes followed by the preps. *y* or *rhag*: cf. text l. 900.

880   *y pedweryd dyd [o] Galan Mei* 'the fourth day from the Calends of May': i.e. 28 April, according to the Roman method of calculating the date; see note 561–2 above. This date is omitted in the RB version.

882   *Ac y darystyngawd y anynat tyngetuen* 'And his dire fate laid him low': the 3 sg. inf. pron. object of *darystyngawd* is fused into the pre-verbal particle, i.e. y['i] darystyngawdd; see *GMW* § 58.

883   *datkanadwy drwy dagreuoed* Lit. 'narratable through tears': Thomas Jones translates, 'which should be narrated with tears', *BT (Pen. 20 trans.)* 76–77.

886   *a gyffelybawd y adwyndra wrth y genedyl* Jones translates, 'made his worthiness match his lineage', *BT (Pen. 20 trans.)* 77.

890–1 *Megys glewder baed koet yn chwyrnu ... velly y dywalhaei ef*: Jones translates, 'Like to the bravery of a forest boar growling ... even so would he rage', *BT (Pen. 20 trans.)* 77. Subordinate clauses introduced by *megys y* 'as' are sometimes followed by [*y*]*velly* in the principal clause: see *GMW* §271.

898   *Ac nyt ryued kwynaw yr angeu*: lit. 'And not strange is the lamenting of the death': Jones translates: 'Nor is it strange that we should lament the death', *BT (Pen. 20 trans.)* 77. For the use of *nyt* before the predicate in a negative copular clause, see *GMW* § 145 N 4.

899   *chwaer y Antropos*: a reference to the three Fates of Greek mythology. Daughters of Zeus and Thetis, the personification of Justice, they are generally depicted as old and ugly. Clotho spins the thread of life, Lachesis determines its length and Antropos, the eldest, cuts it off; her name in Greek means 'inflexible'. It is not clear from this context to which of Antropos's sisters reference is made, but the Latin reads *Antropos sororum seuissima* (probably *seuerissima*) 'the severest of the sisters', with reference to Antropos herself.

900–1 *o gyngoruynus law* 'with envious hand'.

903   *ac odyna y diodefawd mynet dros gof goruchelder y rot*: Jones translates literally, 'and thereupon she (Fortune) suffered to be forgotten the height of her wheel' (*BT (Pen. 20 trans.)* 77). The meaning is that she allowed the height of her wheel to be forgotten. See *Brill's New Pauly. Encyclopedia of the Ancient World* Vol. 5 *s.v* Fortune. The *Rota Fortunae* (Wheel of Fortune) is a concept in classical philosophy which refers to the fickle nature of Fate and is epitomized in Seneca's tragedy

Agamemnon: 'Whatever Fortune raises on high, she lifts to cast down'. (*Tragedies* II 133–34, 133–35). The earliest reference to the Wheel of Fortune, symbolising the endless changes in life between prosperity and disaster, is made by Cicero, *In Pisonem*, *c.* 55 B.C., (see *Pro Milone* 166). For the concept of Fortune adopted by medieval Christian writers, see Boethius *The Consolation of Philosophy II*.

907   *Digrif y ymadrawd* 'Pleasant (was) his speech': the first of a series of nominal sentences.

907   *adurn y weithret*: lit. 'an adornment (was) his deed'.

918–19   *ac yna y perys Llywelyn ap Jorr[werth] mudaw y Beruedwlat a Mon a'y holl da hyt ynyalwch Eryri*: lit. 'and then Ll. ap I. caused to [the people of] Perfeddwlad and Môn and all their goods to move as far as the wilderness of Eryri'. The reading in RB confirms that it was the inhabitants, not the territories themselves, that were moved: *Ac yna y mudawd Llywelyn a'e giwdawt y Peruedwalt a'e da hyt ymynyd Eryri*, 'And then Ll. moved both his people of Perfeddwlad and his goods to the mountain of Eryri' (*BT* (*RB*) 190). Using a territory name to represent the people is common in the work of the Poets of the Princes. The syntax is *perys* (3 sg. pret. of *peri*) + Llywelyn (subj.) + *mudo* (vn. and direct obj. of *perys*) + *i* + Perfeddwlad etc. (indirect objects). To express the notion that X is causing Y to do s.th., *peri* is followed by the prep. *y*; see *GPC s.v. paraf* 3(d).

919   *Peruedwlat*: Y Berfeddwlad indicated the territories in north-east Wales lying between the rivers Conwy and Dee, and comprised the *cantrefi* of Rhos, Rhufoniog, Dyffryn Clwyd and Tegeingl. It was named 'middle country' because of its location between Gwynedd and Powys on one side and between Gwynedd and England on the eastern side. Consequently it was much disputed territory. Although at this stage of his career Llywelyn conceded Y Berfeddwlad to king John, he later regained it. On his death it was conquered by Henry III but was recoverd by Llywelyn's grandson, Llywelyn ap Gruffydd.

919–20   *yn y aruaeth* 'according to his plan': this phrase is omitted from the RB and BS versions.

927   *yw y losgi*: lit. 'to its burning', i.e. to be burned'. For *yw y*, see note 636; for the gender of *dinas*, see note 412–13 and for the passive meaning of the vn. see note 108–9.

928   *a'y brynnu*: Thomas Jones translates, '**but** he was ransomed': *BT* (*Pen. 20. trans.*) 85. For *a* sometimes meaning 'but', see *GMW* § 252 N1.

931   *merch y brenhin*: Joan, natural daughter of King John.

942   *y Mynwy*: *ym Mynwy*; for nasalisation see Introduction, xliv.

942   *abat Llanndefit*: *Landifei* in RB. In Llandyfái (Lamphey) in Pembrokeshire are the remains of a luxurious palace where the medieval bishops of St David's retreated from the demands of their

work. It was established in the thirteenth century and was mainly the work of Henry de Gower, bishop of St David's from 1328 to 1347. See *BT* (*Pen. 20 trans.*) 198.

946   **Gwyl Marthin**: St. Martin bishop of Tours in the 4th century, is regarded as the patron saint of wine-growers on the Loire. His feast day is 11 November.

947–8   **merch Lywelyn**: this is Gwladus Ddu, 'Gwladys the Black', who was subsequently married sometime before 1221 to Reginald de Breos/ Braose and in 1230 to Ralph de Mortimer.

949   **Ac Ieuan vrenhin … a aeth y tu a'r Ardal**: Jones translates 'And king John … went towards The March' (*BT* (*Pen. 20 trans.*) 93). *Ardal* is the name given to the borderlands between England and Wales in the Middle Ages.

955   **damweinnyeu**: the *damweinyeu* 'events' are the failed truce between Henry and the French and the subsequent unsuccessful invasion of Britain by Louis, the son of the King of France.

956–7   **eu hewythyr**: this is Reginald de Breos/Braose, their uncle by his marriage to their father's sister, Gwladys, daughter of Llywelyn the Great, see note 947–8 above.

957   **ymaruoll**: this is a reference to the stance which Reginald had taken the previous year in support of the Welsh princes against King John: see text ll. 941–8.

961   **mynet wrth Aberhodni** 'to attack Brecon': lit 'to go against'. This town later became known as *Aberhonddu*, 'the mouth of (the river) Honddu', so called because of its geographical position at the confluence of the rivers Usk and Honddu. In south Wales <-dn-> sometimes becomes <-ndd-> (/nð/), cf. *cadno* 'fox' > *canddo* (Ifor Williams, *Enwau Lleoedd*, 54). However on the basis of provection occurring before metathesis in the name of the river *Hoddnant* > *Hodnant*, Williams thinks that *Hoddni* (/-ðn-/) preceded *Hodni*, then metathesised to *Honddi*, later > *Honddu*. The ending *–ddu* is probably influenced by the adj. *du* 'black', whereas in reality *–ni* is a common suffix in river names. *Hodd-* may be from the adj. *hawdd* 'prosperous, pleasant', based on the Latin gloss *vallis prospera* 'prosperous valley'; on the other hand the seventeenth-century botanist, linguist, geographer and antiquary Edward Lhuyd called *Honddi* 'an ugly torrent' (Thomas, R. J., *Enwau Afonydd*, 152–53). The English name *Brecon* comes from the Latin *Breconia* for the ancient lordship of *Brycheiniog*, (Owen and Morgan, *Dictionary of Place-names*, 45).

963   **pump wystl**: *pump* can be followed by both lenition and the nasal mutation: see *GMW* §§20, 25(c).

967–8   **A phan weles Reinallt**: cf. RB version, *A [gwedy] gwelet o Reinallt ac o Wiliam Brewys* (*BT* (*RB*), 214). Since *Reinallt* is the sole subject in

BS too, the inclusion of *Wiliam* in RB is probably an error, as Thomas Jones suggests: *BT (Pen. 20 trans.)* 199.

968   *hynny o distrywedigaeth* 'such destruction': see *GMW* § 91 N1.

969-70   *Llywelyn a rodes ydaw kastell Seynenid*: it is not logical that the victorious Llywelyn should concede anything to the defeated Reginald. The RB and BS versions are more accurate and record that Reginald surrendered himself and the castle to Llywelyn: *BT (RB)* 215, *BS* 219. The *Annales Cambriae* and *Cronica de Wallia* locate the castle in *Abertawe* 'Swansea': see *BT (Pen. 20 trans.)* 200 and also Lloyd, *History*, ii, 652 *n* 209.

972   *Blwydyn wedy hynny*: the events of late 1217 -1218 appertaining to Wales and Llywelyn are (i) Llywelyn made peace with the invading Flemings of Pembroke; (ii) William Marshal laid siege to Caerleon and took it in protest against the peace with France, agreed by the regents of the new young king Henry III, who restored their rights to the barons; (iii) Rhys Gryg ('Rhys the Hoarse', fourth son of the Lord Rhys, also known as Rhys Fychan, who ruled part of the Kingdom of Deheubarth and died 1234) overthrew the castle of Seinhenydd and drove all the English away from that land; (iv) the castles of Carmarthen and Cardigan were given to Llywelyn to keep; (v) Rhys ap Gruffudd (son of Gruffydd ap Rhys and Maud de Breos/Braose, 1197–1222), on the advice of Llywelyn, did homage to the king of England.

975   *gwyl Nicloaws* 'the feast of St Nicholas': it is celebrated on 6 December.

978   *Blwydyn wedy hynny*: 'A year after that': the events of the year in question were (i) the seizure of Rhys Gryg by his son, Rhys Fychan, (Rhys the Younger) and his release in return for the castle of Llandovery; (ii) the death of Maredudd, archdeacon of Ceredigion, who was buried in St David's near the grave of his father, the Lord Rhys.

978   *Henri*: King Henry III of England, who succeeded his father King John in 1216.

982   *ac yna drwy greulonyon gyrcheu y eu gelynyon*: 'and then by fierce attacks on the enemy'.

986-9   *A'r brenhin [...] heb vrenhinawl anryded a ymchwelawd y Loegyr* 'And the king ... returned to England without kingly honour': the text of RB reports the king's retreat in stronger terms, *Ac yna yd ymhoedlawd y brenhin y Loegyr* **yn gewilydus** 'And then the king returned **ignominiously** to England.' (*BT (RB)* 228–29).

993   *Blwydyn wedy hynny*: for the purpose of these selections, the most important event recorded for 1236 was the seizure of Morgan ap Hywel's castle, called Machen, in Monmouthshire, by Gilbert, earl of Pembroke. However, he returned the castle through fear of Llywelyn, which is an indication of the power Llywelyn wielded by this time.

993   *arglwydes Gymry ... (Jon oed y henw)* 'the lady of Wales ... (her name was Joan)' : in RB and BS the Welsh forms of her name are given: *Dam Siwan (BT (RB)* 234), *Sioned (BS* 230).

995   *gard gyssegredic* 'sacred enclosure': so named in *BS* 230 but in *BT (RB)* 234 this is a *mynwent newyd*, 'new cemetery'.

996   *Hywel esgob*: in MS Mostyn, this is recorded as *holl esgyb* 'all the bishops'. *BT (RB)* 234 and *BS* 231 agree on *Howel esgob Llan Elwy*. Lloyd maintains that the bishop of St Asaph in 1237 was Hugh (*History*, ii, 686). Nevertheless Thomas Jones, although he agrees that the new burying-ground had been consecrated by Hugh, asserts that the Brut is equally correct in saying that it was Hywel who consecrated a monastery there (*BT (Pen. 20 trans.)* 204).

997   *manachloc y'r Brodyr Troednoeth* 'a monastery for the Barefooted Friars': i.e. the Franciscans, followers of St Francis, who went on their preaching missions barefooted, in obedience to Christ's teaching to his disciples that they should provide no gold, silver, or copper to fill their purses, no pack for the road, no second coat, no shoes, no stick. (Matthew 10.9). According to *BT (RB)* 234 and *BS* 232, the monastery was built in *Llann Vaes y Mon* 'Llanfaes in Anglesey'.

998   *a'y hedeilawd* 'and he (the prince) built it': see *GPC²* s.v. *adeiliaf.*

1000   *Jor[werth] vab Ywein Gwyned*: *BT (RB)* 236 and *BS* 232 omit *vab Ywein Gwyned*. BS names him *Jerwerth Drwyndwn*, a rare example of this epithet.

1002   *Jon* 'Joan': see note 993 above.

1003   *y mis [Mei] racwyneb* 'the following month of May': *Mei* is inserted in the margin; cf. *BT (RB)* 236 *Mis Mei racwynep* and *BS* 232 *A mis Mai racwyneb.*

1005   *A barwnyeit Kymry yr haf wedy hynny*: according to RB and BS the barons accompanied Gruffudd in doing homage to King Henry. Only according to the *Chronica de Wallia* did they do so subsequently: see *BT (Pen 20 trans.)* 204.

1008   *Blwydyn wedy hynny*: in 1245, king Henry III advanced on Wales with a large army, resulting in a huge loss of life.

1010–11   *gwedy nat oed etiued ydaw* 'since he had no heir': *gwedy* normally means 'after' (temporal), but here it has a causal connotation.

1011   *ef a wledychawd yn y ol deu neieint ydaw* 'there ruled after him two nephews of his': Owain and Llywelyn, Gruffudd's two eldest sons, in spite of the fact that Dafydd had pledged that if he died without issue the whole of Gwynedd would come into the possession of his uncle, the king of England. See Smith, *Llywelyn ap Grufudd*, 57.

1012–13   *A'r rei hynny, o gyngor doethyon y wlat, a rannhassant y kyfoeth yn deu hanner y ryngthunt* 'And those, by counsel of the wise men of the land, divided the territory in two halves between them': it would appear that Owain's territories were in the south-west of Gwynedd and those of Llywelyn in the north-east, while both brothers held sway over various parts of Anglesey. Although these territories would have had economic equality, nevertheless, Llywelyn, the younger brother, had the strategic advantage of being in possession of the mountainous stronghold of Gwynedd: see Smith, *Llywelyn ap Gruffudd, 65–67.*

1015–16 *kyuodes teruysc y rwng meibyon Gruffud vab Llywelyn*: by 1252 the third brother, Dafydd, had come of age and was seeking part of his patrimony. In this he was supported by the King of England and his eldest brother Owain, but Llywelyn refused to accept any further division of the already reduced Gwynedd. This disagreement eventually led to the battle of Bryn Derwin in June 1255, from which Llywelyn emerged victorious. There was a fourth brother, Rhodri, but it is not known what part, if any, he played in the events of 1255. By 1272, however, Rhodri had given up all claims to his patrimony and received financial compensation from Llywelyn for his loss of territory. (Smith, *Llywelyn ap Gruffudd*, 68–73.)

1017–18 *Llywelyn ... a arhoes dyuodyat y vrodyr yn y erbyn* 'Llywelyn ...awaited the coming of his brothers against him': both *BT (RB)* 246 and *BS* 240 omit *yn y erbyn* but mention instead that the encounter took place *ym Bryn Derwyn* 'on Bryn Derwin'. Nevertheless, since the location of the battle is not mentioned either in *Cronica de Wallia* or *Annales Cambriae*, Thomas Jones maintains that there is no corroborative evidence to assume that *yn y erbyn* could be an error of transcription for *Bryn Derwyn* (*BT (Pen. 20 trans.*) 208). Lloyd locates Bryn Derwin on the borders of the parishes of Clynnog and Dolbenmaen (*History*, ii, 715 and *n* 127); see also Smith, *Llywelyn ap Gruffudd*, 73.

1019 *ef a delis y vrodyr ac a'y karcharawd*: the Pen. 20 version is in agreement with CW (quoted in *BT (Pen. 20 trans.*), 208) *et predictum Owinum vna cum fratre suo Dauid ... tenuit et in carcerem retrusit*, 'and the aforementioned Owain together with his brother David he held and restained in prison'. According to *BT (RB)* 246 and *BS* 240 only Owain was captured; Dafydd fled: see Lloyd, *History* ii 715 and *n*. 128.

1023 *yarll Kaer* 'The Earl of Chester': in *BT (RB)* 246 and *BS* 240 the full name *Iarll Caerlleon/Kaer Lleon* is given.

1030 *erbynn penn yr wythnos ef a'y gorysgynnawd oll*: *oll* refers to the whole of Perfeddwlad. The text then states that he subsequently took the *cantref* of Meirionnydd into his hands. *BT (RB)* 246 is in agreement, but *BS* 240–41 records a different timescale and maintains that he gained possession of both Perfeddwlad and Meirionydd in one week. Cf. AC *et eam* (*sc.* Perfeddwlad*) infra unam ebdomadam preter duo castra, scilicet Deganho et Dissert, uiriliter occupauit*, 'And that he courageously seized

within one week, except two castles, Deganwy and Diserth' (quoted in
BT (*Pen. 20 trans.*) 209).

1032–3   *a Buellt a rodes y Vared[ud] vab Rys*: according to *BT* (*RB*) 246–48,
247–49, he gave Builth, together with the portion of land in Ceredigion
that was in Edward's possession, to Maredudd ab Owain; to Maredudd
ap Rhys Gryg he restored his territory. This is corroborated in AC: (*BT*
(*Pen. 20 trans.*) 209). Cf. *BS* 240, 241 *a goresgyn i Vredudd ap Rys Gryc
i gyvoeth yntav* 'and he won for Maredudd ap Rhys Gryc his territory
also'.

1036   *Blwydyn wedy hynny*: the year 1257 was a turbulent one: not only was
there internal strife among the Welsh princes but also King Henry
III stayed with a large contingent in Deganwy. Finally, Llywelyn ap
Gruffudd made peace with Gruffudd ap Madoc but dispossessed
Gruffudd ap Gwenwynwyn of his land.

1037   *rodassant lw ar gadw kywirdeb a duhundeb y gyt* 'they gave an oath
to maintain loyalty and agreement together': Pen. 20 is in disagreement
with RB and BS in that it does not specify that the oath of allegiance is to
Llywelyn: cf. *BT* (*RB*) 250, 251, *Y ulwydyn racwyneb y rodes kynnulleitua
o dylyedogyon Kymry lw ffydlonder y Lywelin ap Gruffud dan boen
ysgymundawt* 'The following year an assembly of the magnates of
Wales gave an oath of allegiance to Llywelyn ap Gruffudd under pain
of excommunication'; *BS* 242, 243, *Anno Domini M.CC.LVIIJ. y roddes
tywy[s]ogion Kymry lw drwy ysgymvndod i Lywelyn,* 'Anno Domini
M.CC.LVIIJ the princes of Wales on pain of excommunication pledged
their oath to Llywelyn'.

1040   *Blwydyn wedy hynny*: in the years 1258–64 Llywelyn continued to
expand his territory by ousting some of the marcher lords from their
lands, but although he received homage from other Welsh princes, his
own brother, Dafydd, deserted him.

1040–2   *y teruysc ... yr y vlwydyn kyn no hynny*: the *teruysc* 'strife' is that of
1263 between King Henry III and his son Edward on the one side, with
the barons of England together with some of the earls and the Welsh
on the other. Thomas Jones (*BT* (*Pen. 20 trans.*) 211) says that RB seems
to have misunderstood the original Latin and thinks the *teruysc* refers
to the stuggle of 1264: *y ulwydyn racwyneb y bu gofadwy teruysc rwg
Henri vrenhin ac Edward, y vap, a'e kymorthwyr o'r neill tu a'r ieirll
a'r barwnneit o'r tu arall,* 'The following year there was memorable
strife between King Henry and Edward, his son, and their supporters,
on the one side, and the earls and barons on the other' (*BT* (*RB*) 254,
255). He then continues that *yn hynny* 'during it' the king of England
and his two sons together with the King of Germany and his two sons
came to do battle on the field of Lewes. *BT* (*Pen. 20*) 215 states that the
strife of the preceding year had not been forgotten and that a year later

Henry and his two sons together with their German allies came to fight against the rebellious earls and barons. *BS* 246 omits the temporal phrases of Pen. 20, which refer to the previous year, but plunges in with the annal of 1264: *Anno Domini M.CC.LXIIIJ. y bu vattel rwng Henrri vrenin* ... 'A.D. 1264 there was a battle between king Henry ...'. Thomas Jones observes that the discord of 1263 is given as a separate entry in AC: *Magna fuit discordia inter dominum Eadwardum filium Henrici regis Angliae primogenitum et barones Angliae*, 'There was great strife between Edward, the first born son of Edward king of England, and the barons of England.' (*BT* (*Pen. 20 trans.*) 211). Basing his theory on the fact that the words *teruysc* 'strife' and *bu gofadwy* 'memorable', *heb vynet dros kof* 'not forgotten' occur in both RB and Pen. 20, Jones suggests that this may have been a memorandum in the original Latin which was later incorporated in the main text.

1047   *yr ymchwelawd yr ewyllys dracheuyn*: Thomas Jones translates, 'the purpose was reversed' (*BT* (*Pen. 20 trans.*) 113) but *GPC s.v. ewyllys* 1(c) gives 'fate, fortune' as the meaning of *ewyllys* here.

1055   *Dyw Sul y Blodeu*: BT (*RB*) 268–70 does not record any of the events of 1282 other than the destruction of Aberystwyth castle and the taking of the *cantref* of Penweddig and the commot of Mefenydd by Rhys Fychan ap Rhys ap Maelgwn and Gruffudd ap Mereudd respectively. However following this entry in *BT* (*Pen. 20*) 227 a later hand has added *Hyd yma y cyrraedd y Llyfr Coch o Hergest* 'The Red Book of Hergest extends as far as this'. From this point onwards until the concluding annal in 1332 there is a change of hand. This new hand, according to Thomas Jones, seems to be that of the scribe who edited the main text of Pen. 20 and it closely ressembles that of BS and *Brut y Brenhined* in BM Cotton MS Cleopatra B.V. (*BT* (*Pen. 20 trans.*) 217).

1055   *y torres rwg Llewelyn ap Gruffud ac Edward*: lit 'it broke between Ll ap G and E', i.e. there was a breach... . *Torri* is intrans. here.

1061–2 *ena y gwnaethpwyd brat Lliwelyn en e clochte en Mangor y gan y wyr ef ehvn*: this is an enigmatic remark and it is impossible to tell who the traitors in the belfry were that day, or what their intention was. For a full discussion on the alleged treachery which led to the death of Llywelyn, see Smith, *Llywelyn ap Gruffudd*, 552–61.

1063   *Ac ena er edewys Lliwelyn ap Gruf[ud]...* : Smith (*Llywelyn ap Gruffudd*, 558) points out that Llywelyn's reason for leaving Gwynedd in the safekeeping of his brother and departing for the south himself may have been one of military necessity: a mission to recruit supporters for his campaign.

1069   *a'y orevgwyr* 'and his best men': cf. *BS* 258 *a llawer o'i lu*, 'and many of his retinue'. With regard to the number of this select band of men, there may be a clue in Gruffudd ab yr Ynad Coch's famous elegy to

Llywelyn: *Uched y cwynaf; och o'r cwynaw*! / *Arglwydd llwydd cyn lladd y ddeunaw*, 'How loudly I lament; alas for the lamentation! / Lord of prosperity, before the slaughter of the eighteen' (Parry, *Oxford Book*, 46). Although presented as an earth-shattering event by Gruffudd ab yr Ynad Coch, Pen. 20 makes no further comment on the death of Llywelyn. *BS* 258 however adds, *Ac yna y bwriwyd holl Gymry y'r llawr*, 'And then all Wales was cast to the ground'.

1069   *Damasius*: Pope Damasus I, c. 304–84. His feast day is 11 December.

1069–70 *pethewnos o'r vn dyd kyn dyw Nodoloc* 'a fortnight to the day before Christmas': cf. *BS* 258 *yr vnved dydd ar ddec o vis Ragvyr, duw Gwener*, 'the 11th day of December, Friday'.

GLOSSARY

The arrangement of words in this glossary is according to graphic shape and follows the same order as that used in Modern Welsh dictionaries, namely a, b, c (/k/), ch (/χ/), d, dd (/ð/), e, f (/v/), ff (/f/), g, ng (ŋ), h, i, l, ll (/λ/), m, n, o, p, ph, r, rh (/r̥/), s, t, th, u (/ɨ/), w, (/u/), y (/ə/or /I/). Since <k>, <j> and <v> do not occur in ModW, <k> is recorded under <c>; <j> is recorded under <i>, whereas <v>, which represents /v/, /ɨ/ and /u/, is listed in its usual position in the English alphabet, between <u> and <w>. Wherever confusion may arise with regard to phonetic value, the ModW orthographic equivalent is given in parenthesis. Except in cases where an initial mutation is petrified or in forms which may cause confusion, e.g. *uu* = fu, lexical items are listed under their radical initial consonant. In the case of words which have a high frequency of occurrence, only the first six examples are quoted. The meaning given is that relevant to the context.

Abbreviations

adj	adjective	eqv.	equative	ModW	Modern Welsh
adv.	adverb(ial)	f.	feminine	MW	Middle Welsh
aff.	affixed	fut.	future	*n.*	note
affirm.	affirmative	gen.	genitive	n.	noun
appos.	apposition	impf.	imperfect	neg.	negative
art.	article	imprs.	impersonal	neut.	neuter
asp.	aspirate	impv	imperative	num.	numeral
aux.	auxiliary	ind.	indicative	obj.	object
borr.	borrowing	indef.	indefinite	OFr	Old French
cf.	compare	indep.	independent	ord.	ordinal
coll.	collective	inf.	infixed	part.	particle
conj.	conjunction	interj.	interjection	perf.	perfect
conjunct.	conjunctive	interr.	interrogative	pers.	personal
cons.	consuetudinal	intrans.	intransitive	pl.	plural/
cpd.	compound	Ir.	Irish		plural noun
cpv.	comparative	Lat.	Latin	plpft.	pluperfect
def.	definite	len.	lenition	poss.	possessive
defv.	defective	lit.	literally	pp.	participle
dem.	demonstrative	m.	masculine	pref.	prefixed
Eng.	English	ME	Middle English	prep.	preposition

pres.	present	rel.	relative	subj.	subject
pret.	preterite	sg.	singular	suff.	suffixed
pron.	pronoun	spv.	superlative	trans.	transitive
pronom.	pronominal	*s.v.*	under the word	var.	variation
red.	reduplicated	sub.	subjunctive	vb.	verb
refl.	reflexive	subd.	subordinate	vn.	verbal noun

a

a¹ (+ asp.), **ac** (before vowels) conj. *and* 1, 2, 3, 4, 5, 6; *but* 928*n*.; **ac** . . . **ac** *both . . . and* 545

a² (+ len.) affirm. pre-verbal part. used when subj. or obj. precedes verb etc., (*GMW* § 192) 1, 2, 5, 6, 8, 9

a³ (+ len.) affirm. rel. pron. used with antecedent. as subj. or obj. *who, whom, which, that* 3, 4, 15, 39, 52 , 58; **ac** 364*n*., 389*n*.

a⁴ (à) (+asp.), **ac** (ag) (before vowels) prep. *with* 6, 24, 65, 192, 221, 226; see also **(y) gyt a(c)**

a⁵ (à) (+asp.), **ac** (ag) (before vowels) *as, that* (introducing a comparison) 27, 31, 128, 187, 283, 290

abadeu see **abat**

aball f. *destruction* 264

aballu vn. *to perish, to die* 318

abat m. 941, 942. *abbot*; pl. **abadeu** 361

aberth f./m. *sacrifice* 71

abid, habit m./f. *religious attire* 112, 501*n*., 1001

ac, ag see **a**

ac[h] *pedigree* 721*n*.

achanoctit m. *want, need* 380

achanogyon pl. (m.) *beggars* 735

achavs (achaws) m. (i) *cause, reason* 36, 202, 234; (ii) sexual intercourse (*GPC*² *s.v. achos* (g)) 221; **o achaws** *because of* 632, 635, 912, 922

achuanec see **ychwenec**

achuanegu (achwanegu) vn. *to add to, enlarge* 110, 527 (*GPC*² *s.v. achwanegaf'*)

achub pres. 3 sg. of vn. 'achub' *to seize, possess by force; protect*; 265; pret. 3 pl. **achubassant** 698

a dan, adan see **dan**

adas (addas) adj. *suitable* 185; spv. **adassaf** 408

adav¹, adaw, vn. *to leave, to remain* 156, 220, 294, 297, 299, 509; impf. 3 sg. **adavhei** 176

adav² (addaw) vn. *to promise* 115, 519, 749, 957; pret. 3 sg. **edewis** (eddewis) 768

adeilat¹ m./f. *building* 142

adeilat², **adeylat**, **edeilat** vn. *to build* 50, 54, 181, 572, 845, 926; pret. 3 sg. **edeil(ei) lawd, adeilwys** 10, 998; plpf. 3 sg. **adeilassei** 58

adeilavdyr (adeilawdr) m. *builder* 86

adfet (addfed) adj. *mature* 849

adnabot vn. *to recognise, to have sexual intercourse with,* 32, 160; pret. 1 sg. **adnabum** 216; pres. sub. 3 sg. **adnapo** 335

adoed impf. 3 sg. of 'adfod' *to be* 311

adoli (addoli) vn. *to bow in homage* 147, 234

adolwyn vn. *to beseech* 748; pret. 3 sg. **adolygus** (adolygws) 761

adref adv. *home, homewards* 628

adurn (addurn) m. *ornament, adornment* 453, 907

adurnedic (addurnedig) adj. *decorated* 452, 455, 459

adwyndra, adwynder, (addfwynd-ra,-er) m. *courtesy, nobility, worthiness* 886, 893, 907

aei see **mynet**

aeleu pl. (m./f.) *eyebrows* 724

aelodeu pl. (m./f.) *limbs of body* 725, 732

aerua (aerfa) f. *slaughter* 177, 506, 533, 540

aeth see **mynet**

aflwydyanus (aflwyddiannus) adj. *unsuccessful* 699

afruyd (afrwydd) adj. *difficult* 729*n.*

agatuyd (agatfydd) adv. *perhaps* 671

aghen (angen) m. *need* 364, 369

agheu, angeu m./f. *death* 501, 898

agheuavl (angeuawl) adj. *fatal* 552

aghyurvys (anghyfrwys) adj. *unskilful, untrained* 529*n.*

agori vn. *to open* 348, 539

agwedi (agweddi) m. *dowry* 163*n.*, 164

albryswyr pl. (m) *crossbowmen* 790

allan adv. *out* 506; **o hynny allan, o henne allan** *from then on, thence* 52, 166, 569, 570, 575, 576-7

allaur (allawr) f. *altar* 863

am, y am prep. (i) *about, concerning, with respect to* 101, 161, 251, 252, 306, 648 (ii) *upon* 123, 278, 371, 401, 424, 426 (iii) *for* 766, 861 (iv) *because of* 297, 503, 600, 633, 833, 959 (v) *on* (a date) 924 (vi) + verb to complete meaning 199 (vii) with suff. pers. pron. 1 sg. **amdanaf** 219; 3 sg.m **amdanav** (amdanaw) 306, 553; 3 sg.f. **amdanei** 354; 3 pl. **amdanunt** 449

amdiffyn¹ (amddiffyn) vn. *to protect* 654; pret. 3 sg. **amdiffynnawd** 660

amdiffyn² m. *protection, defence* 182, 905

amdiffynnwr m. *protector* 840, 888, 892

amgen adj. *different, other* 127, 222; **nyd amgen, nyt a.** *namely* 640, 650, 865, 915, 939, 1011

amgylch prep. *around* 923, 975, 1023, 1050

amhyl adj. *profuse, abundant* 46

amlet (amledd) m. *abundance* 413

amliv (amliw) adj. *multi-coloured* 455, 459

amlvc adj. *obvious* 460

amod m. *condition* 706

ampriodoryon pl. adj. *foreign, non-native* 763

amrauael, amravael (amrafael) adj. *various* 418, 434, 455, 529, 809; pl. **amraualyon, amrauaelyon, amravaellyon** 456, 457, 459, 726, 844, 870

amryssony pres. 2 sg. of vn. 'amryson' *to discuss* 202

amser m. *time, season* 31, 44, 50, 63, 119, 334

amserawl adj. *temporal, transient, temporary* 841

amuot (amfod) m./f. *contract* 480

amylder m. *multitude* 949

anadyl m. *breath* 259

andylyedus (anddyliedus) adj. *wrongful, without just cause* 1028

aneiryf, aneirif, m. *countless number* 458, 842 , 878, 1060

anelu vn. *to aim, to direct* 23

anhyedwyr pl. (m./f.) *flatterers, deceitful persons* 247

anhyspys adj. *secret, clandestine* 673n.

annoc (+y) vn. *to urge, to encourage* 524, 532, 1028

annot impv. 2 sg. of vn. 'annod' *to delay* 807; 1 pl. **annodun** (annodwn) 806

annvyleyt, an(n)vyl(y)eit (anwyliaid) pl. (m) *loved ones, servants, members of his household* 68, 70, 341, 405

annvyt (annwyd) f. *disposition* 160

annyan f./m. *nature* 229, 230, 902

anobeithav vn. *to despair* 499

anodun (anoddun) adj. *abysmal* 588

anogedigaeth f. *instigation* 612n.

anorchyuygedic adv. *undefeated* 881

anregyon pl. (m./f.) *provisions, dishes or courses of food* 145, 292, 922

anreith f. *spoil, plunder* 634; pl. **anreithyeu** 649, 843

anreithyaw, anreithyav, (anrheithiaw) vn. *to plunder* 686, 787, 834; impf. 3 sg. **anreithei** 300

anryded (anrhydedd) f./m. *honour, esteem, dignity, rank* 17, 134, 414, 452, 458, 521

anrydedu (anrhydeddu) vn. *to honour* 277, 281, 291, 408, 419; pres. 3 sg. **anrydeda** 642*n.*, imprs. **anrydedir** 274; pret. 3 sg. **anrydedawd, anrydedvys** 153, 871

anrydedus (anrhydeddus) adj. *honourable* 4, 58, 213, 460, 690, 1002

anryuedu (anrhyfeddu) vn. *to wonder at, to be amazed at* 149, 223, 239, 252

ansavd (ansawdd) m. (i) *method, way* 129; (ii) *condition* 45, 355, 461

ansodi (ansoddi) vn. *to array, to organize* 960

antrugaravc adj. *merciless* 540

anudonyl adj. *perjurious* 539

anundeb m. *lack of unity, strife* 100

anuolyannus adj. *infamous* as adv. 699

anuon (anfon) vn. *to send* 211, 275, 297, 684, 691, 693; pret. 3 sg. **anuones, anvones** 653, 757, 930, 1057, 1065, 3 pl. **anuonassant** 365, 1006, imprs. **anuonet** (*GMW* §135) 194, 420; impf. imprs. **anuonyt** (anfonid) 291, 292; plupft. 3 sg. **anuonassei** 476

anvylyeit see **annvyleyt**

anyanavl adj. *innate* 379

anynat adj. *perverse, dire* 882

ar[1] dem. pron. 489*n.* (*GMW* §75); **ar nyd** 671-2*n.*

ar[2] prep. (i) *on, onto* 2, 10, 147, 177, 256, 307 (ii) *to* 9*n.*, 17, 198, 234, 365, 396*n.* (iii) *as a result of* (*GPC s.v.*(6)) 532 (iv) *over* 104*n.*, 111, 747 (v) + vn. or adj. *to complete meaning* 15, 104 (vi) used in various expressions to express manner or condition (*GMW* §204 pp.184 5), listed here under second element: **brys; kyhoed; fo; gwarthaf; hyt; maeth; medyr; talym** (vii) with num. 57 (viii) with suff. pers. pron. 1 sg. **arnaf** 338; 2 sg. **arnat,** 335; 3 sg.m **arnav, arnaw** 10, 120, 148, 171, 343, 351, 372, ; 3 sg.f. **arnei** 51, 159, 355; 3 pl. **arnunt, arnadunt, y arnadunt** 27, 42, 93, 198, 231, 238, 573

arall[1] adj. *other* 61, 338, 344, 410, 435, 454; pl. **ereill** 88, 102, 209, 226, 289, 407

arall[2] pron. *other* 257; pl. **ereill** 1020

arbennic adj. *special* 132, 414

arbet vn. *to spare* 900; pret. 3 sg. **arbedawd** 879*n.*

arch[1] f. *request, petition* 768, 1029

arch[2], **arch-** see **erchi**

archdiagon m. *archdeacon* 849

archescob, archesgob m. *archbishop* 120, 363, 424, 425, 427

archesgobty, archescopty m. *archbishop's house* 416, 426 , 427, 775*n.*

ardaloed (ardaloedd) pl. (f.) *districts* 594*n.*

arderchavc, arderchawc, (ardderchawg) adj. *excellent, fine, splendid, famed for* 417n., 552, 868, 984; supv. **arderchocaf** 358

argluydiau (arglwyddiaw) vn. *to reign, to rule* 754

arglvydiaeth (arglwyddiaeth) f. *lordship* 573

arglvyd, argluyd, arglwyd m. *lord* 152, 215, 221, 237, 243, 248; pl. **argluydi** 747, 763n.

Arglvydes, arglwydes, f. *lady* 557, 563, 632, 993n.

argywedu (argyweddu) vn. *to harm* 380n.

arhos vn. *to await* 305, 513; pret. 3 sg. **arhoes** 1017

arn- see **ar**

aruaeth (arfaeth) f./m. *plan* 920n.

aruaethu (arfaethu) vn. *to plan, to decide* 403, 913, 961, 979

aruavc, aruawc (arfawg) adj. *armed* 139, 324, 949

arueidyawd (arfeiddiawdd) pret. 3 sg. of vn. 'arfeiddio' *to dare* 900

aruer[1] f./m. *practice* 494

aruer[2] (arfer) vn. (+o) *to use, to employ, to enjoy, to wear habitually* 333; impf. 3 pl. **aruerynt** 463n., 464; pret. imprs. **aruerwyt** 596

arueu, arveu (arfeu) pl. (m./f.) *arms* 463, 763, 819, 823, 892, 984

aruoll[1] (arfoll) m. *pledge, oath* 115, 173

aruoll[2] (arfoll) vn. (i) *to invite,* to *welcome* 213n., 283, 403; (ii) *to pledge, to swear on holy relics* 797n.; pret. 3 sg. **arvolles, aruolles** 4, 663, 690, 696

arveu see **arueu**

arvydocaa pres. 3sg. of vn. 'arwyddocáu' *to indicate* 265, 266; impf. 3 sg. **arvydocaei** 263

arvyd- see **arwyd**

arwein vn. (i) *to carry* 409, 431, 439 (ii) *to wear* 501

arwyd (arwydd) m./f. 598n., *sign*; pl. **arvydon, arwydyon** *standards, insignia* 376, 810

aryant m. *silver* 38, 407, 413, 520, 843, 986; as adj 456

assv, assu (asw) adj. *left* 429, 863

at[1] see **gat**

at[2] prep. *to* 933, 950, 1025; with suff pers. pron. 1 sg. **attaf** 218; 2 sg. **at(t)at** 112, 779; 3 sg.m. **atav, attaw** 41, 180, 224, 306, 314, 327; 3 sg.f. **attei** 69, 70; 3 pl. **attadunt** 366

atep m. *answer, reply* 750

atkyweiryawd pret. 3 sg. of vn. 'atgyweirio' *to repair* 975

atnewydhau vn. *to renovate, to renew* 404; pret. 3 sg. **atnewydhavys** (adnewyddhawys) 87

attal vn. *to keep, to retain* 1034

atteb vn. *to reply* 242

atuyd (atfydd) adv. *perhaps* 231

athoed see **mynet**

athraon (i) *philosophers* 418; (ii) *priests* 437, 777

auon see **avon**

aur/avrhon see **awr**

avch (awch) pref. poss. pron. 2 pl. *your* 528, 531

avon, auon (afon) f. *river* 10, 78, 81, 409, 512, 926; pl. **auonoed** 45, 267

avory adv. *tomorrow* 806

awr f. *hour* 1019; adv. *now* **er aur hon(n)**, **yr avrhon**, **yr awr honn** 3, 672, 806

Awst m. *August* 1023

awyr f./m. *air* 817

b

bacwn m. *bacon* 823

baed m. (baedd) *wild boar* 270*n.*, 890

ball f. *pestilence* 568, 588

bar m. *wrath* 300

bard (bardd) m. *bard, poet* 325; pl. **beird** (beirdd) 869*n.*, 873

barwn m. *baron* 765, 1049; pl. **barvnyeit, barwnyeit** 277, 361, 421, 1005n., 1042, 1045

baryf f. *beard* 724

bedin- see **bydin**

bedyd (bedydd) m. *baptism* 159, 525

bei see **bod**[1]

beichogi[1] m. *conception, pregnancy* 357

beichogi[2] see **beychogy**

beichyavc, beichyavc, beychavc adj. *pregnant* 15, 220

beird see **bard**

bendigau vn. *to bless* 852, 853

bendith f. *blessing* 798

berthed (berthedd) m. *treaasure, wealth* 843

beth interr. *what* 150, 151, 180, 191, 241, 262

beunyd see **peunyd**

beychogy, beychogi, beichogi[2] vn. *to impregnate* 12, 71, 72, 357; pret. 3 sg. **beichoges** 232; plpft. 3 sg. **beychogassei** 13

blaen: o ulaen (o flaen) cpd. prep. *in front of* 432; with pref. poss. pron. 3 sg.f. **o'e blaen** 438, 3 pl. **oc eu blaen** 800-1; **en ev blaen** *at their head* 1058

blaenwed, blaenwyd (blaenwedd) cpd. f. *highest pinacle* 17, 893

blinder m. *weariness, tedium* 446

bluyd, blvyd (blwydd) *years old*, denoting age 21, 371

blwydyn, blvydyn (blwyddyn) f. *years* 57, 563, 580, 602*n*., 839*n*., 867; pl.
　　blwydyned, bluydyned (blwyddynedd) 741*n*, 770; **blyned, blyneδ** used
　　with numerals 70, 83, 567, 579, 586, 910

bod¹ see **bot**

bod² see **ryngu b.**

bodi (boddi) vn. *to drown* 80; pret. 3 sg. **bodes** 1060

bodlavn (bodlawn) adj. *pleased* 46

bonhed, boned (bonedd) m. *nobility* 387, 721, 887

bonhedic (bonheddig) adj. *noble* 409, 727, 731; spv. **bonhedicaf, bonhedikaf** 719,
　　885, 964

bonhedigyon, bonhedygyon, bonedigyon (boneddigion) pl. (m.) *noblemen*
　　879, 934, 1024, 1050

bot, bod¹ vn. *to be* 15, 21, 42, 63, 96, 97; pres. ind. 1 sg. **wyf** 779, 781, 784, 2 sg. **vyt,
　　wyt** 203, 333, 781, 3 sg. **mae¹** 156, 208, 241, 321, 618, 682, **mae²** (as copula at
　　beginning of a noun clause) (*GMW* §148 (b)) 677, **yw, ydyw, yu, yv** (yw)
　　154, 216, 299, 315, 333, 672, **oes²** 318, 322, rel. **syd, ys(s)yd** (ysydd) 108*n*.,
　　208*n*., 247, 264, 321, 806, 2 pl. **ywch²** 530, 3 pl. **maent, ynt** 529, 671, 786;
　　cons. pres./fut. 2 sg. **bydy** (byddi) 110, 3 sg. **byd** (bydd) 273, 274; impf. 1 sg.
　　yttoedvn (ydoeddwn) 217, 3 sg. **oed, oet, adoed, ydoeδ, ytoed** (ydoedd)
　　3, 22, 26, 34, 35, 36, 2 pl. **oedoch** (oeddoch) 624, 3 pl. **oydynt, oedynt,
　　oedent,** (oeddynt, -ent) 22, 609, 610, 629, 857, imprs. **oedet** (oeddet) 426,
　　436; cons. impf. 3 sg. **bydei** (byddei) 464, 3 pl. **bydynt, bydunt,** (byddynt)
　　248, 345, 853; pret. 3 sg. **bu, bv,** 19, 33, 58, 69, 72, 84, 3 pl. **buant** 47; plpft.
　　3 sg. **buassei, bvassei** 119, 167, 568, 590, 690, 691, 3 pl. **bvessynt** (buesynt)
　　688; pres. sub. 2 sg. **bych** 336, 3 sg. **bo, boet** 113, 320, 335, 336, 378, 379; impf.
　　sub. 3 sg. **bei, pei, ryffei** 88, 189, 325*n*., 345, 349, 382

bradvr, bratvr, bratwr m. *traitor* 476, 511, 526, 539, 541

brat m. *treason, treachery* 831, 1061

brathedic adj. *wounded* 985

brathei impf. 3 sg. of vn. 'brathu' *to stab* 535, imprs. **brethyt** (brethid) 536; pret.
　　imprs. **brathvt** (brathwyd) 552

bravt, braud, brawd, brawt, m. *brother* 161, 666, 691, 947, 1063; pl. **broder,** 387*n*.,
　　brodyr 108, 610, 650, 997*n*., 1018, 1019.

brawhau vn. *to take fright* 631

breich f. a*rm* 893

breid (breidd) adv. *hardly, scarcely, with difficulty* 830; **o ureid** (o freidd) 118

breinhavl adj. *noble, regal* 412

breint f. *status, right, special right* 422*n*., 431*n*., 438

brenhin, brenin see **brenhyn**

brenhinaeth, brenhinyaeth f. *sovereignty, kingship* 105, 111, 116, 129, 136, 384

brenhinolyon see **brenhynavl**

brenhinyn m. *kinglet, petty king 755n.*

brenhyn, brenhin, brenin m. *king* 4, 5, 6, 9, 26, 29; pl. **brenhined, brenhyned** (brenhinedd) 34, 402, 410, 420, 439, 746

brenhynavl, brenhinavl, brenhinawl, brenhinyaul, brenhinyawl adj. *royal, regal* 9, 117, 145, 204, 214, 376; pl. **brenhinolyon** 449

brenhynes, brenhines f. *queen* 76, 436, 448, 450, 458, 498

brethyt see **brathei**

broder, brodyr see **bravt**

bron f. *breast, heart* 24; **rac bron** *before, in front of, in the presence of* 212; with pref. poss. pron. 1 sg. **rac y mron** 238, 2 sg. **rac dy vronn** 779-80, 3 sg.m. **rac y uron** 240

brvydyr, brvyder, bruydr, brwyder f. *battle* 487, 507, 543, 728, 806, 813

bryd see **bryt**

brys m. *haste* 511; **ar vrys** (ar frys) *in haste* 759

bryssyav vn. *to hasten, to approach quickly* 264

bryt, bryd m. *mind, disposition, accord* 521, 802

Brytannec f. *Brittonic language, British* 53

bu, bu- see **bot**

buched, bvched f. *life* 8, 841

budugaul (buddugawl) adj. *victorious* 809, 827

budugolyaeth, budygolyaeth (buddugoliaeth) f. *victory, supremacy* 169, 683, 873, 940; pl. **bvdugolaetheu** 842

buelin (buelin) m. *buffalo,* adj. *of buffalo* 457

bugeil m. *shepherd* 176

bv, bv- see **bot**

bva (bwa) m. *bow* 23

bvched see **buched**

bvdugolaetheu see **budugolyaeth**

bvrn (bwrn) m. *crowd, group* 196.

bvryassant see **bwrw**

bvystuiled (bwystfiledd) pl. (m.) *beasts* 46

bvyt, bwyt (bwyd) m. *food* 274, 734, 920

bvyta (bwyta) vn. *to eat* 145

bwrdeissyeit pl. (m.) *burgesses* 962

bwrw vn. *to cast down, to throw* 953; pret. 3 sg., **bwryawd** 904, 3 pl. **bvryassant** 573

bwyeill pl. (f.) *battle-axes* 810n.

bwyt see **bvyt**

bych see **bot**

bychan adj. *small* 143*n*.; pl. **bychein** 620, 621

bychydic *a little, a few* 1067

byd¹, byd- see **bot**

byd² see **byt**

bydavl (bydawl) adj. *worldly* 559

bydin (byddin) f. *army* 523, 538, 807, 825; pl. **bydinoed, bedinoed** 518, 519, 532, 545, 809; **yn y vedin gentaf** *in the vanguard* 825

bydinauc (byddinawg) adj. *drawn up in battle array* 788

bydinav (byddinaw) vn. *to march to battle* 505

bynnac see **pa, peth, pvy**

byssed (bysedd) pl. (m.) *fingers* 725, 733

byt (byd) m. *world* 374, 410, 562; **yn y byd** *at all, ever* 219, 320, 322, 707

byv (byw) adj. *alive, living* 215*n*., 534

c, k

cad f. see **cat**

cadarn adj. *strong, mighty* 183; pl. **kedyrn** 887; see also **cadarnleoed**; spv. **cadarnhaf** 181, 182, 308

kadarnhau, cadarnhau, vn. *to fortify, to ratify* 305, 497, 1007; pret. 3 sg. **cadarnhavs** (cadarnhaws) 560

cadarnleoed, lleoed cadarn pl. (m.) *strongholds* 172

cadeir f. *chair* 871

cadv, cadw vn. *to keep, to maintain* 571, 1037, 1039; impf. 3 sg. **catwei** 324

caedic adj. *closed* 321

cael see **caffael**

kaer f. *fortress, fortified town or city* 1, 55*n*., 58, 210, 411, 423; pl. **kaeroed** (caeroedd), **kaeryd** (caerydd) 87, 888

caffael, kaffael, cahel vn. *to obtain, get, reach, beget, find, discover, come by/ across* 7, 14, 118, 128, 129, 135; pres. 1 sg. **caffaf, cahaf** 316, 319, 2 sg **ceffy** 244, 3 pl. **cant** 671; impf. 3 sg. **kaffei** 133, 182, 312, imprs. **ceffyt** (ceffid) 225; pret. 3 sg **kafas, kauas** 71, 96, 170, 305, 357, 492, 3 pl. **cavssant, kawssant** 162*n*., 405, 625, imprs. **caffat** 120, 232*n*.; plpft. 3 sg. **kawssei** 696; **c. beychogi** *to become pregnant* 71

cah- see **caffael**

Kalan Awst *the first of August* 924-5

Calan Mei *Mayday* 561-2*n*., 582, 880*n*.

calaned (calanedd) pl. (m.) *corpses* 510

calch m. *lime* 192, 193

calet (caled) adj. *hard* 487; spv. **caletaf** 543

call adj. *wise* 571, 734

callon (calon) f. *womb, heart* 217, 557

kam[1] adj. *crooked, wrong* 53*n.*

cam[2] m. *a wrong* 646

can[1], **cant** num. *hundred* 556, 563, 964; **canwr** *a hundred men* 515*n.*

can[2] conj. *since, because* 182, 214, 306; with negative **cany, canyd, canyt** 26, 178, 318, 349, 354

kanhaiaf (cynhaeaf) m. *harvest, autumn* 1056

canhiat, canhyat, kannyat f./m. *permission* 49, 118, 294, 297, 299*n.*, 976

canhorthwy, canhorthuy, kanorthvy (canhorthwy) m. *aid, assistance, support* 271, 748, 749, 767, 780, 802

kanlyn, kanlhyn vn. *to follow* 22, 441

kanmoledic adj. *praiseworthy* 671

kannyat see **canhiat**

canonwyr pl. (m.) *canons* 416, 433

canorthuyav, kanorthuyav (canorthwyaw) vn. *to aid, assist, support* 761; impf. 3 sg. **kannorthwyei** 708; pret. 3 sg **cannorthwyawd** 901

canorthuywr (canorthwywr) m. *supporter* 769

kanorthvy see **canhorthwy**

canpunt f. *a hundred pounds* 702

cant[1] see **can**[1]

cant[2] see **caffael**

cantref, kantref m. *hundred* (division of land) 597, 958, 1031; pl. **cantrefoed** (cantrefoedd) 593*n.*

canu vn. *to sing, chant; to state, to say* 418*n.*, 434; impf. imprs. **kenit** 445

canwr m. *hundred men* 515

cany, canyd, canyt, see can[2]

canys, kanys (i) < *can* + *ys*, pres. 3 sg. of *bot* + mixed or abnormal order (*GMW* § 261 (b) (1)), *SW*, 327) 59, 101, 127, 129, 134, 203 (ii) as simple conj. before verb (*GMW* § 261 (c)) 251, 646, 885

car m. *kinsman* 555

karcharu vn. *to imprison* 171; pret. 3 sg. **karcharawd** 1019, imprs. **karcharwyt** 985

cardodus adj. *charitable* 735

karedyc adj. *beloved* 34

carei impf. 3 sg. of vn. 'caru', *to love* 88, 296, 374; pret. 3 sg. **karvys** 166

carned f. *cairn, tumulus* 837

carrec f. *stone* 321, 323, 324

carw m. *stag* 22, 24

caryad, **caryat** m. *love, infatuation* 67, 150, 289, 313, 315, 318

caryatwragedd pl. (f.) *sweethearts* 739

castell, **kastell** m. *castle* 181, 185, 307, 308, 311, 320, 970*n*.; pl. **kestyll** 171, 303, 305, 572, 681*n*., 926

cat (cad) f. *battle* 506

catwedigaeth (cadwedigaeth) f. *keeping* 970

catwei see **cadv**

kau-, **cav-**, **kaw-** see **caffael**

kaur (cawr) m. *giant* 813; pl. **kevri** (cewri) 45, 47, 48

ked, **ked-** see **kyd**, **kyd-**

kedernyt m. *might, power, strength* 372, 766, 893, 896, 979; *warranty, oath confirmed by surety* (*GPC s.v. cadernid* (2)) 173

kedymdeith m. *companion* 314, 415; pl. **kedymdeitheon**, **kedymdeithyon**, **kydmeithyon** 161, 505, 649, 688, 722

kedymdeithas see **kydmeithas**

kedymdeithessei pl. (f.) *female companions* 218

kedymdeithocau vn. *to accompany* 381

kedyrn see **cadarn**

kefneu pl. (m.) *backs* 816*n*., 826

kefnitherw f. *female cousin* 610

kefynderw see **keuynderv**

ceff- see **caffael**

cegin f. *kitchen* 454

cein(n)yadaeth f. *music, singing* 434, 443

keinyawc f. *penny* 921

keis- see **keyssyav**

keithiwet see **keythywet,**

cel: **a dan gel** *secretly, stealthily* 832

celadwy adj. *concealed* 710

celuydyd (celfyddyd) f. *art, science* 334; pl. **celuydodeu** 333, 342, 418

celwyd (celwydd) *lie, falsehood* 239

celwydawc adj. *lying* 246

kemryt see **kymrut**

kenadwri m. *errand* 713

kenedyl, **kenedel** f. *nation, kinsmen; descent, lineage* 30*n*., 32, 41, 51, 103, 228; pl. **kenedloed** (cenhedloedd) 551, 747; *categories* 870.

kenit see **canu**

kenna(a)deu pl. (m.) *messengers, delegates* 138, 195, 197, 204, 210, 276

kennhadawd pret. 3 sg. of vn. 'kenatau' (caniatáu) *to grant* 936

kentaf see **kyntaf**

keny neg. conj. *if not, though not* 189

ker, ger llaw see **llav**

kerd (cerdd) f. *music,* **k. music** *the craft of music* (*GPC s.v.* cerdd (b)) 870

kerdet, kerded vn. *to march, walk, traverse* 23, 445, 668, 803; **k. mor** *to sail* 752-3; pres. 3 pl. **kerdant** 787; pret. 3 sg **kerdus** (cerddws) 745, 764, 776, 799, 801; 3 pl. **kerdassant** 796

kestyll see **castell**

ket see **kyt**

cetwis see **cadv**

kethiwet see **keythywet**

keu adj *hollow* 249

keueillyon (cyfeillion) pl. (m.) *friends* 797

keuynderv, kefynderw m. *male cousin* 565, 609

kevri see **kaur**

kewilyduus adj. *disgraceful* 509

keyssyav, keissyav, keissyaw vn. *to try* 24, 105, 184, 191, 194, 199; *to possess* 748; impf. 3 sg. **keissyei** 907; pret. 3 sg. **keissyawd** (ceisiawdd) 874, 3 pl. **keissasant** 624; impv. 2 pl. **keisswch** 645

keythywet, keithiwet, kethiwet m. *captivity* 29, 31, 43, 577, 1026

kic m. *meat* 922

kigleu see **clybot**

cilid (cilydd) as pron. *other* 258; **pwy gilyd, pvy g.** *from one . . . to another* 445-6, 590

kilyav vn. *to retreat* 178

kiwdawd, kiudaut, kivdaut f./m. *people* 675, 685, 836; *armed band, troop, army* 727*n.;* pl. **kiwdawdwyr, kivdavtwyr** *natives* 175, 705

clad (cladd) m./f. *hole dug in the ground* 245

cladu (claddu) vn. *to bury, dig* 244, 502, 510, 1001; pret. imprs. **cladwyt, cladvyt, cladwt, kladpwyt,** 58, 90, 838, 863, 995, 1010

clas m. *monastic community* 777

clavstyr (clawtyr) m. *cloister, monastery* 127

cledyf (cleddyf) m. *sword* 431, 814; pl. **cledyueu** (cleddyfeu) 539

cleuychvs (clefychws) pret. 3 sg. of vn. 'clefychu' *to become ill* 561

clochte (clochty) m. *belfry* 1061

clod, clot m. *renown* 36, 40, 1034

clotuavr (clodfawr) adj. *famous, celebrated* 462, 491; cpv. **clotuorach** 466; spv. **clotuorhaf** 358

klybot vn. *to hear* 605; impf. 3 sg. **clyvei** (clywei) 374; pret. 3 sg. **kigleu** 114, 204, 310 607, 617, 744, 3 pl. **klywssant** 682, imprs. **clywyt** (clywyd) 334, 819; plpft. imprs. **clywssyt** ar(clywsid) 372*n*.

clyv-, clyw-, klyw- see **klybot**

cnaut (cnawd) m. *complexion* 725

coch, cohc adj. *red* 257*n*., 264 , 266

koet, koedyd pl. (f.) *woods, forests* 46, 890

cof m. *memory* 598, 817; **mynet dros kof/gof** *to be forgotten* 903, 1040 **dwyn ar gof** *to recall* 598

coffadwy adj. *recorded (GPC s.v)* 883

coffau (cofféu) vn. *to recall, remember* 313; pret. 3 sg. **koffaawd** 1006

cohc see **coch**

colomen f. *dove* 440

kolledus adj. *fraught with loss* 884

collet (colled) f. *loss* 648, 898

kolli vn. *to lose* 503, 923; pret. 3 sg. **colles, kolles** 575, 582; plpf. 3 sg. **collas(s)ei** 183, 504; pres. sub. 1 sg. **collvyf** (collwyf) 316

corff m. *body* 732, 850, 995, 1009, 1010, 1011

coron f. *crown* 98, 123, 278, 370, 401, 424

cost f./m. *expense* 998

credu (y) vn. *to believe* 250, 253, 355; pret. 3 pl. **credassant** 652

kreiryeu pl. (m./f.) *relics* 797*n*.

creuyd (crefydd) f. *religion* 1001

creu[1] m./f. *blood* 557

creu[2] vn. *to create, to kindle* 259; pret. 3 sg. **crevys** (crewys) 216

creulavn, creulawn adj. *cruel* 727, 912; pl. **creulonyon** 982; cpv. **creulonach** 925; spv. **creulonaf** 899

creulonder m. *cruelty* 471

creuyd (crefydd) f. *religion* 121, 1001

crevys see **creu**[2]

cristonogaeth f. *Christianity* 268

cristonogyon pl. (m./f.) *Christians* 485, 557

kroget (croged) pret. imprs. of vn. 'crogi' *to hang* 990

crvydrav (crwydraw) vn. *to wander* 183

crwnn adj. *round* 724, 725

crythoryon pl. (m.) *fiddlers* 870

cudyavc (cuddiawg) adj. *secret* 69

kuunfan see **kvynuan**

cvnstabyl m. *constable* 210

kvplau vn. *to celebrate* (*GPC* s.v. *cwplâf*) 447

cvuenhoed (cwfennoedd) pl. (m./f.) *convents, religious communities* 433

cvymp (cwymp) m. *fall* 268

kvynav, kwynaw vn. *to complain, to lament* 746, 898

kvynuan, kuunfan, kwynvan (cwynfan) vn. *to lament* 534*n.*, 861, 884

cwbyl as adv. *completely* 627, 914, 961

kwyn- see **kvynav, kvynuan**

kychwyn, kychuyn, kychvyn vn. *to set out* 210, 386, 427, 502

kydmeithas, kedymdeithas f. *company, presence, comradeship* 707, 832

kydmeithyon see **kedymdeith**

kydtirogyon pl. (m.) *fellow / neighbouring landowners* 643

kyduarchogyon see **kytuarchavc**

kydyav vn. *to copulate* 220, 231

kyf- see also **kyu-**

kyfleoed pl. (m.) *precincts* 687*n.*

kyfnessaf m./f. *kinsman* 555

kyfnewid m. *merchandise* 665

kyfodi vn. *to rise* 957; pret. 3 sg **kyuodes** 100, 452, 454, 1015; 3 pl. **kyuodassant** 257; impf. 3 sg. **kyuodei** 669, imprs. **kyuotit** 188

kyfreithus (cyfreithus) adj. *law-abiding, just* 735

kyfruch[1] (cyfrwch) vn. *to meet* 759

kyfruch[2] (cyfrwch) m. *encounter meeting, consultation* 764, 795

kyffelip (cyffelyb) adj. *similar* 813

kyffelybu vn. *to compare, match* 462; impf. imprs. **cyffelybit, cyffelypit** (cyffelybid) 140, 412; pret. 3 sg. **cyffelybawd** 886*n.*

kyffelyprwyd (cyffelyprwydd) m. *likeness, similarity* 855*n.*

kyffes f./m. *confession* 846

kyffroi vn. *to be moved; to array* 612, 959

kyffrowr m. *instigator* 889

kyghor, kyngor, kynghor, m. *advice, counsel*, dsicretion 116, 127, 134, 305, 317, 320; *council* 764; **bod vrth gyngor** *to submit to counsel* 110

kyghoret (cynghored) pret. imprs. of vn. 'cynghori' *to advise* 181

kynghorwr (cynghorwr) m. *counsellor* 887; pl. **kyghorwyr** 131*n.*

kynghorwreic f. *counsellor* 734

kyngor see **kyghor**

ky(n)goruynnu (cyngorfynnu) (+wrth) vn. *to envy, bear hatred* 5; pres. 3 sg. **kyghoruynna** 643

kyngoruynnus (cyngorfynnus) adj. *envious* 900

kyngreir m./f. *truce* 694

kyhoed: ar gyhoed *openly, publicly* 710

kyhudaw (cyhuddo) vn. *to accuse* 677

kyhyt (cyhyd) eqv. based on a noun (*GMW* § 41 (a) (3)) *as much as* 31

kylch: am gylch cpd. prep. *about* 946; **yg kylch/ynghylch** *around* 505, 613, 616, 803; with pref. poss. pron. 3 sg.m. **en e gylch, yn y kylch** 619*n.*, 824; 3 sg.f **yn y chylch** 437; 3 pl. **yn eu kylch** 206, 498

kylchynu vn. *to surround* 311, 615

kyllellauc (cyllellawg) adj. *armed with knives* 811

kymedraul (cymedrawl) adj. *moderate* 723

kymeint see **kymeynt**

kymell (**ar**) vn. *to drive; to urge, to compel* 65, 171, 260, 261, 493, 508 impf. 3 sg. **kymellei** 364

kymeredyc (cymeredig) adj. *acceptable* 34

kymerth see **kymrut**

kymeynt, kymeint, eqv. based on a noun, 'of the same size' (GMW § 41 (a) (3)) *so great, so much* 27, 33, 128, 187, 284; **yn g. a(c)** *in as much as* 290, 461-2, 920-1

cymhell see **kymell**

kymhennach cpv. degree of adj. *wiser, fairer, more accomplished* 494

kymodi vn. *to reconcile* 951; pret. 3 sg. **kymodes** 934

kymorthyeit (cymorth(w)yeid) pl. (m.) *supporters* 1041

kymot m. *reconciliation, agreement* 959

kymperved m. *middle* 822

kymraec m./f. *Welsh* 91

kymrut, kymryt, kymmryd, kemryt vn. *to take, to receive* 26, 116, 123, 137, 144, 173; *to feel, to experience*; pres. 1 sg. **kymeraf** 338; impf. 3 sg. **kymerei** 120; pret. 3 sg. **kymerth, kymyrth** 60, 61, 62, 79, 174, 283, 396

Kymry[1] see Index of Place Names

Kymry[2] pl. see Index of Personal Names

kymun m. *holy communion* 846

kymvt (cymwd) m. *commot, district* 716

kymynnvs (cymynnws) pret. 3 sg. of vn. 'kymynnu' *to bequeath* 555

kymyrth see **kymrut**

kymysgu vn. *to mix* 192

kyn(n) prep. *before* 390; **kyn(n)/gynn no** (*GMW* § 46 N 3) 52, 167, 251, 372, 665, 782

kyndared (cynddaredd) f. *rage* 792, 930

kyneuyn (cynefin) adj. *habitual* 530

kyneuynau (cynefinaw) vn. *to acquaint oneself* 33

kyn(n)al vn. *to hold, keep* 428, 590, 636; *sustain* 342, 542; impf. 3 sg. **kynhalyei** 705; pret. 3 sg. **kyn(n)helis** 586, 867

kynnennu *to quarrel*, quarrelling 200*n*.; pres. 2 sg. **kynnenny** 203

kynneuavt (cynefawd) f. *custom* 460

kyn(n)helis see **kynnal**

kynnoessoed pl. (f.) *bygone days* 838

kyn(n)ullaw, kynnullav vn. *to assemble* 77, 185, 302, 385, 565, 843; pret. 3 sg **kynnullawd, kynnvllus** 771, 912, 3 pl. **kynnullassant** 652

kynnvryf (cynnwryf) m. *motion, disturbance* 819

kyntaf, kentaf ord. num. *first* 574, 778, 813, 825; **gyntaf** adv. 444

kyrcheu pl. (m.) *attacks* 911, 982

kyrchu vn. *to set out* 506, 952; *to make for* 497, 613, 960; *to attack* 302, 537; impf. 3 pl. **kyrchynt** 444; pret. 3 sg. **kyrchawd, kyrchus** (kyrchws) 655, 656, 663, 813, 913, 1029; 3 pl. **kyrchassant** 653, 655, 662, 664

kyrn m. pl. *drinking-horns* 456

kysgu vn. *to sleep* 55, 250, 350, 615; pret. 3 sg. **kysgvs** 66, imprs. **kysgvyt** 165

kyssegru vn. *to ordain, to dedicate, to consecrate* 121, 363, 370, 845; pret. 3 sg. **kyssegrawd** 996

kyssygredig adj. *sacred* 851, 995

kystal see **da**

kyt, ket, ked conj. *although* 88, 379, 491, 493, 984

kytdoluryav (+a) vn. *commiserate* 370

kytduhun adj. **yn g**. *in unity* 981

kytgyghor m. *mutual agreement* 162, 405

kytsynhyav vn. *approve of* 159

kytsynhyedigaeth f. *consent* 362

kytuarchavc m. *fellow-knight* 314; pl. **kyduarchogyon** 39

kythreul m. *devil* 612

kyuanhed m./f. *habitation* 50

kyuanhedu vn. *to inhabit* 45

kyuarch, kyvarch guell vn. *to greet* 148, 760

kyuarvv pret. 3 sg. of vn. 'kyfarfod' *to meet* 661

kyuedychwyr m.pl. *banqueters, revellers* 156

kyueilles f. *kinswoman* 608

kyueillyach m. *friendship* 642

kyuliv, kyfliw adj. *the same colour* 347*n*., 832

kyuod- see **kyfodi**

kyuoeth, kyfoeth, kywoeth m. (i) *land, territory* 112, 180, 183, 300, 308, 521, 646 (ii) *people or subjects of a realm* 735 (iii) *power* 9, 111, 253 (iv) *wealth* 413, 461

kyuoethocaf (cyfoethocaf) spv. degree of adj. *very rich* 407

kyuoethogi (cyfoethogi) vn. *to enrich* 383

kyuotit see **kyfodi**

kyuranc (cyfranc) f. *story* 225

kyureith (cyfreith) f. law 472; pl. **kyureithyeu** 1045

kyurvys (cyfrwys) adj. *experienced, skillful* 530

kyuryv (cyfryw), **kyfryw** adj. *such* 195, 901;   **neb kyuryw** (*GMW* § 100 (b)) 322

kyuyawn (cyfiawn) adj. *just* 908

kyuyng (cyfyng) adj. *narrow* 323

kyvarch guell see **kyuarch gwell**

kyvoedyon (cyfoedion) pl. (m./f.) *contemporaries* 35

kyvun (cyfun) adj. *agreeing, in agreement* 795

kywarsangedic (cyfarsangedig) adj. *oppressed* 269

kywersengir (cyfersengir) pres. imprs. of vn. 'cyfarsangu' *to trample underfoot),* *to oppress* 266

kyweiryaw (cyfeiriaw) vn. *to direct, to equip, repair* 54, 673

kyweithas f./m. *company* 685

kywilyd (cywilydd) m. *shame* 647

kywir adj. *true, faithful* 636; spv. **kywiraf** 649

kywirdeb m. *loyalty* 1037

kywoeth see **kyuoeth**

kywreint adj. *clever, skilful* 726

ch

'ch inf. pron. 2 sg. 643

chu- see **chw-**

chuaer, chwaer, f. *sister* 393, 899*n.*

chue, chuech num. *six* 515, 516, 517, 968; ch. canwr see **can**[1]

chuechant, chwechant num. *six hundred* 517, 579

chwedyl f./m. *report, account, news* 631*n.*; pl. **chuedleu** 498

Chwefrawr *February* 995

chwi[1] indep. pron. 2 pl. 339, 649; **chuitheu** indep. conjunct. pers. pron. 2 pl. 529

chwi[2], **chui** aff. pron. 2 pl. 246, 528, 623, 641; **chwitheu** aff. conjunct. pers. pron. 2 pl. 644

chwyrnu vn. *to growl* 890

chwys m. *sweat* 820

d

da[1] adj. *good* 342, 557, 671, 724, 734, 740; eqv. **dahet, kystal** 445, 921; cpv. **gwell** 1027; spv. **goreu** 367, 733, 922; **da gennwch** see **gan**[vi]

da[2] n. *goods* 377, 382, 857, 919

daear see **dayar**

daearavl (daearawl) adj. *earthly* 296

daearty m. *underground room, cellar, cave* 67

daeony, daeoni m. *goodness* 36, 95, 373, 382

dagreuoed, dagreu pl. (m.) *tears* 883, 1026

dangos vn. *show* 1025; pres. 3 pl. **dangossant** 359

dahet see **da**

dala, daly vn. *hold, to capture* 401, 426, 625, 927, 992, 1046; impf. imprs. **delit** 983; pret. 3 sg. **delis** 1019, 1047; impv. 2 pl. **delywch** 645

damgylchynu vn. *to surround* 48

damunav (dymunaw) vn. *to desire* 130, 333

damunedic adj. *desired* 351

damunet (dymuned) vn. *eagerly wait for* 760n.

damwein f./m. *misfortune, mishap* 130, 309n.; pl. **damweinnyeu** *events* 955n.

damweyney impf. 3 sg. of vn. 'damweinio' *to chance, to happen* 38n.; pret. 3 sg. **damweinnyawd** 658n.

dan, a dan, adan, tan prep. (i) *under* 24, 29, 244, 247, 271; (ii) *as far as* 395; (iii) with vn. it forms a participle which expresses an action simultaneous with that of the main vb. but usually separate from it 807 (*GMW* § 237); **tan yr amod hwnn** *on this condition* 706; **a dan gel** see **cel**

danhed (dannedd) pl. (m.) *teeth* 822

darfcy see **daruod**

darmerth m. *provision* 419

daroed see **daruot**

darparu vn. *to prepare* 400, 405; plpf. 3 pl. **darparassei** 282

daruot, daruod, darvot (darfod) vb. (i) *to finish* 1, 442, 502, 605, 701, 831 (ii) *to happen, to occur* 588 (iii) also used as auxiliary verb, *happen that* (*GMW* § 154 N.1) 145, 200, 395, 447, 519, 531; impf. 3sg. **daroed** (daroedd) 368, 569, 756; cons. past. 3 sg. **daruydei** (darfyddei) 188; pret. 3 sg. **darvu** 835; impf. sub. 3 sg. **darfey** 16n.

darystung, darystwng vn. (i) *to submit, surrender* 820 (ii) *to subdue* 979; pres. 3 pl. **darystyngant** 272; pret. 3 sg. **darystyngawd** 882

darystyngedigyon pl. adj. *subjected, subjugated, vanquished* 888

datcanu vn. *to declare; to tell, recite* 225, 535; pres. sub. 3 sg. **datcano** 274

datkanadwy adj. *narratable* 883*n*.

dathoed see **dyuot**

dav see **dyuot**

davn (dawn) f. *prowess* 34

dayar, **daear** f. *earth* 16, 188, 189, 228, 229, 244

dec num. *ten* 910; **deng mil** *ten thoussand* 1050

dechreu[1] vn. *to begin* 187, 255, 258, 302, 311, 507; pret. imprs. **dechreuyt** (*GMW* § 135) 49

dechreu[2] m. *beginning* 902

dechrynv (dechrynu) vn. *to fear*, *to be scared* 808

dechymygedic (dychymygedig) adj. *devised* 352

deffroi vn. *to wake* 616

deng see **dec**

deheu m. and adj. *right* 428

deheubarth m. *southern part, South Wales* 776*n*., 881

Deheuwyr pl. (m.) *men of the South* 801

dehol vn. *to banish* 28; pret. 3 sg. **deholes** 25; pl. **deholassant** 591

deissyuyt (deisyfyd) adj. *quick, sudden, unexpected* 142*n*., 561

deledogeon see **dylyedogyon**

delei see **dyuot**

delis, **delit**, **delywch** see **dala**, **daly**

deu num. *two* 92, 195, 201, 249, 250, 309; **deu can**, **deucant**, **deukant** *two hundred* 417, 910, 928, 999; **deu ugein**, **deugein**, **deugeint** *forty* 83, 556, 586, 936, 999

deu- see **dyuot**

deuavt, **deuaut**, **deuawt** (defawd) f. (i) *custom, practice, manner,* 156, 827 (ii) *law, ordinance, decree* (*GCP s.v. defod* (b)) 1006; pl. **deuodeu** (defodeu) *marks of character* 372, 740 (*GPC s.v. defod* (a))

deucant, **deukant** see **deu**

deuδecved, **deudecuet**, ord. num. *twelfth* 561*n*., 582

deueit (defeid) pl. (f) of 'dafad' *sheep* 176

deugein(t) see **deu**

deunav *eighteen* 138

deuodeu see **deuavt**

deuryw *two kinds* 868

deuvinyauc (deufiniawg) adj. *double edged* 811*n*.

devred, **dewred** m. *courage* 36, 506, 896

devyn- see **dewin**, **dewyndabaeth**

dewin m. *soothsayer* 224; pl. **dewinyon, dewynyon, devynyon** 13, 190, 191, 235, 238, 240

dewr adj. *brave* 766; spv. **dewrhaf** 37

dewred see **devred**

dewynav (dewinaw) vn. *to prophesy* 14

dewyndabaeth, devyndabaeth (dewindabaeth) f. *vaticination, prophecy* 17, 18

di see **ti²**

dial see **dyal**

diang vn. *to escape* 675; pres. 3 sg. **diang** (=diainc) 622; pret. 3 sg. **diengis** 621, 623, 662, 830

diannot adj. *immediate, without delay* 117, 163, 211, 348

dianrydedu *to dishonour* 527

diawt f. *drink* 906

diawul (diafwl) m. *devil* 158; pl. **dieuyl** (diefyl) 229

dibryder adj. *without worry* 339

dichellion pl. (m.) *wiles* 678

diengis see **diang**

dieithyr adj. *strange, foreign* 705

diergrynnedic as adv. *fearlessly* 1017

dieuyl see **diawul**

diffeith adj. *deserted* 44, 676

diffeithyaw vn. *to destroy* 669, 681, 686

digoded (digodded) adj. *without harm* 662

digrif adj. *pleasant* 907

digriuet (digrifed) eqv. adj. used as n. *delight* 443

diguydedigaeth (digwyddedigaeth) m./f. *death* 861

digvydaf (digwyddaf) pres. 1 sg. of vn. 'digwydd' *to fall, fall in battle* 780; pret. 3 pl. **digvydassant, dygvydassant** (*GPC s.v. digwyddaf* 2(a)) 488, 544, 824

digyuoethi, digyfoethi vn. *to dispossess* 527, 913

digyffro *unperturbed* 1018

diheu adj. *sure* 316; cpv. **diheuach** *more certain* (*GPC s.v. diau¹*) 554

dihewyt m. *whole-hearted devotion, earnest desire, ardent wish, zeal* 130, 291

dileir pres. imprs. of vn. 'dileu' *to annihilate* 268

dillat see **dyllat**

dim¹ m. *anything* 115, 189, 296, 354, 679; **o dim** adv. *at all* 290

dim² adj. *any* 1020

dimeu f. *halfpenny* 921

dinas see **dynas**

dineu vn. *to pour* 193

diodef (dioddef) vn. *to endure* 930, 1027; pret. 3 sg. **diodefawd** 903

diogel adj. *safe, sure* 905

diogelwch m. *safe conduct* 933

dioluch (diolwch) vn. *to thank* 750n.

diot vn. *to deprive* 136

dirann adj. *without a share* 97

direbud (dirybudd) adv. *without warning* 1068

dirgel adj. *stealthy, secret* 68

dirperei impf. 3 sg. of vn. 'dirper' *to befit, become* 457

diruavr, diruawr, diruaur, dirvaur, dirvavr, dyruawr adj. *very great* 282, 400, 441, 492, 507, 511, 803n.; pl. **diruawryon** 702

disbydu vn. *to drain* 249, 251

disgynnassant pret. 3 pl. of vn. 'disgyn' *to descend, come upon* 786

distein m. *steward* 1066

distryv see **dystryw**

distrywedigaeth f. *destruction* 968

ditheu see **titheu**[2]

diua (difa) vn. *to destroy* 685; pret. imprs. **diuawyd** 662; plpf. 3 pl. **diuaassant** 682

diuetha (difetha) vn. *to destroy* 657, 660, 914

divlanedic (diflanedig) adj. *faded* 783

diwed, dywet (diwedd) m. *end* 269, 273, 508, 667, 771, 847; **d. dydyeu** *last days* 855; **y diwed hvnn** *lately, recently* 786; **o'r diwed** *at last* 16, 103, 105, 184, 220

diweirach cpv. adj. *more chaste* 466

diwyll m. *cult, worship* 268

diwyllyav (diwylliaw) vn. *to cultivate* 49, 572

diwyrnaut see **dywyrnavt**

dodi vn. *to place, put, give* 123, 219, 616; plpf. 3 sg. **dodassei** 351; pret. imprs. **dodet** 490; **d. ar** *put a name on, gave a name to* 10, 20, 72, 73, 81

doeth[1] adj. *wise* 18, 524, 571, 734; pl. **doethon, doethyon** *wise men* 37, 180, 226, 731, 1013; cpv. **doethach** 494; spv. **doethaf** 37, 848

doeth[2] see **dyuot**

doethant, doethost see **dyuot**

doethineb, doethinab, doethinap m. *wisdom* 221, 252, 254, 849, 897

dolur m. *pain* 884

dolurus adj. *painful* 535

doluryav vn. *to grieve* 260, 331

dos see **mynet**

dosparth (dosbarth) m. *reason* 894

dothoed, dothoet see **dyuot**

dracheuyn, drachevyn see **tracheuyn**

drav (draw) adv. *yonder. beyond* 368; **tu drav** *the other side* 478

drech m. *appearance, form* 218n., 231, 335, 338, 343, 346 (*GPC s.v drych* 3(a))

dreic f. *dragon* 250, 257, 259, 261, 264, 265; pl. **dreigeu** 261

dros, dros- see **tros**

drvs see **drws**

drvy, drwy see **trvy**

drwc see **dryc**

drws m. *entrance, doorway* 618; **yn drvs** *in front of the gate* 197n. (*GPC s.v.*)

dryc, drwc adj. *bad, evil* 309n.; **bod d. gan** *to be sorry, to grieve* 631

drycysprydawl adj. *evil-spirited* 684

drygyrferthassant pret. 3 pl. of vn. 'drygyrferth' 860

drythyll adj. *luxurious, comfortable* 740

drythyllwch m. *luxury* 461

duc-, dug- see **dvyn**

duhundeb see **duundeb**

duunav (duunaw) vn. *to unite, to bring together, to agree* 483; impf. 3 pl. **duunynt** 103

duundeb, duhundeb m. *unity* 571, 1037

Duv, Duw *God* 227, 556, 563, 750, 845, 865; pl. **dwyweu** 71

Duw Merchyrgweith *one Wednesday* 1044

duy see **dvy**

dvwavl (dw[y]fawl), **dvywavl** adj. *supernatural; divine, holy* 253, 447

dvy, duy, dwy f. num. *two* 250, 257, 414, 442, 444, 556

dvylav see **llav**

dvyn, dwyn vn. *to bring, take* 186, 223, 238, 240, 243, 396; *lead*; **d. ar gof** *to recall* 598; pret. 3 sg. **duc** 620, 910, imprs. **ducpvt** 552; plpft. 3 sg. **dugassei, dugassey** 30, 526, imprs. **dugessit** 234

dvywavl see **dvwavl**

dw- see also **du-, dv-**

dwaythaf (diwethaf) spv. *last* 581

dwyssav (dwysaw) vn. *to press hard on* 820

dwyvronn (dwyfron) f. *breast. chest* 895

dy pref. poss. pron. 2 sg. 108, 112, 220, 238, 243, 326

dyal, dial vn. *to avenge, take revenge* 30; + **ar** *on, upon s.o.* 639

dyblygawd pret. 3 sg. of vn. 'dyblygu' *to duplicate* 886

dybryt adj. *serious, monstrous, terrible* 509

dyd (dydd), **dyδ** m. *day* 187, 423, 446, 502, 537, 561; pl. **dydyeu, dyewed** (diewoedd) 8*n.*, 714, 745, 855, 1015; **lliw dyd goleu** *in broad daylight* 673

dyewed see **dyd**

dyffygyawl adj. *tired, exhasuted, weary* 198

dygrynoes pret. 3 sg. of vn. 'dygrynhoi' *to benefit, to avail* 568

dygvydassant see **digvydaf**

dyheurvyd (diheurwydd) m. *assurance* 14

dylyedogyon, deledogeon pl. (m.) *noblemen, rightful owners* 284, 397, 453, 599

dylyet f./m. *right, claim, entitlement* 279*n.*, 385, 387, 396, 422*n.*, 431*n.*

dylyy pres. 2 sg. of vn. 'dlyu, dylyu' *ought, owe; to have a right to* 153; imprs. **dylyir** 670; impf. 3 sg. **dylyei** 151, 384, 389, imprs. **dylyit** 278

dyllat, dillat pl. *clothes* 39, 118, 905

dyn m. *human being, man* 203, 878; pl. **dynyon** 206, 226

dynas, dinas f./m. *city, stronghold* 10, 55*n.*, 195, 197, 210, 412*n.*; pl. **dinassoed, dinessyd** 87, 88, 171, 303, 572, 593*n.*

dynavl (dynawl) adj. *human* 229, 230

dynessau vn. *to approach, come close* 198, 258, 275; pret. 3 sg. **dynessahawδ** *succeeded, followed* 584

dynyadawl adj. *human* 902

dyoer adv. *certainly* 315, 794

dyrchauael, dyrchavael (dyrchafael) vn. *to raise, to exalt* 9, 76, 119, 125, 205, 752; pres. 3 sg. **dyrcheif** 643; pret. imprs. **dyrchauwyt** 817

dyred see **dyuot**

dyro see **rodi**

dyruawr see **diruavr**

dysc m./f. *learning, training* 127, 494, 530

dyscassei plpft. 3 sg. of vn. 'dysgu' 127; impf. 3 sg. **dysgei** 384

dystryw, distryv m. *destruction* 1, 30, 367, 569, 954

dyuod[1], **dyuot** (dyfod) vn. *to come* 18, 141, 143*n.*, 144, 146, 147; as adj. 763*n.*; **dyuot ac** vn. *to bring* 118; pres. 1 sg. **deuaf** 339, 3 sg. **dav** (daw) 17; impf. 3 sg. **deuei** 69; pret. 2 sg. **doethost** 760, 781, 3 sg. **doeth**[2] 63, 83, 184, 232, 486, 498; 3 pl. **doethant** 2, 284, 347, 497, 566, 624; plpft. 3 sg. **dathoed** (dathoedd), **dothoed, dothoet** (dothoedd) 286, 366, 444, 665, 768; impf. sub. 3 sg. **delei** 598, 749; impv. 2 sg **dyred** 619

dyuod[2] see **dywedud**

dyuodedygaeth (dyfodedigaeth) f. *coming, arrival* 57

dyuodyat (dyfodiad) m. *coming, arrival* 1018

dyuynnu (dyfynnu) vn. *to summon* 276, 327

Dyw Damasius Pap *Pope Damasius's Day, 11 December* 1069

Dyw Gwener *Friday* 1070

Dyw Nodolic *Christmas Day* 1070

Dyw Sul y Blodeu *Palm Sunday* 1055*n*.

dywal adj. *cruel, ferocious* 538, 567

dywalder m. *ferocity* 270, 273

dywalhaei impf. 3 sg. of vn. ' dywalu' *to rage* 891

dywededic adj. *said, afore-mentioned* 606, 884, 1028; pl. **dywededigyon** 804

dywedvyt, dywedud, dywedut, vn. *to say, mention* 13, 107, 151, 264, 332, 353; pres. 3 sg **dyweit** 227, 553; impf. 3 sg. **dywedei** 352, 3 pl. **dywedynt** 237, 722, 731; pret. 3 sg. **dywaut, dywavt, dyuod** (dywod) (*GMW* §8 (a)) 151, 154, 202, 215, 225, 235, 618, 3 pl. **dywedassant** 15, 207, 239, imprs. **dywetpvt, dywetpwyt** 439, 588; plpft. 3 sg **dywedassei** 150, 251; impv. 2 pl. **dywedvch** 246

dywet see **diwed**

dywygyat m./f. *dress, attire* 463

dywyrnavt, diwyrnaut (diwrnawd) m. *day* 21, 803*n*.

e

'e see **'y**

e see **y**[1, 2, 4, 5]

e hun see **ehun**

ebostol m. *apostle* 851*n*.

ebryuygvs (ebryfyngws) pret. 3 sg. of 'ebryfyngu', *to discount, ignore* 122

edeilat see **adeilat**[2]

edewis see **adav**[2]

ediuarwch (edifarwch) m. *repentence* 846

edrych vn. *to inspect* 142, 1023; + prep. **ar** *look at* 198, 205

ef[1] indep. pron. 3 sg. 2, 6, 134, 304, 311, 427*n*.

ef[2] aff. pron. 3 sg. 12, 39, 42, 61, 63, 91

ef a part. 701, 738 (*GMW* § 191, *SW* 297-8); *he and*, i.e. *with* 799, 828

effeiryeid, effeirieit, pl. (m.) *priests* 684, 850

efferen f. *mass* 425, 435, 438, 441; pl. **efferenneu** 447

eg see **yg**

eglur adj. *illustrious* 885

eglurder m. *lustre* 893

eglvys, egluys, eglwys f. *church* 209, 414, 427, 432, 435, 437, 777*n*.; pl. **eglwysseu** 269, 845

egylyon (engylion) pl. (m.) *angels* 230

ehebawc m. *falcon* 929

ehedec vn. *to spread* 40

ehelaeth adj. *ample* 872

ehouyn (ehofyn) adj. *bold* 339

ehun, e hun, ehvn pron. 3 sg *himself, herself, itself* 58, 105, 122, 126, 129, 137; pl. **ehunein, e h.** 572, 573, 687, 700, 830

eidav, eidau, eidaw (eiddaw) stressed poss. pron. 3 sg. *one's own* 768, 859*n.*, 1031; 3 pl. **eydynt** (*GMW* § 57) 390

eigyavn m. *ocean* 272

eil ord. num. *second, like* 412, 894, 1001; used as a noun *the second one*, i.e. *an equal* 140

eilenwi (ail-lenwi) vn. *to refill, replenish, satisfy* 318

eilweith adv. *a second time* 246

eirchyeit pl. (m.) *suppliants* 873

eiryoet, eryoet adv. *ever* 189, 216, 221, 334

eiryf m. *number* 484, 560

eissoes, eissyoes adv. *however, nevertheless* 88, 96, 121, 169, 170, 303

eissyeu m. *want* 379, 920

eisted (eistedd) vn. *to sit* 198, 240, 256, 451

eithavoed, eithauoed (eithafoedd) pl. (m.) *extremities* 260, 373

eithyr prep. *apart from* 44, 70, 679, 687, 938, 958; **eithyr mod** see **mod**

ell (ill) occurs with numerals in apposition after pers. pron. 3 pl. (*GMW* §107(c)) 309

ellwng see **gellvng**

em, em- see **ym, yma**

emadrodes pret. 3 sg. of vn. 'ymadrawdd' *to relate, to speak* 778

eman adv. *here* 255

emchuelassant see **ymchwelud**

emdangosses (ymddangos) pret. 3 sg. of vn. 'ymddangos' *to appear* 833

emdeith (ymdeith) f. *journey* 803*n.*

emdirgelu (ymddirgelu) vn. *to hide* 784

emdivnav (ymddyunaw) vn. *to reach an agreement* 798*n.*

emennyd (ymennydd) m. *mind, brain* 723

emlynvs (ymlynws) pret. 3 sg. of vn. 'ymlid' *to chase* 828

emwnaethant (ymwnaethant) pret. 3 pl. of 'ymwneud' *to become* 797

emwrthlad (ymwrthladd) vn. *to withstand* 815

emylyeu (ymyleu) pl. (m./f) *borders* 178

emys pl. (m.) of 'amws' *horses* 936

en, en- see **yn**[1, 2, 3]**, yn-**

ena, ene see **yna**

endav see **yn**[3]

eneit m./f. (i) *soul* 216*n*,, 864, 998; (ii) *life*; pl. **eneidieu** *souls* 865

engirolaeth f. *cruelty* 80

enni (ynni) m. *strength* 291, 761

ennynnu vn. *to light a fire, to kindle* 616

ennyt m./f. *a short space* (*of time*) 1019

enryded see **anryded**

enw, henv, m. *name* 56, 60, 61, 62, 81, 89, 165*n*.; pl. (**h**)**enweu** 593, 596

enwavc (enwawg) adj. *famous* 766

enwir adj. *unjust* 754*n*.

enys, ynys f. *island* 48, 49, 51, 54, 57, 60; pl. **ynyssed, enyssed** 271*n*., 529 , 876

er¹ see **y¹**

er² see **yr²** prep. *since, from specified time; despite*

erbynn prep. *by* 1030; **yn erbyn** *against* 178, 484, 486, 528, 531, 629

erbynneit vn. *to receive* 283

erchy, erchi (+y) vn. *to ask for, request* 13, 42, 80, 155, 162, 211; pret. 3 sg. **erchis** 191, 262, 834, 3 pl. **archassant** 236, 362; impv. 2 sg. **arch** 238, 243, 248

erchyruynu (erchyrfynu) vn. *to strike* 900

ereill see **arall**

ergyd, ergyt f./m. *blow* 25, 78

ermynwisc f. *robe of ermine* 452

eruynnyeit (erfynieid) vn. *to beg for, entreat* 951

eryoet see **eiryoet**

escob, escop, esgob, eskob, m *bishop* 120, 123, 638, 683, 776*n*., 798; pl. **esgyb** 361, 437

escor vn. *to give birth* 19

esgeiryeu pl. *legs* 726, 733

esgynnu, esgynnv (+ar) vn. *to ascend, to reach; to embark* 741, 752

essewydyon (eisiwydion) *needy ones* (GMW § 36) 906

estravn (estrawn) adj. *foreign* 747; pl. **estronyon** 270, 271, 1028

etiued see **etyuet**

etwa adv. *still* 91, 515, 740

etyuet, etiued (etifedd) m. *progeny, descendents* 28, 817, 946

etholedigyon pl. adj. *chosen* (GMW § 36) 139

ethrykyg m. (ethrycyng) *headland* 323

ethrylith m. *ingenuity* 136

eu, ev pref. poss. pron. 3 pl. *their* 17, 18, 42, 56, 63, 93

euo (efô) indep. red. pron. 3 sg. *he, him* 133, 412

eur m. *gold* 38, 146, 407, 413, 520, 843; adj 456

eureit adj. *golden* 431

ev see eu

ewch see mynet

ewined (ewinedd) pl. (m./f.) *nails* 733

ewyllys, ewyllis m. *desire, wish, pleasure, fortune* 135, 162, 212, 318, 1047

ewythyr m. *uncle* 94, 484, 506, 527, 957*n.*, 1004

eydynt see eidav

f = /v/

fegis lenited form of **megis** 861

f, ff

fals (ffals) adj. *false* 351

figur (ffigur) m./f. *shape, form* 230

flemychedic (fflemychedig) adj. *inflamed, raging* 503

fo, ffo vn. *to escape, put to flight* 48, 493, 509, 514, 779; as n. *flight* 495; impf. 3 sg.
   ffoei 654; pret. 3 sg foes 1, 542, 784*n.*; plpft. 3 sg. foassei (ffoasei) 681; **ar fo**
   (*to be*) *on the run, in flight* 65, 827

foedic (ffoedig) adj. *on the run* 783

ford (ffordd) *road, way, reason, means* 320, 322, 512, 632*n.*, 634; pl. **fyrd** 539

foresteu (fforestau) pl. (f.) *forests* 411

fos (ffos) f. *ditch* 614*n.*

froeni (ffroeni) vn. *to snort* 792

frydyeu, frydeu (ffrydieu) pl. (f./m.) of 'ffrwd' *streams* 249, 821

furyfhau (ffuryfheu) vn. *to arrange* 987

fydlavn (ffyddlawn) adj. *faithful, loyal* 797

fydlonaf (ffyddlonaf) spv. 649

fyrd see ford

ffuryf f. *form, way* 695, 932

g

gadav, gadaw vn. (i) *to leave, to abandon* 509, 1052, 1066 (ii) *to allow, to permit*;
   pres. 3 sg. gat 242, 244, 380*n.*; impf. 3 sg. gadavhei, gadei 176, 707; pret. 3
   sg. gadawd 696, gedewys 1063, imprs. gadpwyd 634

gaflachauc (gaflachawg) adj. *armed with javelins or spears* 811

galv, galw vn. *to call, to name* 51, 180, 314, 401, 640; pres. 3 sg. geilw 836, 1
   pl. galwnn 228, 3 pl. galweint 597, imprs. gelwir 3, 60, 61, 78, 91, 667;
   impf. imprs. gelwit 44, 53, 89, 90, 201, 423; pret. 3 sg. gelwis 62, 152, 3 pl.
   galwassant 594, 595, 600, imprs. gelwyt 52

gallu[1] m. *might* 1007

gallu[2] vn. *to be able* 930; pres. 1 sg. **gallaf** 335, 2 sg. **gelly** 339, 2 pl. **gellwch** 645, 646, 3 pl. **gallant** 230, 531; impf. 2 sg. **gallut** 326, 3 sg. **gallei** 129, 136, 182, 224, 319, 330, 3 pl. **gellynt** 367, imprs. **gellit** 93, 462; pret. 3 sg. **gallawd, gallvs, gallvys** 77, 242, 674, 3 pl. **gallasant** 542, 566, 576, imprs. **gallvt** 186, 295; pres. sub. 1 sg. **gallvyf** 317, 3 sg. **gallo** 109, imprs. **galler** 322

gan, y gan prep. (i) *by, with* 49, 55, 66, 113, 165, 177 (ii) *from* 696, 702, 874 (iii) *because of* 818 (iv) + vn. to perform function of participle, 175, 263, 350, 471, 478, 505 (v) denoting possession 378 (vi) *in the opinion of* 34, 464; **bod da gan** *to please* 669, **bod drwg gan** *to be sorry, to grieve* 631, **bod gwell gan** *to prefer* 1027; (vii) *namely* (*GMW* § 208) 476, 526, 539, 541 (viii) with suff. pers. pron. 1 sg. **genhyf** 316, 318; 3 sg.m. **(y) gant(h)av, (y) ganthaw,** 30, 64, 67, 143, 174, 185; sg.f. **genthi** 627; 2 pl. **gennwch** 669; 3 pl. **ganthunt, gantunt, gantwynt** 26, 138, 139, 921, 1018, 1068

ganassei see **geni**

ganedic adj. *innate, natural* 374

ganedigaeth f./m. *extraction, origin* 214, 226

ganet see **geni**

gant-, ganth- see **gan**[(viii)]

gard (gardd) f. *garden, enclosure* 995n.

garwder m. *sturdiness* 895

gat see **gadav**

gawr f. *shout* 616, 617; pl. **geuri** (gewri) 817

gedewys see **gadav**

geilw see **galv**

geiryeu pl. (m.) *words* 293, 352, 674

gelw- see **galv**

gelynolyon pl. adj. *hostile* 889

gelynyon pl. (m.) *enemies* 618, 728, 767, 815, 820, 855

gellwch see **gallu**[2]

gellvng (gellwng) vn. *to release, to let in* 23, 172, 173, 349; pret. 3 sg. **gyllyngawd** 637, 1051, imprs. **gellygvyt** 174; impv. 2 sg **gyllwg** (gyllwng) 636

geneu pl. (f.) *mouth, jaws* 273

geni vn. *to be born, to beget* 556, 563; pret. imprs. **ganet** 10, 55, 73, 357, 715; plpf. 3 pl. **ganassei** (*GMW* § 167) 207

genn- see **gan**[(viii)]

ger llav see **llav**

geu lenited adj. after dual; see **cen**

geuri (gewri) pl. of **gawr**

girat adj. *bitter, severe* 258, 588

glan f. *bank, edge* 78, 256, 307, 486; cpd. prep. **yglan** *at the end of* 996

glawawc adj. *rainy* 1008

gleinnyon pl. adj. *holy* 560

gleiuyauc (gleifiawg) adj. *bearing a spear* 812

glevder, glewder m. *courage* 372, 890, 895

glin m. *knee* 148; pl. **glinyeu** 780

glynneu, glynnyeu pl. *valleys* 267, 268, 828

gnotaedic adj. *customary* 827

godef (goddef) vn. *to endure* 577

godyneb (godineb) m. *adultery* 11

gogled (gogledd) adj. *north* 62

gogonedus (gogoneddus) adj. *victorious* 86

gogonyant m. *glory, victory* 891

gogoueu (gogofau) pl. (f.) *caves* 48, 265

gogwydedic (gogwyddedig) adj. *fallen* 229

gohir[1] m. *delay* 301, 759

gohir[2] vn. *to delay* 510

gohodeist see **gwahawd**

goleu adj. *light* 673

goludoed (goludoedd) pl. (m./f.) *riches* 407

golvython (golwythion) pl. (m./f.) *portions of meat* 291

gorchymyn[1] m. *order, command* 704, 851

gorchymyn[2] (+y) vn. *to command, order, to entrust to* 341, 854; pret. 3 sg. **gorchymynnawd** 654, 970, imprs. **gorchymynnvt** (gorchymynw(y)d) 425; plpft. 3 sg. **gorchymynassei** 659

gorchyuygei (gorchfygei) impf. 3 sg of vn. 'gorchfygu' *to outshine, surpass* 288, 399

gorchyuygwr (gorchfygwr) m. *conqueror, victor* 887; pl. **gorchyvigwyr** (gorchfygwyr) 871

gorderch (gordderch) m./f. *lover, mistress* 465, 626; pl. **gorderchwraged** pl. *sweethearts, lady loves* 463n

gorderchu (gordderchu) vn. *to commit adultery* 11

gordethol (gorddethol) adj. *select* 518

goresgyn, goresgin vn. *to overcome, vanquish, gain possession, rise to supremacy, get the upper hand, prevail* 368, 390, 589, 958, 1059, 1064; pret. 3 sg. **goresgynaud, gorysgynnawd** 1020, 1030, 1065, 3 pl. **goresgynassant** 1058; plpft. 3 sg. **goresgynnasei** 402, 420

goreu see **da**

goreureit adj. *gilded* 412, 457

gorevgwyr (goreugwyr) pl. (m.) *noblemen* 1069

gorfowys (gorffwys) m. *respite* 814

gorffei see **goruod**

gorffwysso pres. sub. 3 sg. of vn. 'gorffwyso' *to rest* 864

gormeswyr pl. (m.) *oppressors* 792

gorthrum, gorthrwm adj. *sad; serious, very severe* 744*n.*, 945

goruc, gorug- see **guneuthur**

goruchel adj. *very high, supreme* 720; spv. **goruchaf** 658

goruchelder m. *supremacy, height* 17, 903

gorulvch (gorflwch) m. *goblet* 146; pl. **goruleheu, gorulycheu** (gorflycheu) 292, 456; see Introduction xxxviii

goruod (gorfod) vn. *to be victorious, compel* 6; impf. 3 sg. **goruydei** (gorfyddei) 520; pret. 3 sg **gorvv** (gorfu) 873, 985; impf. sub. 3 sg. **gorffei** 514

goskethloyu (gosgeddloyw) cpd. adj. *of wondrous appearance* 732*n.*

gosper m. *vesper, evening* 806

gossot (gosod) vn. *to place, to set* 67. 187, 307, 451, 523, 871; pret. 3 sg. **gossodes** 343, 868

goual (gofal) m. *care* 306

gouyn, govyn (gofyn) (often + y^4) vn. *to ask (of), inquire (from)* 150, 180, 190*n.*, 206, 214, 224; pret. 3 sg. **gouynnvs** (gofynws) 241

gre f. *herd of horses* 679

grvndwal (grwndwal) m. *foundation* 187, 193

grymm m. *strength* 815

grymus adj. *strong* 725, 732, 888

gu- see also **gv-, gw-**

guaet, gvaet, gwaet m. *blood* 192, 193, 236, 268, 821

guahavd, gwahavd, gwahawd vn. (i) *to invite* 141, 420, 603 (ii) *to recall* 295; pret. 2 sg. **gohodeist** 265

gualcheid (gwalchaidd) adj. *like a hawk, fine, noble excellent* 732

guarandav (gwrandaw) vn. *to listen* 443

guare[1] (gware) vn. *to play* 197, 200

guare[2] m. *play* 198

guaret y am (gwared) vn. *to divest* 448

guastat (gwastad) adj. *constant* 494

guedi (gweddi) f. *prayer* 796; pl. **gwedieu** (gweddieu) *pleas, entreaties* 702

guedus, gwedus (gweddus) adj. *fine, beautiful* 724

guehynedic (gwehynedig) adj. *drained* 256

guehynnu (gwehynnu) vn. *to pour out, lay bare* 263

gueirglodyeu (gweirgloddieu) pl. (f./m.) *meadows* 411

gueith[1](gweith) m. *work* 144, 188, 194, 236, 241, 242

gueith[2] f. *time* 465; as adv. **(g)weithieu, (g)weithyeu** *sometimes* 729

gueithret, gweithret m./f. *deed, act, action* 122, 325, 907; pl. **gweithredoed** (gweithredoedd) 274, 359

guelet see **gwelet**

guerni (gwerni) pl. (f./m.) *swamps, damp meadows* 828

guerydon (gweryddon) pl. (f.) *virgins* 415

guirodeu, gwirodeu pl. (m./f.) *strong drinks* 292, 457

guneuthur, gvneithur, gvneuthur, gwneuthur vn. *to do, make, to prepare, hold (a feast), to cause* 50, 71, 93, 101, 103, 109, 245; pres. 1 sg. **gwnaf** 795; impf. 3 sg. **gwnae, gwnaei** 178, 181, 191*n.*, 617; pret. 3 sg. **goruc, gorug, gwnaeth, gunaeth** 6*n.*, 12, 13, 23, 32, 48, 3 pl. **gorugant, gwnaethant** 205, 247, 496, 625, 627, 667, imprs. **gwnaethpwyd, gwnaethpwyt, gwnaethput, gwnaethpvt, gunaethpv(y)t** 8, 85, 93, 186, 329, 427; plpft. imprs. **gwnathoedyt** (gwnathoeddid) 142; impf. sub. 3 sg. **gwnelei, gwneley, gwnelhei** 27, 115, 898, 3 pl. **gwnelynt** 187

guraged see **gwreyc**

gurandav (gwrandaw) vn. *to listen* 233

guraul (gwrawl) adj. *brave* 815, 854

guressauc (gwresawg) adj. *lively* 723*n.*

gurthlad see **gvrthlad**

gurthladedic (gwrthladdedig) adj. *expelled* 783

gurthwynebu see **gvrthvynebu**

gurthuynepwyr (gwrthwynebwyr) pl. (m.) *enemies* 814

guryogaeth (gwrogaeth) m. *homage* 795*n.*

guynn, gvynn (gwyn) adj. *white* 257, 725

guyrda see **gvr**

guys (gwys) m. *summons* 280*n.*

gv- see also **gu-, gw-**

gvahanedic (gwahanedig) adj. *dispersed* 764

gvahanredaul (gwahanredawl) adj. *special* 722

gvallt pl. (m.) *hair* 723

gvant (gwant) pret. 3 sg. of vn. 'gwanu' *to strike* 24

gvarchadv, gwarchadv, gwarchadw vn. *to guard* 68, 341, 1063

gvas, guas, gwas m. *boy* 11, 22, 206, 872; **guas ystauell** *chamberlain* 338; pl. **gweissyon, gueissyon** 196, 200

gvassanaethu, gwassanaethu vn. *to serve* 68, 453, 455

gveled, gvelet, gwelet, guelet vn. *to see* 5, 12, 47, 134, 176, 283; pres. 1 sg. **gwelaf** 109, 2 sg. **gwely** 249*n.*, 2 pl. **gwelvch** 528; impf. 1 sg. **guelvn** (gwelwn) 218, 3 sg. **guelei** 345, 349, 374, 3 pl **guelynt** (gwelynt) 196; pret. 3 sg. **gweles, gveles** 28, 149, 288, 956, 967*n.*, 3 pl. **guelsant** 809

gvelygord (gwelygordd) m. *retinue* 28

gverthed (gwerthed) m. *value* 843

gvlad, gvlat, gulat, gwlad, gwlat, f. *country, land* 2, 3, 420, 562, 603, 653; pl. **gwladoed, gwladoet, guladoed** 16, 40, 272, 389, 785, 844 .

gvr, gur, gwr m. *man* 27, 132, 165, 216, 218, 294; pl. **gwyr, guyr, gvyr** 131, 145, 345. 450, 502, 504; **gwyrda, guyrda** *noblemen* 101, 133, 276, 286, 360, 421; **y gwr, y gvr** as antecedent to rel. 4*n*, 86, 491, 650, 659

gvravl, gwraul adj. *brave* 542, 815

gvrhau (gwrhau) vn. *to do homage* 482; pret. 3 pl. **gwrhassant** 1005

gvrtheb (gwrtheb) m. *answer* 151, 153

gvrthlad, gurthlad (gwrthladd) vn. *to expel, drive away, drive back* 259, 762; pret. imprs. **gwrthladwyt** 874

gvrthvyneb (gwrthwyneb) m. *opposition* 113

gvrthvynebu, gurthwynebu (gwrthwynebu) vn. *to oppose* 531, 854; pres. 3 sg. **gvrthvynepa** (gwrthwynepa) 270

gvybot, gwybod, gwybot, vn. *to know* 14, 70, 164, 189, 293, 330; as n. *knowledge* 253, 614; pres. 1 sg. **gvnn** 334; impf. 3 sg. **gvydat, gvydyat** (gwydd(y)at) (*GMW* § 132(b) (ii)) 178, 214, 538, 3 pl. **gwydynt, gvydynt** (*GMW* §157, 3) 207, 443; pret. 1 sg. **gvybum** 216; pres. sub. 3 sg. **gwypo** 336; impf. sub. 1 sg. **gvypvn** (gwypwn) 222, 3 sg. **gvypei** 345, 349; impv. 3 sg. **gvybydet** (gwybydded) 220

gvylua, gwylua (gwylfa) f. *feast day* 275, 281, 408, 423

gvyllt (gwyllt) adj. *wild* 46

gvynt (gwynt) m. *wind* 752, 774

gw- see also **gu-, gv-**

gwae m. *woe* 264

gwaedwch see **gweidi**

gwaelavt (gwaelawd) m. *bottom* 249

gwallav (gwallaw) vn. *to serve* 457

gwalltwenn cpd. adj. *fair-haired* 732

gwar adj. *gentle, polite* 908

gwaradvydus (gwaradwyddus) adj. *disgraceful* 514

gwaradwyd (gwaradwydd) m. *shame* 923

gwarchadv, gwarchadw see **gvarchadv**

gwarchae vn. *to besiege, hold (in captivity)* 312; plupf. 3 sg. **gvarchayssey** 31

gwarder m. *kindness, compassion* 96

gwarthaf: ar warthaf *on top of* (*GMW* § 206 (h)) 823

gwarthec pl. (m.) coll. n. *cattle* 935

gwasgarassei plpft. 3. sg. of vn. 'gwasgaru' *to scatter* 844; **gwasgaressit** plpft. imprs. 703

gwasgaredicyon pl. adj. *scattered* 496

gwassanaeth m. *service* 446, 447, 460

gwassanaethu see **gvassanaethu**

gwassanaethwyr pl. (m.) *servants* 459

gwastat, gwastad adj. *continual* 380; **yn w.** *continually* 567, 577, 635

gwed (gwedd) f. *manner, way* 136, 262, 315, 519, 528, 537

gweda (gwedda) pres. ind. 3 sg. of vn. 'gweddu' *to be proper* 672; impf. 3 sg. **gwedei** 678

gwediav (gweddiaw) vn. *to pray, plead* 766; impv. 1 pl. **gwediun** (gweddiwn) 864

gwedieu see **guedi**

guedy, gvedi, gvedy, gwedy, wedy prep.; (i) *after* 86, 89, 358, 491, 561, 602 (ii) *since* 1010*n.* (iii) + vn. to form a temporal clause (*GMW* § 217) 1, 5, 7, 9, 11, 12 (iv) adv. *afterwards* 544 (v) **gwedy na(t), guedy na,** conj. with subord. negation 103, 299 (vi) **gwedy nas** conj. with subord. negation + inf. pron. 3 sg. (*GMW* § 58) 625

gweidi (gweiddi) vn. *to shout* 622; pres. 2 pl. **gwaedwch** (gwaeddwch) 623

gweilgi f. *sea, ocean* 321; **kerdet g.** *to sail* 765

gweissyon see **gwas**

gweithret see **gueithret**

gweithwyr pl. (m.) *workers* 243

gwelioed (gwelioedd) pl. (f./m.) *wounds* 553

gwell, guell see **da**; also **kyuarch g.**; **hanbych well**; **g. gan** see **bot**

gwenn adj. f. *white* 261, 265, 267

Gwener see **Dyw G.**

gwerthit impf. imprs. of vn. 'gwerthu' *to sell* 921

gwestyteir pres. imprs. of vn. 'gwastatáu' *to level, subdue* 267

gwibyaw vn. *to forage about* 679

gwin, gvin (gwin) m. *wine* 147, 155

gwir, guir adj. *true* 224, 251, 345

gwisc, guisc f. *dress, raiment* 428, 436, 453; pl. **gwisgoed** (gwisgoedd) 449, 455, 459

gwisgav, guisgav vn. *to wear, to put on* (*clothing / armour*), *to clothe* 117, 278, 370, (+am) 401, 424, 426; pret. 3 sg. **gwisgvs** (gwisgws) 575

gwisgedic adj. *wearing* 436

gwled (gwledd) f. *feast* 285, 402, 406, 419, 603, 604

gwledychawd (gwledychawdd) pret. 3 sg. of vn. 'gwedychu' *he ruled* 1002, 1011

gwraged see **gwreyc**

gwreyc, gwreic, gwreig, gureic f. *woman, wife* 7, 55, 287, 289, 296, 331; pl. **gwraged, guraged** 231, 284, 288, 289, 399, 439*n.*; **gwreigda** (gwreigdda) f. *noble woman* 232

gwrhassant see **gvrhau**

gwrogaeth f. *homage* 988, 1004, 1066

gwrthwynebed (gwrthwynebedd) m. *opposition* 1021

gwychyr adj. *fierce* 762, 820, 855; spv. **gwychraf** 728

gwyd-, gvyd-, see **gvybot**

Gwydelec (Gwyddeleg) adj. *Irish* 716

gwyl f. *feast day* 946*n.*, 975*n.*

gwylwyr pl. (m.) *sentries* 614

gwynnuydic (gwynfyddig) adj. *blessed* 997

gwyp-, gvyp- see **gvybot**

gwyrda see **gvr**

Gwyry see Index of Personal Names *s.v.* **Meir**

gwyssyaw vn. *to summon* 914

gwystyl m. *hostage* 963*n.*; pl. **gwystlon** 934

gyllwg, gyllyngawd see **gellvng**

gynn no see **kyn(n)**

gynt adv. *of old, of yore* 590, 838, 854

gyrru vn. *to drive, send* 814, 1033; impv. 2 pl. **gyrrwch** 646

gyt see **(y) gyt**[1, 2]

h

habit see **abid**

haeach see **hayach**

haearnaul (haearnawl) adj. *hard* 811

haedu (haeddu) vn. *to earn* 642

haelder m. *generosity* 36, 95, 377, 379, 381

haelyoni m. *generosity* 893

haeth see **myned**

haf m. *summer* 1005

hagen conj. *however* 45, 287, 510, 515, 554, 836

hanbvyllei (hanbwyllei) impf. 3 sg. of vn. 'hanbwyllo' *to take an interest in, concern oneself with* 290

hanbych well see **hanuot**

handenvs pret. 3 sg. of vn. 'handdenu, hamddenu' *to concern oneself with* 510*n.*

hanner m. *half* 794, 857, 1013*n.*

hanuot (hanfod) vn. *to descend from* 214; pres. 1 sg. **hanvyf** (hanwyf) 204, 3 pl. **henynt** 529; impf. 3 sg. **hanoed, hanoet** 41, 397, 885, 3 pl. **hanoydynt** 387; **hanbych well** pres. sub. 2 sg. *greetings* 778*n.*

hardhau (harddhau) vn. *to adorn, to beautify* 376

havd (hawdd) adj. *easy* 377, 489

hayach, haeach adv. *almost, well nigh* 548, 783

heb[1], heb yr, hep, hep e, hep y defv. vb. *said* (*GMW* § 170) 108, 152, 202, 207, 208, 215

heb[2], hep prep. *without* 159, 164, 188, 191, 203; **hep eu llav** see **llav**

hediw (heddiw) adv. *today* 82, 155, 597, 601

hedwch (heddwch) m. *peace* 699, 956, 1053

hedychu (heddychu) vn. *to appease, make peace* 629, 931, 963; impf. 3 sg. **hedychei** 695; pret. 3 sg. **hedychawd** 937, 943, imprs. **hedychwyd** 674

hefyt see **heuyt**

heibyav adv. *past* 313

heil m./f. *service in a banquet* 293

heilyav vn. *to serve, wait at table* 148

heint m./f. *disease* 561, 945

helaethrwyd m. *abundance* 906

hely vn. *to hunt* 22

hen adj. *old, former* 396, 461; **hynaf, hynhaf** spv 59, 86, 107, 131

hendat m. *grandfather* 74

heneint m. *old age* 847

henne see **hynny[1]**

henuryeit (henurieid) pl. (m.) *elders* 180

henv, henw see **enw**

henynt see **hanuot**

hep see **heb**

herwyd (herwydd) prep. *according to* 594, 851; *because of* 96, 895; **yn herwyd** (*GMW* §245(*h*)) 431, 438, 451-2, 460

herwyd y(d) conj. *according as* (*GMW* §268) 457

heuyt, hefyt adv. *also* 126, 131, 193, 414, 527, 739

hi[1], hy[1] indep. pers. pron. 3 sg. f. 44, 152, 264, 320, 583

hi[2], hy[2] aff. pers. pron. 3 sg. f. 69, 140, 154, 163, 164, 215

hir adj. *long* 63, 200; pl. **hiryon** 725, 733; cpv. **hvy** (hwy) 514

hitheu[1] indep. conjunct. pers. pron. 3 sg. fem. 451, 619

hitheu[2], hythev aff. conjunct. pers. pron. 3 sg. fem. 73, 151, 215, 260, 294, 356

holl adj. *all, the whole* (*GMW* § 107(*b*)) 125, 130, 136, 180, 186, 288

hon(n) dem. pron. f. *this* 232, 350, 357; **yr hon(n), er honn** in appos. to ante. 3*n.*, 60, 61, 62, 265, 266

hon(n)o dem. pron. and adj. f. *that* 30, 72, 81, 156, 165, 170

huaudel (huawdl) adj. *eloquent, fluent* 726, 734

huolder m. (variant of *huodler*) *eloquence* 897

hun¹, hunein see **ehun**

hun² m. *sleep* 617

hundy m. *bedroom* 218

hunnv, hvn(n)v, hwnnw dem. pron. m. *that, that one* 3, 11, 15, 25, 44, 84

hvn, hwnn, dem. pron. m. *this* 217, 706; **yr hvn, yr hwnn** in appos. to ante. 317, 330. See 3*n*.

hvy see **hir**

hvyntev (hwynteu) conjunct. aff. pron. 3 pl. 464

hwch m. *pig* 824

hwndrwt m. *hundred, a division of land* 597

hwnn, hwnnw see **hvn, hunnv**

hwy aff. pron. 3 pl. 134

hwyllyeu (hwylieu) pl. (f.) *sails* 752, 773; for <ll> = /l/ see Introduction xl

hy see **hi¹, ²**

hyd see **hyt**

hyduf (hydwf) adj. *fine, handsome, well-grown, developed* 731, 733

hygar adj. *kind, beloved* 902; as adv. 664

hyn(n) dem. pron. neut. sg. *this* 104, 107, 148, 154, 217, 641; **yr hyn(n)** as ante. to rel. 153, 874 see 3*n*.

hynaf, hynhaf see **hen**

hynavs, hynaws adj. *pleasant* 734, 908

hynawster m. *pleasantness, gentleness* 895

hynny¹, henne dem. pron. neut. sg. *that* 5, 13, 31, 35, 37, 39; **o henne allan** see **allan**; **yr hynny** *from then* 81, 596, 601, *in spite of that* 66; **ymhlith henne** 742*n*.; **en h.** *in the meantime* 770, 821

hynny² dem. pron. neut. pl. *those* 231, 233, 356, 498, 674, 697

hynt f. *journey, course* 346, 966

hyrwyd (hyrwydd) adj. *favourable* 774

hyspyssach see **yspys**

hyt, hyd, prep. (i) *as far as* 64, 186, 195, 235, 685, 777 (ii) *until* 82, 155, 497, 501, 596 (iii) **hyt ar** *up to, as far as* 65, 211, 260, 402, 512, 765 (iv) **hyd, hyt y(d), h-yg, h- ym, h- yn, h- en** *as far as* 2, 28, 41, 77, 106, 118 (v) **ar hyt** *all over, all along* 54, 323 (vi) (**o**) **hyd nos, hyt n.** *by night* 614, 668 (vii) **en hyt e nos/dyd**, *throughout the night/day* 829 (viii) **hyt rac bron** *up to* 147

hyt pan conj. (i) *until,* 193, 382, 533, 544, (ii) *so that* 864*n*.; **hyt na(t)** introducing neg. sub. clause of consequence 335, 377, 443, 874; introducing sub. clause of purpose 815*n*.

hythev see **hitheu**

i, j

i^1 prep. see y^4

i^2, **ui**, **vi** aff. pron. 1 sg. 216, 238, 315, 335, 779, 781

idaw, idav, idi see y$^{4(v)}$

ieirll see **yarll**

jeua(n)g see **yeuanc**

igyon vn. *to gasp, to sob* 807*n.*

innheu conjunct. aff. pers. pron. 1 sg. 109

ir adj. *green, fresh* 822

irav, irau (iraw) vn *to smear, to annoint* 192, 236, 850

istoriaeu pl. (f.) *reports* 226

it see y$^{4(v)}$

ll

llad (lladd) vn. *to kill* 6, 24, 27, 65, 79, 100; impf. 3 sg. **lladei** 15, 536, imprs.
    lledit 176, 536; pret. 3 sg. **lladawd, lladavd, lladavt,** 19, 25, 650, 878, 3 pl.
    lladassant 170, 599, imprs. **llas** (*GMW* §135(b)) 508, 541, 545, 548, 549,
    825, 826

lladedigyon (lladdedigion) pl. adj. *slain* 502

llall pron. *other* 201, 415, 428; pl. **lleill** 542, 747*n.*, 826

llas see **llad**

llauassei (llafasei) impf. 3 sg. of 'llafassu' *to dare* 713; **llauassvs** (llafasws) pret. 3
    sg. 303

llaur, llawr m. *floor, ground* 822, 890, 904, 953

llauur, llavur (llafur) m. *labour* 492, 820

llav, llaw f. *hand* 126, 129, 146, 432, 440, 893; pl. **dvylav** (dwylaw) 219; **ker llaw, ger**
    llav prep. *near, nearby* 90, 775; **rac llaw, ragllau** *thereafter, later* (*GMW* §
    235 p. 208) 598, 853; with pref. pron. 3 pl. **hep eu llav** *past them* 23

llaver see **llawer**

llavn (llawn) adj. *full* 139, 772

llavrwyd (llawrwydd) f. *laurel* 437

llavur see **llauur**

llaw see **llav**

llawen adj. *joyful* 283, 750, 801*n.*

llawenhau vn. *to rejoice* 114

llawer, llaver adj. *many* 16, 88, 169, 183*n.*. 226, 491; pl. **llaweryon** 841

llawr see **llaur**

lle m. *place* 41, 47, 106, 182, 184, 185, 798*n*.; pl. **lleoed** 183, 184; **en y lle, yn y lle** *immediately* 32, 149-50, 210, 263, 327, 495-6; **yn lle** *instead of* 122, 490; **ymhob lle** *everywhere* 625

lledradavl adj. *stealthy, secret* 11

lledrat (lledrad) adj. *stealthy* 353

lledu hwyllyeu (hwyliau) vn. *to set sail* 773

lleng f. *legion* 518

llei cpv. adj *less* 304

lleihavys (lleihawys) pret. 3 sg. of vn. 'lleihau' *to diminish* 67

lleill see **llall**

llesteiryav vn. *to hinder* 241

llestri pl. (m.) *vessels* 456

lleuat m. *moon* 228, 829

llew m. *lion* 538, 814, 890

llewenyd, llywenyd m. *joy* 278, 400, 404, 441, 939; cf. **llawen**

llidyav see **llydyav**

llin f./m. *lineage* 109, 204, 885; pl. **llinyoed** 720

llit m. *anger* 295, 300, 301, 503, 891

llithrant pres. 3 pl. of vn. 'llithro' *to flow, to slide* 268; impf. 3 sg. **llithrei** 378*n*.

lliw m. *colour* 724; **lliw dyd goleu** *in daylight* 673

llong f. *ship* 138, 664, 752; pl. **llongeu, llogheu** 2, 409, 487, 566

lloneit m. *full(ness)* 146

llosgi vn. *to burn* 302, 627, 680, 688, 927, 953

llu m. *force, host* 77, 302, 327, 484, 492, 493; pl. **lluoed** 532, 652, 786

lluchyadennaul (lluchiadenawl) adj. *flashing* 814

lludedic (lluddedig) adj. *tired, exhausted, weary* 198

lluesteu pl. (f.) of **lluesty** *quarters, billets for soldiers* 804

lluneithu see **llunyeithu**

llunyeith m./f. *shape* 355

llunyeithu, lluneithu, vn. *to organise* 382, 395, 519

lluossogrwyd (lluosogrwydd) m. *multitude* 879

llvyn, llwyn m. *grove* 347, 832; pl. **llwyneu, llvyneu** 411, 828

llw m. *oath* 1037*n*., 1038, 1039

llwith (llwyth) m. *burden* 1060

llwyn see **llvyn**

llwyr adj. *complete* 132

llyaws (lliaws) m./f. *large number* 845

llydyav, llidyav (llidiaw) vn. *to grow angry* 5, 76, 260, 294, 297; pret. 3 sg. **llidyawd** 959

llygat m. *eye* 893; pl. **llygeit** 724

llygatvras (llygatfras) cpd. adj. *with big eyes* 732

llyges, llyghes, llynges f. *fleet* 64, 366, 772, 1057

llygru vn. *to corrupt* 685

llynges see **llyges**

llyngcu vn. *to swallow* 188

llymder m. *keenness* 896

llynn[1] m. *lake* 244, 247, 249, 251, 252, 256

llynn[2] m. *drink* 734

llys m. *court* 294, 297, 299, 398, 746, 868

llysyeu pl. (m.) *vegetables* 822

llyuyr (llyfyr) m. 553*n*. *book*; pl. **llyureu** (llyfreu) 225

llyvodraeth see **llywodraeth**

llyw m. *tail* 891

llywenyd see **llewenyd**

llywodraeth, llyvodraeth f. *government* 79, 125, 659

llywyav (llywiaw) vn. *to reign over, to rule* 127; pret. 3 pl. **llywyassant** 699

m

'm inf. pron. 1 sg. 217, 220, 807

mab m. *son* 2, 8, 10, 15, 19, 21; pl. **meyb, meibyon, meibeon** 55*n*., 59, 84, 97, 133, 167

mae, maent see **bot**

maedu (maeddu) vn. *to beat* 890

maen m. *stone* 249, 250; pl. **mein** (*GMW* § 30) 186, 192, 838

maes m. *battle ground* 506, 509, 1044, 1046

maeth: ar uaeth *in fosterage* 20*n*. 74

magei impf. 3 sg. of vn. 'magu' *to rear, to breed; to cause, to produce* 446; pret. imprs. **magwyt** 716; plpft. imprs. **magadoed** 398

magyat m. *upbringing* 740

mal conj. *as* 80, 160, 333, *so that* 534; **mal na** conj. with subord. negation 312

mam(m) f. *mother* 15, 19, 27, 394, 609, 717; used adjectivally 435

mamvaeth (mamfaeth) f. *wet-nurse* 717*n*.

man f./m. *place* 497

man- see **myn-**

marchavc, marchauc, marchawc m. *knight* 462, 969; pl. **marchogyon** 139, 142, 144, 277, 361, 378

marv, marw vn. *to die* 19, 24, 58, 75, 85, 90; **en varw** *dead* 822

marvolaeth, marwolaeth f. *death* 364, 579*n*., 877

marwavl adj. *deadly* 568

mavr, maur, mawr adj. *great, large* 302, 315, 366, 520, 568, 580; **yn uawr** adv. *greatly, very much* 114, 223, 261, 331, 499

mavrvrydrwyd (mawrfrydrwydd) m. *magnaminity, heroism, bravery* 894

mavrvryt *magnaminity, nobility, heroism* 894, 897

Mawrth *March* 1008

medgell (meddgell) f. cpd. *mead cell* 456

medu (meddu) vn. *to possess, rule over, control* 574; fut. 3 sg. **medhavt** (*GMW* § 129 (d) (3)) 272; impf. 3 sg. **medei** 134

medvl, medwl (meddwl) m. *mind, purpose, intention,* 290*n.*, 315, 326, 405, 887

medwi (meddwi) vn. *to be drunk* 158

medyant (meddiant) m. *possession, power, claim, control* 111, 128, 520

medylyav, medylyaw (meddyliaw) vn. *to think* 129, 135, 513, 639

medyr: ar vedyr *on the point of, with the intention of* 1046

megis, megys[1] prep. *as, as if, like* 538, 585, 608, 613, 770

megys[2] conj. *just as* 175, 222, 278, 281, 358, 583; **megys ket** *as though* (*GMW* § 262 N.3) 247-8; **megys y bei** *in order that* (*GMW* § 271) 182; **megys na(t)** *so that . . . not* 132, 344-5

Mei month of May 562, 1003

meib- see **mab**

mein see **maen**

meint m. *extent, size* 331, 354, 413, 723; adj. *so great, such a great* 898

meirch see **meyrch**

meirv pl. adj. *dead* 534

melyn adj. *yellow* 723

melldigedic adj. *accursed* 684

men- see **myn-**

merch, merhc f. *girl, woman, daughter* 7, 66, 72, 80, 139, 208, 947*n.*; pl. **merchet** 285, 736, 737, 738, 858

Merchyrgweith see **Duw M.**

merhc see **merch** and Introduction p. xxxviii

merthyr m. *martyr* 415

messur see **muy**

meun, mewn see **myvn**

meyrch, meirch pl. (m) *horses, steeds* 39, 520, 818, 922

meythryn vn. *to rear* 21

mi indep. pron. 1 sg. 219, 220, 238, 326, 334

mil num. *thousand* 453, 454, 485, 516, 517, 910; pl. **milyoed** 541, 550, 826

milvryaeth see **mylwryaeth**

milltir f. *mile* 717

minheu, **minneu** indep. conjunct. pers. pron. 1 sg. 111, 203, 336, 338, 649

mis m. *month* 995, 1003, 1008

miui, **mivi**, **myuy** (myfi) red. indep. pron. 1 sg. 202, 619, 807

mod (modd) m. *way* 952; **eithyr mod** *beyond measure* 76-7; **o nep ryw uod** *in any way* 816

moesseu pl. (f.m.) *manners* 908

moli vn. *to praise* 144, 506

molyant m. *praise, fame* 95, 379, 381; pl. **molyanheu** 491

mor¹ m. *sea* 321, 486, 590, 774, 842

mor² adv. (+ **a**) *as … as* 132, 673

morc m. *mark* (coinage) 964

mordwyaw vn. *to sail* 688

morvyn, **morwyn** f. *maiden* 14, 15, 81, 146, 149, 150, 155

mudaw vn. *to move* 918

mur m. *wall* 614*n*.; pl. **muryoed** 87

music see **kerd m.**

mut (mud) adj. *dumb* 248

muy, **mvy**, **mwy**, cpv. adj. *more, bigger* 35, 88, 166, 189, 306, 493; spv. *most, greatest* **mwyaf**, **muyaf**, **mvhaf mvyhaf** 77, 508, 656, 848; **mwy no messur** *beyond measure, exceedingly* 166

mvnugyl m. *neck* 725

mylwryaeth, **milvryaeth** f. *military prowess, battle* 36, 465

mynach, **manach** m. *monk* 106, 136, 847; pl. **mynych** 433

mynaches, **manaches** f. *nun* 209, 500; pl. **mynachesseu** 209, 438, 500

mynachloc, **manachloc** f. *monastery* 415, 416, 850, 997*n*.

mynechtit f. *monkhood, monastery* 117

mynet, **myned** vn. *to go* 106, 122, 310, 312, 313, 340; impf. 3 sg. **aei** 71; pret. 3 sg. **aeth**, **haeth** 28, 308, 450, 1064; plpft. 3 sg. **athoed** 629, 709; impv. 2 sg. **dos** 618, 2 pl. **ewch** 644

mynegi, **menegi** vn. *to express, to proclaim* 190, 315, 347, 405, 1026; impf. 3 sg. **managei** 742*n*., imprs. **mynegit** 875

mynnu¹ n. *desire, will* 333, 356

mynnu² vn. *to want* 657, 900; pres. 2 sg. **mynnu**, **mynny** 332, 636, 807; 3 sg. **mynn** 336, 1 pl. **mynnwn** 644, 2 pl. **mynnwch** 641; impf. 3 sg. **mynhei**, **mynhey**, **mynnei** 40, 102*n*., 115, 3 pl. **mynnynt** 101*n*., 103; pret. 3 sg. **mynnwys**, **mynnvs**, **mynnvys** 51, 96, 3 pl. **mynnassant**, **manassant** 173, 668, 952, 1059; pres. sub. 3 pl. **mynnont** 230

mynych, **menych** adj. *frequent* 293, 577, 819, 911

mynychau vn. *n. to frequent* 69

mynychet m. *frequency* 511*n*.

mynyd, menyd (mynydd) m. *mountain* 804, 836, 837; pl. **mynyded** 48, 184, 267, 829, 927

mynygleu pl. (m.) of 'mwnwgl' *necks* 271

myuy (myfi) see **miui**

myvn, mywn, y meun, o uyvn prep. *in, inside* 67, 249-50, 411, 624, 696, 863; **o vewn,** adv. *from within* 622 **y myvn** adv. 349 *inside*

n

na[1], **nac** conj. *or, nor*; (*GMW* §254) 335, 531, 554; *and* 203*n*.; **na(c) . . . na(c)** *either . . . or* 38, 39, 203*n*., 535, 543-3; *neither . . . nor* 295, 312, 705

na[2], **nad, nat** sub. neg. part. (*GMW* §194 (a), (b)) 207, 216, 221, 316, 336, 345; **nas** neg. + inf. pron. 3 sg. 625, 707, 708

na[3] with impv. (*GMW* §195) 618

nachaf interj. *lo* 22, 145, 196

namyn prep. *except* 67, 70, 97, 116, 122, 171

nav (naw) num. *nine* 523

nawd (nawdd) m./f. *patronage, protection, sanctuary* 681*n*., 683, 685, 905

neb, nep indef. pron. *anyone , any, the one* 35, 70, 299, 312, 335, 345; **n. kyfryw** see **kyfryw**; **n. ryw uod** see **mod**

nef f. *heaven* 562

neges f. *mission, business* 199, 924

nei m. *nephew* 470*n*., 489, 766, 1033; pl. **neieint** 858, 1011*n*.

neidyav vn. *to jump* 158

neill *one* (of two or more) 201, 408, 428, 1016, 1041

neilltuedic adj. *chosen, appointed* 524

neithoryeu pl. (f./m.) *marriage feast* 472

nep see **neb**

nerth m. *strength, support* 372, 708, 780, 962; pl. **nerthoed** (nerthoedd) *reinforcements, support* 671 (*GPC s.v.* (d))

nessau vn. *to approach* 233

neu[1], **nev** conj. *or* 53, 514, 577, 890

neu[2], **neur** affirmative pre-verbal part. (*GMW* §188) 188*n*., 483*n*., 623

neuad (neuadd) f. *hall* 450, 458

newyd (newydd) adj. *new* 143*n*., 144, 334

newyn m. *famine* 569, 588

newynavc (newynawg) adj. *hungry* 538

ni[1] aff. pron. 1 pl. 229

ni², **ny**, **nid**, **nyd**, **nyt** neg. part. (*GMW* §194) 17, 67, 92, 96, 109, 120; **nys** neg. + inf. pron. 3 sg. 374, 682, 952; negation in relative clause *that . . . not* 242, 334

ninheu conj. aff. pers. pron. 1 pl. 864

niuer, **nifer** f. *host* 141, 143, 304, 485, 493, 495

no, **noc**, **nogyt** conj. used after cpv. degree of adj. *than* (*GMW* §46) 35, 88, 127, 189, 222, 304

Nodolic *Christmas* 604*n*., 867

nodua (noddfa) f. *refuge* 784

noeth(y)on pl. adj. *unsheathed* 432, *naked* 905

nogyt see **no**

nos f. *night* 165, 350*n*., 356, 497, 668

ny, **nyd**, **nyt** see **ni²**

nyth f. *niece* 12

o

o¹, **oc**, **og** prep. (i) *from* 41, 43, 51 60, 61 62 (ii) *of* 14, 16, 28, 31, 35, 44 (iii) *by. by means of* (GMW §231) 78, 321, 530, 634, 691*n*., 814 (iv) *because of, as a result of* 25, 94, 162, 357, 506 (v) *with* (expessing manner) 117, 130, 135, 521, 634, 816 (vi) *concerning, about* 227, 418 (*GPC s.v. o* (9)) (vii) *in accordance with* 362 (viii) *with regard to, in respect of* 372, 407, 413, 418, 734, 849 (ix) *to* (= *y*) 13, 39, 119 (x) preceding vn. to perform function of a participle 282, 760, 814, 964, 1028 (xi) marking agent of vn. (*GMW* §§ 181 (a)) 5*n*, 12, 32, 47, 128, 134 (xii) with suff. pers. pron. 3 sg. m. **ohanav, ohonav, ohonaw** 33, 183, 257, 312, 405, 513, 3 sg. f. **ohenei** 56, 3 pl **onadunt** 14*n*, 109, 134, 187, 201, 258 (xiii) **o achaws** see **achaws**; **o barthet** see **parthet**; **o bleit** see **pleit**; **o dim** see **dim**; **o hyd** see **hyd**; **o ulaen** see **blaen**; **o ureid** see **breid**; **o vewn, uyvn** see **mywn**

o² conj. *if* 110, 332, 636, 830; **os** + pres. 3 sg. of 'bod' *if it is* (*GMW* §272 (b) (1)) 336, 669

o'r a o¹ + dem. pron. 'ar' + rel. 'a' *of those who, of that which* 40*n*., 41, 115, 173, 186, 253 (*GMW* § 75)

oblegyt prep. *because of* 204

oc see **o¹**

och interj. *alas* 891, 905, 906

odyna, **odena** (oddyna) adv. *from there, from then on* 214, 346, 501, 628, 695, 903

odyno (oddyno) adv. *from there, afterwards, then* 450, 552, 966

oed, **oed-** see **bot**

og see **o¹**

oes¹ f. *time, age* 392, 589, 591; **oes oessoeδ** *for ever and ever* 865*n*.

oes² see **bot**

oet¹, oyd (oed) f./m. *time, age* 18, 92, 579, 849, 910, 999

oet² (oedd) see **bot**

ofyn, m. *fear* 632; **rac ofyn/ouyn** *for fear of* 295, 944

ofynhau, ofynhav vn. *to fear* 617, 831; pres. 3 sg. **ouynhaa** (ofynha) 273

ohan-, ohen-, ohon-see **o¹⁽ˣⁱⁱ⁾**

ol *track*: cpd. prep. **yn ol** *after* 83, 297-8, 584, 1002, 1011; **oc eu hol** *behind them* (*GMW* § 245 (q)) 774

olew m. *oil* 851; **olew ac ygen** (yngen) *extreme unction* 846

oll adj. *all* 39, 133, 183*n.*, 451, 686, 701, 1030*n.* (*GMW* §107(a))

onadunt see **o¹⁽ˣⁱⁱ⁾**

ony conj. *unless, if not* 316; **onys** (+ inf. pron. 3 sg.) 318, 645

organ f./m. *organ, instrumental music* 435, 443

os see **o²**

ouer (ofer) adj. *futile*; as adv. *in vain* 623

ouyn, ouyn- see **ofyn, ofyn-**

oyd, oydynt see **oet¹**

p

pa interr. adj. *what, which* 129, 136, 202, 207, 234, 355; **pa beth** *what* (*thing*), *why* (GMW § 82) 247, 768; **pa beth bynnac** *whatever* (*thing*) (*GMW* § 90) 38; **pa ffuryf b.** *whatever way* 695, 932; **pa ryu** *what kind of* 853; **pa wed** (wedd) *what way* 136

pab see **pap**

padriarch m. *patriarch* 853*n.*

paganes f. *pagan woman* 159

paganyeit pl. (m.) *pagans* 485, 525

palualu (palfalu) vn. *to grope* 823

pan conj. *when* 90, 92, 114, 149, 188, 204, 230*n.*

pap, pab m. *pope* 560, 944

paraf see **peri**

paratoes pret. 3 sg. of vn. 'paratoi' *to prepare* 602, imprs. **paratoet** 418

parawt adj. *ready* 906

parhau vn. *to continue* 301

parth m. *part, side* 169, 321, 368, 408, 410, 428; **parth a(c)** *at towards* 112, 178, 310, 346, 386, 427

parthet: o barthet prep. *on the part of* 831

Pasc m. *Easter* 275

paub, pavb, pawb pron. *all, everyone* 39, 41, 133, 134, 253, 276

pebyllu vn. *to encamp* 667; pret. 3 sg. **pebyllawd** 967, 981

pechodeu pl. *sins* 846

pedeir f. num. *four* 439

pedrus adj. *faltering* 273

pedrusder m. *doubt* 318

pedryuannoed (pedryfannoedd) pl. *four quarters* 410

pedwar m. num. *four* 431; **pedwar ar dec** *fourteen* 613-14; **pedwar vgein, petwar ugeint, petwar vgein** *eighty* 485, 563, 579, 862

pedweryd (pedwerydd) ord. num. m. *fourth* 880; f. **petwared** (pedwaredd) **ar ugeint** *twenty fourth* 57

pedyt (peddyd) m. *infantry* 818

pei see **bot**

peleu pl. (f.) *pellets, bullets* 811*n.*

pellaf spv. adj. *furthest, most distant* 95

pen(n) m. *head* 123, 278, 371, 401, 425, 437; *top* 321; *end* 1030; *chief* 882; as adj 452, 454; in cpd. prep. **am ben, amben** *against* 503, 911; **ar ben** *on top of* 321; **ym pen, ympen** *at the end of* 56, 75, 502

penhaf, pennaf sup. ending + noun *topmost, supreme, chief* 657, 689, 746, 785

pennaduryaeth f. *sway, dominion* 586

pennkenedyl cpd. m. *head of kindred* 885

perffeith adj. *perfect, extreme, mature* 847

perffeithyaw vn. *to fulfil, to complete* 924

peri vn. *to cause* 159; pres. 1 sg. **paraf** 112; pret. 3 sg. **peris, perys** 871, 918

personolaeth f./m. *personage* 901

perthynei impf. 3 sg. of vn. 'perthyn' *to belong* 392, 937

perued (perfedd) m. *centre, middle* used as adj. 60

peryglawd pret. 3 sg. of vn. 'peryglu', *to endanger* 967

perygleu pl. (m.) of 'perygl' *dangers* 842

petwared see **pedweryd**

peth m. *thing* 14, 217, 242, 864*n.*; see also **pa b., pob p.**; pl. **petheu** 697

pethewnos (pythefnos) m./f. *fortnight* 1069

peunyd (peunydd) adv. *every day* 742, 786

peunydyavl (peunyddiawl) adj. *daily* 494, 530

pibydyon pl. (m.) *pipers* 870

pleit: o bleit *on behalf of* 211

plith, plyth: cpd. prep. amongst them, **ymplith, ymplyth, ym plith, ymhlith** *amongst* 37, 156, 209, 217, 286, 289, 852; with pref. poss. pron. 3 pl. 34

pob pronom. adj. *each, every* 41, 169, 194, 258, 276, 280; **pob peth** *everything* 54, 115, 126, 135, 173, 252; **ymhob lle** *everywhere* 625

pobyl f. *people* 65, 112, 118, 177, 179, 369

pont f. *bridge* 1059, 1060

pori vn. *to graze* 822

porth[1] m. *gate* 90, 197; pl. **pyrth** 348

porth[2] m./f. *aid, support* 306, 366, 478

porth[3] m./f. *harbour* 486, 753; pl. **porthloed** (porthloedd) 857

porthavr m. *janitor* 348

pressvylav, pressvyllyav vn. *to dwell, inhabit* 47, 228, 744

priavt, priaut, priawt adj. *rightful, lawful* 401, 575, 856n., 947, 973, 974

priodaur (priodawr) adj. *with hereditary rights, rightful* 762; pl. **pryodoryon** 177

prior m. *prior* 850n.

processio Lat. borr. *procession* (*GPC s.v. prosesio*) 434, 442

profaf (+ar) pres. 1 sg. of vn. 'profi' *to prove to s.o.* 238

proffvydolyaeth (proffwydoliaeth) f. *prophecy* 255

proffwydassei plpft. 3 sg. of vn. 'proffwydo' *to prophecy* 583n.

prouedic (profedig) adj. *proven, experienced* 379, 465

prudder (prudd-der) m. *wisdom* 220

prydydyon (prydyddion) pl. (m.) *poets* 869n.

prynnu vn. *to buy, to redeem, to ransom* 928; pret. 3 sg. **prynnawd, prynvs** (prynws) 557, 701

pryodoryon see **priodaur**

pryt[1] m. *appearance, comeliness* 149, 287, 398, 896

pryt[2] conj. *when, since* 320

pu- see also **pv-, py-**

purwynnyon pl. adj. *pure white* 440n.

pvy, puy, pwy interr. pron. *who* 13, 206, 215, 216, 319, 768; **pvy bynnac** *whoever* 378; **pvy/pwy gilid** see **cilyd**

pym, pymp, pump, num. *five* 556, 590, 592, 963; **pymp ar (h)ugein(t)** *twenty five* 825, 1049; **pym cant** *five hundred* 556

pymet ord. num. *fifth* 719n.

pymtheg num. *fifteen* 21, 371

pyrth see **porth**[1]

pyscavt pl. (m.) *fish* 45

ph

phioleu f./m. *goblets* 456

r

'r[1] see **y**[1]

'r[2] perf. part. (*GMW* §185) 13*n.*

'r[3] dem pron.: **o'r a** *of those who* 41, 115, 173, 186, 253, 349; **y'r a** 274*n.*

rac prep. (i) *because of* 140, 354, 443, 444, 891 (ii) *lest, for fear of* 308, 660 (iii) *for the sake of* 998 (iv) *against* 324 (v) *from* 1053 (vi) with suff. pers. pron. 3 sg.m. **racdav** 730*n.*, 799; (vii) **rac bron** see **bron**; **rac llaw/ragllau** see **llav**; **rac ofyn/ouyn** see **ofyn**; **rac wynep** see **wyneb**

raccw adv. *yonder, over there* 528

racrymhaa pres. 3 sg. of vn. 'racrymhau' *to prevail* 269

rad m. *graciousness, goodness* 373

ragllau see **llav**

randir *territorial unit varying between 16 and 312 acres* 857; pl. **randiroed** 593*n.*, 601

ra(n)n f. *part* 60, 229, 592, 656, 698*n.*, 719

rannv (rhannu) vn. *to divide, share* 755; pret. 3 pl. **ranhassant, rannassant** 592, 1013, imprs. **rannvyt** (rhanwyd), **rannvt** 49, 59*n.*

rat (rhad) m. *goodness* 373

redegauc (rhedegawg) adj. *running* 821

reeni, ryeni pl. (m./f.) *parents, ancestors* 721, 817

rei pron. *those, some* 37, 101, 231, 257, 388, 389

reid see **reit**

rein pron. *those, some* 228*n.*

reit, reid m. *necessity* 333, 377, 495, 670

rifav (rhifaw) *to count* 489

rith, ryth m. *guise* 70, 337, 344

rithaf pres. 1 sg. of vn. 'rhitho' *to form by magic* 337

riuedi (rhifedi) m. *number* 800

rodi, rody (rhoddi) vn. *to give* 97, 115, 161, 162, 171, 279; **r. vrth** *to add to* 325–6; pres. 1 sg. **rodaf** 649, 794, 3 sg. **ryd** (rhydd) 270; impf. 3 sg. **rodei, rodey** 39, 793, 3 pl. **rodynt** 816; pret. 3 sg. **rodes** 125, 164, 172, 390, 392, 394, 3 pl. **rodassant** 826, 1037, imprs. **rodet** 163, 325; **rodet ar** *was entrusted to* 20, 74; plpft. 3 sg. **rodassei** 373, 772, imprs. **rodessit** 393; impv. 2 sg. **dyro** 317

rodyon (rhoddion) pl. (f./m.) *gifts* 692, 872, 906

rot (rhod) m. *wheel* 903

rung, rvng see **rwg**

ruthraf pres. 1 sg. of vn. 'rhuthro' *to storm* 808

ruthrwr m. *attacker* 889

ruthyr m. *attack* 540

rvysc (rhwysg) m./f. *majesty, dignity, glory, splendour, pomp, ostentation* 463*n.*

rwg (rhwng), **y rwng, y rvng, y rung** prep. *among, between* 59, 100, 200, 228, 869, 873; **y rvng . . . a** *both . . . and* 484, 551; with suff. pers. pron. 3 sg.m. **y ryngthaw** 707, 987, 3 pl. **ryngthunt, rygthunt, y rygthvnt** 301, 404, 571-2, 592, 599, 700

rwyd (rhwydd) adj. *easy* 729*n.*

ry[1] adv. *too* 108

ry[2] perf. part. 121*n.*, 131*n.*, 297, 353, 460, 503

ryd[1] (rhyd) f. *ford* 667

ryd[2] (rhydd) see **rodi**

ryd[3] (rhydd) adv. *free* 933

rydhau (rhyddhau) vn. *release* 43

rydit (rhyddid) m. *freedom* 985, 1025, 1027

ryeni see **reeni**

ryffei see **bot**

ry(n)gt- see **rwg**

ryngu bod (rhyngu bodd) vn. *to give pleasure* 641

rysswr m. *hero, soldier* 838

ryth see **rith**

ryued (rhyfedd) adj. *strange* 898

ryuel (rhyfel) m./f. *war* 382, 691, 1027; pl. **ryueloed** 842, 892

ryuelu (rhyfelu) vn. *to wage war* 77, 567

ryv, ryw pron. used adjectivally *kind of* (*GMW*, §99 (b)) 184*n.* 226*n.*, 228, 285, 372, 419

s

Saesnec adj. m./f. *English* 91

saeth f. *arrow* 23, 24, 79

sarhaed m. *insult* 633*n.*, 639, 647; pl. **sarhaedeu** 298*n.*

sathru vn. *to trample* 1027; pres. 3 sg. **sathyr** 271

sauei (safei) see **seuyll**

savl (sawl) pron. *such, those* 378*n.*, 503

sef, ysef *it is this, thus* substantival 23*n*, 56, 104, 140, 154, 165; adjectival 36*n.*, 403, 555; *sef* adverbial 141, 159, 177, 197, 263, 305 (*GMW* §55(f))

sein f. *sound* 818

seinnyav (seiniaw) vn. *to sound* 818; impf. 3 sg. **seinnyei** 819

seint pl. (m.) of 'sant' *saints* 560, 687, 845

seiri pl. (m.) of 'saer' *masons* 186

seith num. *seven* 70; **seith gant** 563*n.* *seven hundred*

sentens m. *sentence* 1037

serch m. *love* 331, 351, 612

seuyll (sefyll) vn. *to stand* 237*n*., 242, 245, 521, 531, 543; impf. 3 sg. **sauei** (safei)
194

sorres pret. 3 sg. of vn. 'sorri' *to be offended, to take umbrage* 834

ssire m./f. *shire* 597

Sul see **Dyw Sul**

Sulgvyn, Sulgwynn *Whitsun* 403, 923

svllt m. *treasure* 383

svyd see **(s)swyd**

svydwr, swydwr m. *officer, steward* 452*n*., 606, 633, 638, 648, 694

swm m. *sum* 986

swmerev (swmereu) pl. (m./f.) *sumpters, pack horses* 967

(s)swyd, svyd (swydd) f. *county, shire, province* 163, 164, 597; pl. **sswidev**
(swyddeu) 593*n*.

syberv (syberw) adj. *proud, fine* 569

syberwyt (syberwyd) m. *pride, courtesy* 414

sychedigyon pl. *thirsty* 906

syd see **bot**

symvdassant (symudasant) pret. 3 pl. of vn. 'symud' *to change* 592, 596*n*. (*GPC
s.v. symudaf* (c))

syrthvs (syrthws) pret. 3 sg. of vn. 'syrthio' *to fall* 169

t

tad see **tat**

tadaul (tadawl) m. *paternal* 747

tagnefedwr (tangnefeddwr) m. *peacemaker* 840

tagnheued, tangneued m./f. *peace* 404, 571, 987

tagnheuedus (tangnefeddus) adj. *peaceful* 54, 63, 774

tangneuedu (tangnefeddu) vn. *to restore peace, to pacify* 474

tal m. *end*: **ar tal y deu glin** *on her knees* 148; **ar dal vy glinyeu** *on my knees* 780

talu *to pay, redeem* 634, 964

talym m. *period of time, interval* 380

tan[1] (tân) m. *fire* 259, 616

tan[2] see **dan**

tanu vn. *disperse, to put to flight* 814

tareanauc (tarianawg) adj. *bearing a shield* 812

taryan (tarian) f. *shield* 892, 1009

tat, tad (tad) m. *father* 12, 16, 22, 24, 25, 27

tebygaf pres. 1 sg. of vn. 'tebygu' *to believe, suppose* 326

tec (teg) adj. *fair* 45, 724, 726, 908; cpv. **tegach** 513; spv.**teccaf** 219, 406

teccau vn. *to make beautiful* 411

teccet eqv. adj. used as noun *beauty* 140, 149, 413

tegach see **tec**

tegvch, tegwch m. *beauty, splendour* 288, 398, 892, 896

tei see **ty**

teilvng, teilwng see **teylvng,**

teilygdavt (teilyngdawd) m. *worthiness* 396

teir f. num. *three* 465

telynoryon pl. (m.) *harpists* 869, 872

teneu adj. *thin* 733

tennu see **tynnu**

teruyn (terfyn) m. *boundary, territory* 395; pl. **teruyneu** 42, 591

teruynawd (terfynawdd) pret. 3 sg. of 'teruynu' *to end, to die* 839

teruysc (terfysg) m. *strife, confusion* 983, 1015n., 1040

teruyscu (terfysgu) vn. *to cause a disturbance, to harass* 911

tervynedic (terfynedig) adj. *ended* 764

teulu m. *retinue* 383, 824

teuydle (tefydle) m. *heir, offspring* 19n.

tewi vn. *to be silent* 247

teylvng, teilvng, teilwng adj. *worthy* 26, 285, 419, 464n., 884

teyrnas, tyrnas f. *kingdom, kingship* 59, 79, 97, 99, 101, 123; pl. **teyrnassoed, tyrnassoed,** 95, 404

teyrnwisc f. cpd. *regal garment* 424

ti[1] indep. pron 2 sg. 152, 244, 249

ti[2]**, di** aff. pron. 2 sg. 108, 152, 202, 203, 221, 238, 243

tir m. *land* 487, 492, 521, 706, 708, 842; pl. **tired** (tiredd) 50, 323, 572, 1020, 1023

tiryon adj. *gentle* 293

titheu[1] indep. conjunct. pers. pron. 2 sg. 336

titheu[2]**, ditheu** aff. conjunct. pers. pron. 2 sg. 109, 110, 112, 153, 781

tlodyon pl. *poor* 905

torrei impf. 3 sg. f. vn. 'torri' *to break* **torrei** 1037; pret. 3 sg. **torres** 1055n., 1060

toruoed, torvoed (torfoedd) pl. (f.) *crowds, hosts* 445, 809, 889, 960

tra[1] conj. *while* 301

tra[2] pref. *excessive* 637, 1060

tracheuyn, dracheuyn, drachevyn adv. *again* 261, 295, 633, 634, 681, 703

traet pl. (f.) of 'troed' *feet* 271, 726, 733

traeth m. *shore* 307, 996

traetha pres. 3 sg. of vn. 'traethu' *to speak, declare* 227

tragywydavl, tragywydawl adj. *everlasting* 559, 562, 937; as adv. *for ever* 642

trallodus adj. *grievous* 1026

trannoeth, drannoeth adv. *the next day* 188, 676, 829, 969

tref f. *town, township* 208, 696, 961, 964, 965; pl. **trefi, treui** 303, 593*n*.

tref tad f. *patrimony, inheritance* 743, 748, 761, 767, 946

treftadavl (treftadawl) adj. *patrimonial, hereditary* 385

trengi vn. *to die, to draw to a close* 807

treiglav see **treyglav**

treis m. *rape* 632*n*.

treissyaw vn. *to rape* 627

treiswyr pl. (m.) *oppressors* 744

tremygu vn. *to scorn* 670

treulyav (treuliaw) vn. *to spend* (time) 537; impf. imprs. **treulit** 446

treyglav, treiglav (treiglaw) vn. *to traverse, turn, revolve* 16, 290*n*.

tri num. *three* 55, 166, 387, 424, 717*n*., 757; **tri ugeint, triugein, trugeint** *sixty* 515, 517, 567

trig- see **trygyav**

trist adj. *sad* 745

troednoeth adj. *barefooted* 997*n*.

troi vn. *to turn, move* 741

tros, dros prep. (i) *over* 40, 95, 280, 614 (ii) *for the sake of* 964, 985 (iii) with suff. pers. pron. 3 sg. m. **drostav** *on his behalf* 793

trosses pret. 3 sg. of vn. 'trosi' *to turn, to make one's way* 711*n*., 966

truan adj. *unfortunate, pitiful* 131, 177, 534

truanu vn. *to take pity* 749

trueni m. *pitiful condition* 369

trugarauc (trugarawg) adj. *merciful* 727, 735

trugeint see **tri ugeint**

trullyat m. *cup-bearer* 454

trvy, trwy prep. (i) *through, throughout* 63, 276, 404, 446, 620, 787 (ii) *by, by means of* 89, 115, 249, 317, 330, 334 (iii) *with* 278, 400, 403, 456, 492, 493 (iv) *because of* 300, 945 (iv) *in the form of* (GPC s.v. (f)) 523 (v) *as a result of* 611 (vi) preceding vn. to perform the function of a participle 845, 911, 913, 934 , 979, 1017

trwydet (trwydded) m. *guest, person permitted to stay at a court* (*GPC s.v. trwydded*) 770

trychut pret. imprs. of vn. 'trychu' *to cut* 821

tryderan (trydeδ + ran) *third part* (*GMW* §52) 369

trydyd (trydydd) ord. num. m *third* 416, 502, 626; *one of three* (*GMW* § 52) 339

trygyav, trigaw vn. *to dwell, live* 32, 682; impf. 3 sg. **trigei** 704

trywyr *three men* 324

tu m. *side* 61; in cpd. prep. **tu a(c)** *towards* 689, 913, 926, 949-50, 966

turyf (twryf) m. *tumult, roar* 818

tvyllasei see **tvyllws**

tvyllodrus, twillodrus (twyllodrus) adj. *deceitful, deceptive* 352, 598

tvyllwr (twyllwr) m. *deceiver*; pl. **tvyllwyr** 246, 526, 539

tvyllws (twyllws) pret. 3 sg. of vn. 'twyllo' *to deceive, to disappoint, to be misleading* 17; plpft. 3 sg. **tvyllasei** 351

twillodrus see **tvyllodrus**

twll m. *hole* 620

ty m. *house, dwelling place; building* 272, 615, 616, 620; pl. **tei** 50, 412, 413, 616, 680

tygheduenavl (tynghedfenawl) adj. *fated, destined* 203

tyngetuen, Tynghetuen, Tynghetven (tyngetfen) f. *fate, Fate* 882, 899, 902

tygu (tyngu) vn. *to swear* 299

tymestawl adj. *stormy* 899

tymestyl f. *pestilence* 568, 878

tymhestylus adj. *stormy, troublesome* 588

tynnu, tynnv, tennu vn. *to remove, draw, divest* 112, 117, 121*n.*

tyrn- see **teyrnas**

tyroed (tyroedd) pl. (m.) of 'twr' *towers* 87

tysta pres. 3 sg. of vn. 'tystio' *to bear witness* 721*n.*

tywyssavc, tywis(s)auc, tywyssawc m. *prince, leader* 42, 366, 574, 585, 840, 881; pl. **tywyssogyon** 35, 402, 421, 517, 524, 544

tywyssogyaeth f. *principality, rule, reign, sovereignty, supremacy, leadership* 389

th

'**th** inf. pron. 2 sg. 108, 109, 113, 221, 334, 337

u

'**u** see '**v**

ual see **val**

uch prep. *above* 189

uchot, vchot, uchof adv. *above* 439, 589, 805*n.*

udunt see $y^{4(v)}$

ugein, ugeint, vgein num. *twenty* 57, 83, 935

ugeinwyr cpd. *twenty men* 800*n.*

ui (fi) see i^2

un, vn num. *one, anyone* 89, 103, 120, 132, 217, 231, 257, 777*n.*; *same* 453, 463, 824, 864, 1070

urdas (urddas) m. *rank*; *monastic order* 113; pl. **urdassoed** 434

urdasseid (urddaseid) adj. *ordinate* 427

urdav (urddau) vn. *to exhalt, to crown* 124

urdavl (urddawl) adj. *dubbed* 277, 361, 421

urth- see **vrth**

uu (fu < bu) see **bot**

uy (fy) see **vy**

v

'v, 'w, 'u inf. pron. 3 sg. 68, 190, 258, 341, 350, 405, 461

val¹, ual¹ (fal) prep. *as, like* 107, 148, 267, 332, 595, 641

val², ual² (fal) conj. *as, while* 22, 261, 275, 590, 657; *so that* 93, 887

vchot see **uchot**

vdunt see $y^{4(v)}$

velly, yuelly, yvelly, yuelly, y velly adv. *so, thus* 19, 22, 25, 63, 69, 123

venyd: y venyd adv. *up* 804

vgein see **ugein**

vi (fi) see i^2

vn see **un**

vnyaun (uniawn) adj. *straight* 726

vrth, wrth, urth, y urth (wrth) prep. (i) *because of, as a result of* 89, 93, 95, 110, 120, 280, 296 (ii) a context denoting obedience, consent 110, 116, 127, 135, 161, 316 (iii) *to* 202, 246, 319, 528, 746, 805 (iv) *at* 435, 438, 441, 848 (v) *by, with the aid of* 829 (vi) *from* 717 (vii) *about* 181 (viii) *in order to, for the purpose of* 47, 108, 424 (ix) *against* 961*n.* (x) preceding vn. to perform function of participle 47, 105, 108, 277, 355, 424 (xi) with suff. pers. pron. 3 sg.m. (**y**) **urthav, vrthav, wrthaw** 107, 152, 189, 235, 332, 618; 3 sg.f. **wrthi, vrthi** 155, 353, 392; 2 pl. **wrthywch** 644; 3 pl. (**y**) **wrthun, vrthunt** 569, 641

vu, vv- (< bu, bv-) see **bot**

vwch (uwch) cpv. adj. *higher* 643

vy, uy (fy) poss. pron. 1 sg. *my* 216, 235, 316, 318, 636; **vyg, uyg, vym, vyng-** 217, 636, 794 see Introduction. xliv

vylav (wylaw) vn. *to weep* 264

vyneb, wyneb, wynep m. *face* 112*n.*, 205, 280, 723, 908; **rac wyneb** *following* 1003

vyt (wyt) see **bot**

vyth, wyth num. *eight* 566, 586; **vyth gan** *eight hundred* 481; **wyth ugeinwyr** *8 x 20, i.e. 160 men* 800; **vythuet** (wythfed) ord. num. *eighth* 562

vythnos, wythnos f. *week* 313, 1030

w

'w see **'v**

wedy see **guedi**

wrth, wrth- see **vrth**

wu (fu < bu) see **bot**

wuy (fwy) see **mwy**

wy¹, wynt¹, vynt¹ indep. pers. pron. 3 pl 15, 32, 47, 284, 370, 490

wy², wynt², vynt² aff. pers. pron. 3 pl. 18, 207, 208, 668, 676, 677

wy³ m. *egg* 921

wy⁴ see **mwy**

wyf see **bod¹**

wyneb, wynep see **vyneb**

wynt see **wy¹'²**

wynteu¹, vynteu¹ conjunct. indep. pers. pron. 3 pl. 206, 545, 624, 652

wynteu², conjunct. aff. pers. pron. 3 pl. 751; **vynteu²** 365, 382

wyt see **bot**

wyth see **vyth**

wythnos see **vythnos**

y

'y, 'e inf. pron. 3 sg. and 3 pl. 12, 13, 16, 27, 31, 35

y¹, yr, er, 'r def. art. *the* 1, 2, 3, 4, 7, 11

y², yd (ydd) affirm. preverbal part. (*GMW* §190) 3, 10, 16, 19, 20, 21

y³, yd (ydd) rel. pron. 106, 311, 317, 320

y⁴, i, e prep. (i) *to* 11, 18, 39, 57, 68, 70 (ii) *for* 495, 524, 672, 678, 768, 781 (iii) to denote possession 12, 84, 107, 167, 393, 626 (iv) with adj./verb to complete meaning 47, 150, 155, 190, 206, 341 (v) with suff.pers. pron. 1 sg. **i mi, ym** 221, 236; 2 sg. **it, yt(t), yti** (iti) 320, 333, 636, 794, 795; 3 sg. **idaw, idav, ydav, ydaw** 7, 10, 13, 16, 35, 38; 3 sg.f. **idi** (iddi) 72, 73, 140, 151, 154, 215; 1 pl. **y ni**

672; 2 pl. **y chwi, yvch** 531, 649; 3 pl. **udunt, vdunt** 145, 171, 172, 180, 227, 241, 710*n*.

y^5, **e** pref. poss. pron. 3 sg. *his, her, its* 2, 8, 12, 15, 19, 22

y^6 predicative/adverbial part. (*GMW* §§ 21 (d), 222) 23, 296, 366; see also $yn^{1, 2}$

y^7 prep. *in*; see also yn^3 217, 334, 691, 862, 943, 1008

y^8 = *y* + *y* 58, 89, 90, 716, 882.

y am see **am**

y gan see **gan**

(y) gyt^1 **a(c)**, **(y) gyd a(c)** (prep. + asp) (i) *together with* 2, 32, 253, 287, 339, 350 (ii) **bod gyd a** denotes possession *to have* 672 (iii) **y gyt a hynny** *at that, besides, moreover* 38, 352, 440, 551, 794;

y gyt^2 adv. *all, together* 309, 484, 653, 844, 1036

y mewn, y meun, y mywn see **myvn**

y rwng, y rung, y rvng, ryng- see **rwg**

y urth- see **vrth**

yachau vn. *to heal* 553

yarll m. *earl* 104*n*., 165, 286, 293, 348, 349; pl. **yeirll** 276, 361, 421, 691*n*., 1042, 1045

yarllaeth f. *earldom* 98, 392

yavn (i) *right, due* 279*n*., 422*n*. (ii) *amends, satisfaction* 298

yavnder m. *justice* 383*n*.

ych pref. poss. pers. pron. 2 pl. 644

ychwenec, achuanec *in addition* 479, 483

ychydic adj. and adv. *a little, a few* 44, 50, 607*n*., 613, 674, 688, 782

yd, yδ see y^2

ydau pl. (m.) *crops* 680

ydav, ydaw see $y^{4(v)}$

ydoed, ydoeδ, ydyw see **bot**

yeirll see **yarll**

yeith f. *language* 52, 153, 594; pl. **yeithyoed** (ieithoedd) 727*n*.

yeithyd (ieithydd) m. *interpreter* 150, 152

yeuanc, jeua(n)g, yeuang adj. *young* 219, 232, 872, 984; pl. **yeueinc** 108, 197

yeuengtit m. *youth* 385, 741, 903

yg, eg, yg- see yn^3

ygen see **olew**

yglan see **glan**

ygyd see **y gyt**

ym^1 see $y^{4(v)}$

ym^2, **em** see yn^3

yma, ema adv. *here* 244; with article + noun acts as dem. pron; **y. . . yma** *this* 208

ymadav (ymadaw) vn. *to leave, depart* 75; pret. 3 sg. **ymedewis** 558

ymadnabot (+ **a**) vn. *to get to know, become acquainted* 33

ymadravd, ymadrawd (ymadawdd) m. *expression, speech* 114, 239, 527, 907, 908; pl. **ymadrodyon** 205, 233, 356

ymaruoll (ymarfoll) vn. 957*n. to pledge, to join in a pact*; pret. 3 sg. **ymaruolles** 944, 1036

ymaruollwyr (ymarfollwyr) pl. (m.) *contenders* 1044

ymborth m. *sustenance* 859, 905

ymchwelut, ymchwelud (ymchwelyd) vn. *to return, turn back, to turn, change* 138, 295, 628, 680, 686, 944; pres. 1 sg. **ymchuelaf** 111*n.*; impf. 3 sg. **ymchuelei** 299; pret. 3 sg. **ymchwelawd** 709, 711, 922, 925, 940, 989, 3 pl. **emchuelassant** 827

ymderbynnyeit (ymdderbynieid) vn. *to resist* 962

ymdiffynawd see **amdiffyn**

ymdiret (ymddired) vn. *to trust* 1017

ymdynnv (ymdynnu) vn. *to withdraw* 832

ymdyrchauael (ymddyrchafael) *vn. to be exalted, to flourish* 94

ymdywynnic (ymdywynig) pres. 3 sg. of vn. 'ymdywynygu' *to appear* 269

ymdywynygrwyd (ymdywynigrwydd) m. *brilliance* 894

ymedewis see **ymadav**

ymeith adv. *away* 630, 646, 1033

ymerbynneit (+ac) vn. *to encounter, meet in battle* 304

ymgaffael (+a) vn. *to obtain* 320

ymgaru vn. *to make love* 219

ymgeled (ymgeledd) m. *care* 354

ymgelu vn. *to conceal oneself* 242, pret. 3 sg. **ymgclawd** 693

ymgerydu (ymgeryddu) vn. *to reproach oneself* 677

ymgydyaw (ymguddiaw) vn. *to lurk, to hide onself* 709

ymgydmeithyaw vn. *to associate* 678

ymgyfaruot (ymgyfarfod) vn. *to meet* 78

ymgyghor (ymgyngor) vn. *to consult* 161

ymgymynu vn. *to slay, fight* 533

ymgymysgu vn. *to mingle* 532

ymgynullav (ymgynullaw) vn. *to assemble* 279, 423, 496; pret. 3 sg. **ymgynnullawd** 981, 1043; 3 pl. **ymgynnullassant** 41, 360, 703

ymhlith see **plith**

ymhob see **pob**

ymlad¹, emlad (ymladd) vn. *to fight* 6, 64, 262, 311, 494, 521

ymlad² (ymladd) m. *battle, fighting* 258, 342, 529, 530, 542, 1019; pl. **ymladeu** 1

ymladgar, emladgar (ymladdgar) adj. *belligerent, warlike* 37, 818

ymladwr, emladwr m. *fighter* 813, 888; pl. **emladwyr** 817

ymlenwy, ymlenwi vn.*to complete, to become full* 8, 150, 289

ympell adv. *afar* 819

ympen see **pen(n)**

ymplith, ymplyth see **plith**

ymrody, ymrodi (ymroddi) vn. *to devote oneself, submit, to surrender* 11, 342, 350, 376; pret. 3 sg. **ymrodes** 126, 969

ymrwymaw vn. *to pledge oneself* 935

ymrysson m. *contest* 869*n*.

ymvrthodes a (ymwrthodes â) pret. 3 sg. of vn. 'ymwrthod â' *to reject, to withdraw from* 558

ymweled (+a) vn. *to visit* 607

ymwnaei impf. 3 sg. of vn. 'ymwneuthur' *to become* (*GPC s.v. ymwnâf* (b)) 466

ymwrandav (+ am) vn. *to listen out for, pay attention to* 199

yn¹, en¹ pred. part. 7, 15, 21, 22, 23, 42

yn², en², ym (before m-) adv. part. 4, 35, 46, 54, 58, 63

yn³, en³, yg, eg, yg-, yng-, ym prep. (i) *at, in, into* 3, 4, 29, 31, 48, 58 (ii) *according to* 919 (iii) **en e** *when* 764*n*. (iv) with suff. pers. pron. 1 sg. **ynof** 315, 3 sg.m **yndav, endav** (ynddaw) 47, 146, 158, 254, 311, 321; 3 sg. f **yndi** (ynddi) 415, 416, 665, 926; 3 pl. **yndun, yndunt, yndynt** 46, 229, 282, 292, 410, 418 (v) cpd. preps. **yghyfrwg** (yn + cyfrwng) *in the midst of* 697; **yghylch** (yn + cylch) see **kylch**, **yghysswllt a** (yn +cyswllt) *attached to* 620 (vi) **yglan** see **glan**

yna¹, ena, ene adv. *then* 5, 7, 18, 31, 49, 54; with article + noun acts as dem. pron.: **yr. . . yna** *that* 533

yna² adv. *there* 284, 419

ynd-, yng- see **yn³**

ynnill (ennill) vn. *to win* 842

yno, eno adv. *there* 69, 71, 165, 186, 235, 347, 387*n*.

ynoethach *much less, to say nothing of*; variant of *anoethach* (*GPC²* s.v. *anoethach*) 374

ynt see **bot**

ynteu¹, enteu¹, entev indep. conjunct. pers. pron. 3 sg. 225, 308, 453, 455

ynteu² yntev enteu²aff. conjunct. pers. pron. 3 sg. 8, 28, 59, 62, 69

ynteu³ conj. *or* (*GPC s.v. ynteu, yntau²*) 53, 514, 577, 890

yntuy (wyntwy) indep. red. pron. 3 pl. 860

ynuydu (ynfydu) vn. *become mad* 534

yny[1], **eny** conj. (i) *until* 497, 512, 668, 694, 822 (ii) *so that* (GMW §278) 34, 95

ynyalwch m. *wilderness* 919

ynys see **enys**

yr[1]see **y**[1]

yr[2], **er** prep. (i) *for the sake of* 172, 173, 299, 354, 559, 604 (ii) *in spite of* 121, 170, 303, 541 (iii) *since, from specified time* 155, 392, 596, 601 (iv) *for (the value of), with* 557, 702, 921, 928

yr[3] variant on **ry**[2] 131*n.*, 156, 167, 207, 234, 366

yrwng, rung, rvng, rygt- see **rwg**

ys (y[2] + inf. pron. 3 sg) 176*n.*

ysbeilyaw see **yspeilyaw**

yscol f. *school* 417*n.*

Yscotyeit see Index of Personal Names

yskrin f. *tomb* 863

ysef variant of **sef**

ysgavnder (ysgafnder) m. *levity* 160

ysgavyn (ysgafn) adj. *light* 449

ysgolheigyon pl. (m.) *clerics* 433, 850

ysgriuennu (ysgrifennu) vn. *to write* 535

ysguboryeu pl. (f.m.) *barns* 680

ysgymun, ysgymvn adj. *accursed* 159, 169, 177, 179, 476, 526

ysgymundawt m. *excommunication* 1038

ysgymunedic adj. *accursed* 525

ysmalha adv. *earnestly* 748

yspeiliaw, ysbeilyaw vn. *to despoil, deprive* 626, 1025, 1033

yspeit f./m. *space of time, respite* 75, 313

yspryt m. *life, spirit* 263

yspys adj. *clear, certain* 622; cpv. **hyspyssach** *more certain* 554

ys(s)yd see **bot**

ystauell (ystafell) f. *room, chamber* 146, 992; **ysteuyll bychain** *closets, privies* 620

ystryvus (ystrywus) adj. *scheming* 160

ystrywav (ystrywaw) vn. *to plot* 130

ystus m. *jusctice* 658

yt(t), yti see **y**[4(v)]

yttoed, yttoedvn see **bot**

yu, yv, yw see **bot**

yuet (yfed) vn. *to drink* 155

yuelly see **velly**

yw y 636*n*., 927
ywch[1] see y[4(v)]
ywch[2] see **bot**

INDEX OF PERSONAL NAMES

Achel Achilles. In Greek mythology he is the son of Peleus, king of Myrmidon and Thetis, a sea nymph. As a baby he is dipped in the River Styx to make him immune to wounds but his heel, by which he is held by his mother, is untouched by the river water and left vulnerable. He is the greatest of the Greek warriors in the Trojan war; he kills Hector and is in turn killed by Paris. 895, 1001

Achel urenhin (frenin) **Denmarc** One of Arthur's allies in the battle against Medrod. 549

Ajax A Greek warrior renowned for his bravery. He offends Minerva during the sack of Troy by committing an act of violence against Cassandra and is punished with shipwreck and drowning on his return home. 897

Avloed (Afloedd) Maternal grandfather of Gruffudd ap Cynan. 718*n.*

Angharat (Angharad) Wife of Gruffudd ap Cynan, d. 1162; daughter of Ewein (Owain) vab Edwin. 730, 856

Angharad Daughter of Maredudd ab Owain ap Hywel Dda; wife of Cynfyn ap Gwerystan; mother of Bleddyn and Rhiwallon ap Cynfyn. 611

Albanactus Son of Brutus; rules over Yr Alban (Scotland) as his share of his inheritance. 56, 62, 65

Amlavd Wledic (Amlawdd Wledig) Father of Eigr, (see below). He is not mentioned in HRB but in the Welsh tale 'Culhwch and Olwen' the form of his name is *Anlawd*; he is said to be Culhwch's maternal grandfather. (See *Culhwch and Olwen*, ed. Bromwich and Evans, 1992, p. 44*n.*). 287

Anna Sister of Arthur and mother of Medrod. 393

Annest Daughter of Gruffudd ap Cynan. 738

Antropos One of the three Fates of Greek mythology. 899*n.*

Apulenis Lucius Apuleius (c. 124–170) was born in the city of Madaura (near modern Madourouch in Algeria) in the Roman province of Numidia, during the reign of Hadrian. He was a Platonic philosopher but his greatest influence on Western writing was through his *Metamorphoses*, the only surviving novel in Latin, which has provided a model stylistically, thematically, and structurally, for many of the great writers of Europe and America. 227

Araun uab Kynuarch (Arawn fab Cynfarch) Auguselus in HRB, brother of Lleu and Urien; Arthur restores to him his kingdom, which had been lost to the Saxons. 388, 391, 429, 488

Aron Companion of Julius the martyr, to whom a church in York is dedicated. 415

Arthur Son of Eigr and Uthr Pen Dragon; succeeds his father as King of Britain; marries Gwenhwyfar; betrayed by his nephew Medrod; falls in the battle of Camlan and taken to Afallon (Avalon) to recover from his wounds. 357, 363, 370, 371, 381, 390

Ascanius Son and heir of Aeneas; founds a city on the shores of the river Tiber; father of Sylvanus and grandfather of Brutus. 2, 8, 9, 12

Asser son of Merwyd, one of three envoys sent by Gruffudd ap Cynan to negotiate with the men of Môn and Arfon. 758

Auarwy (Afarwy) Androgeus in HRB; elder son of Lludd; inherits the earldom of London and Kent on his father's death; betrays his uncle Caswallon to the Romans and goes to Rome with Julius Caesar; brother of Teneuan (see below). 93, 97

Bedwyr One of Arthur's knights, chief cup-bearer. 454

Beli Mavr (Mawr) Beli the Great, ruler of Britain after Manogan. 83*n*.

Bledyn(t) (see Cadwgawn).

Brewys, Gilys Giles de Breos/Braose, Bishop of Hereford 1200–15; son of William de Breos/Braose and Maud de St Valery. With his brother Reginald he engages in open war with King John for lordships in Wales, which the king had confiscated in 1211 on the death of their father. 943

Brewys, Gwiliam William de Breos/Braose (1) the father of Giles, Bishop of Hereford and Reginald (see Brewys, Gilys and Rheinallt). He expands his Welsh territories, with the blessing of King John, but in 1207 he suddenly falls from favour and flees to Ireland, where he is pursued. His wife and eldest son are captured and starved to death at Windsor. William himself escapes to France, where he dies 9 August 1211. 943

Brewys, Gwilym William de Breos/Braose (2), the Younger; born 1197; succeeds his father, Reginald, as Lord of Abergavenny, Builth and other Marcher lordships in 1227. Imprisoned by Llywelyn ap Iorwerth in 1228 during King Henry III's campaign against the Welsh, but ransomed and released after ceding Builth as a dowry for his daughter Isabella on her betrothal to David, son and heir of Llywelyn; married to Eva Marshall, daughter of William Marshall, Earl of Pembroke. Hanged in 1230 by Llywelyn after he discovers his adulterous relationship with his wife Siwan (Joan), natural daughter of King John. 983, 990

Brewys, Jon John de Breos/Braose; married to Margaret, daughter of Llywelyn ap Iorwerth. 973, 976

Brewys, Reinallt (Rheinallt) Reginald de Breos/Breose, died 1228. With his brother Giles he takes an active part in the barons' war against King John. Married to Gwladus Ddu, daughter of Llywelyn ap Iorwerth. 946, 950, 955, 960, 968, 984

Brutus First king of the Britons; son of Sylvius, grandson of Ascanius and great grandson of Aeneas; when he is fifteen years of age, he accidentally kills his father with an arrow while hunting, as prophesied; banished from Italy; flees to Greece and is invited by the Trojans, who were enslaved there, to lead them out of bondage. After leaving Greece, he visits Diana's temple and is told by the goddess to found a second Troy in an island beyond France, which is inhabited by giants. He intimidates the giants, settles in the island and names it Brytaen/Prydein (Britain), and the people of Prydein he calls Brytannyeit (Britons), after himself. On his death the island is divided among his three sons, Locrinus taking Lloegyr (Lloegr, England), Kamber taking Kymry (Cymru, Wales), and Albanactus taking Yr Alban (Scotland). 20, 23, 26, 32, 33, 49

Brodyr Troednoeth Barefoot friars, Franciscans. 997*n*.

Brytannyeit, **Brytannyeid** (Brytaniaid) Britons. 52, 266, 367, 551, 570, 573, 581

Brythael One of Gorlois's servants whose image Myrddin assumes on the night of Eigr's seduction. 344

Cadvr (Cadwr) Earl of Cornwall; rears Gwenhwyfar; sword bearer at the ceremony in Caer Lleon. 398, 430

Cadvr Llymenic (Cadwr Llymenig) One of Arthur's allies in battle against Medrod. 550

Kadwaladyr vab Kadwallawn see **Catwaladyr Uendigeit**

Cadwallavn Llavhir (Cadwallon Llawhir) King of Gwynedd and sword bearer at the ceremony in Caer Lleon. 429

Cadgawn (Cadwgan) Abbot of Llandyfái (Lamphey), becomes Bishop of Bangor in 1215; ends his days as a monk. 942

Kadgawn ap Bledynt (Cadwgan ap Bleddyn) Father of Owain, ravisher of Nest. Cadwgan was a first cousin to Gwladus, daughter of Rhiwallon ap Bleddyn, grandfather of Nest. 602, 608, 628, 631.

Kamber (Camber) Son of Brutus, rules over Cymru (Wales) as his share of the inheritance. 56, 61

Caradauc m. Grufud (Caradog m. Gruffudd) King of Gwynllwg, part of Glamorgan; his influence increases after the death of Gruffudd ap Llywelyn in 1063; he plans further expansion of his territories, allying himself with the Normans, if it is to his advantage; is killed in the battle of Mynydd Carn. 788

Caswallavn (Caswallon) Cassivelaunus. Succeeds his brother Llud (Lludd) as king of Britain, because Lludd's sons are both minors at the time of their father's death; fights against Julius Caesar but is eventually defeated. 84, 94

Casswallavn One of Arthur's allies in battle against Medrod. 550

Catwalader (Cadwaladr) Son of Gruffudd ap Cynan. 737

Catwaladyr Uendigeit (Cadwaladr Fendigaid) Cadwaladr the Blessed, son of Kadwallawn, the last king to hold sway over the ancient Island of Britain;

escapes to Britanny from the ravages of a plague and dies in Rome before he can re-establish his rule. 558, 580, 584, 589

Catwallavn (Cadwallon) Son of Gruffudd ap Cynan, killed in 1032 in the commote of Nanheudwy near Llangollen doing battle with the army of Powys; this put a halt to the expanson of Gwynedd for many years. 737

Kei (Cai) One of Arthur's knights. 452

Kenwric vab Riwallavn (Cynwrig fab Rhiwallon) Usurper of the kingdom of Gwynedd. Although described in HGK as a kinglet of Powys, he is said in *EWGT*, 119 to originate from Maelor. 755

Celdeic One of Medrod's Saxon allies. 545

Colgrim Saxon prince vanquished by Arthur in battle near York. 366

Cendelu m. Conus (Cynddelw mab Cwnws) His family's pedigree is traced as far back as Cunedda Wledig. In *EWGT* p. 111 he is named as one of Gruffudd ap Cynan's supporters in the Battle of Mynydd Carn. 800

Constans Eldest son of Custennyn Uendigeit; becomes a monk in the monastery of Amphibalus but is persuaded by Gwrtheyrn to leave the monastic life to become king; assassinated by one of Gwrtheyrn's Pictish agents. 106, 108, 114, 123, 125, 136

Corineus Leader of a group of Trojans whom Brutus meets during his exile in Greece. He joins forces with Brutus and being a formidable giant slayer, he helps him overpower his enemies and gain domination of Britain; rewarded with the province of Cornwall, which takes its name from him. He subsequently puts pressure on Brutus's son Locrinus to marry his daughter, Gwendoleu (Gwenddolau), in spite of his preference for the German princess, Estrildis (Esyllt). 66, 74, 75, 80

Krist Christ 579, 841, 910, 999

Kuhelyn Guithelinus, Archbishop of London; died before he could anoint Constans as king, therefore Gwrtheyrn (Vortigern) undertakes this episcopal task himself. 119

Curialius One of the famous men to whom the Lord Rhys is likened; probably Eurialius or Euryalus, who with the help of his friend Nisus, wins a race in the funeral games, described by Vergil in Aeneid V. 896

Custennyn uab Cadvr (Custennyn fab Cadwr) Arthur's successor as King of Britain, allegedly in AD 542. 555

Custennyn Uendigeit (Custennyn Fendigaid) Custennyn the Blessed; comes from Brittany to the rescue of Britain at the request of Kuhelyn (Guithelinus) Archbishop of London; is crowned king, marries and has three sons, Constans, Emrys Wledig and Uthr Pen Dragon; is knifed to death by a Pict. 100, 107

Kymry Welsh people 570, 860

Kyndeyrn (Cyndeyrn) One of Gwrtheyrn's sons by Rhonwen. 167

Kynuyn (Cynfyn) Great grandfather of Nest, married to Angharad, daughter of

Maredudd ap Owain, son of Hywel Dda (Hywel the Good). 611

Kynuarch (Cynfarch) Father of Lleu, Urien and Arawn, who are compensated by Arthur for being deprived of their territories under the Saxons. 388, 389, 391, 429, 488, 490

Daenysseit Danes, supporters of Gruffudd ap Cynan. 773, 799

Dafydd escob Bangor Consecrated as Bishop of Bangor in 1120 and was there at least until 1137; present at Gruffudd ap Cynan's deathbed. 849

Damasius Pab Pope Damasus I, c.304-384. 1069

Dauid/Dauyd (Dafydd) (1) Son of Llywelyn Fawr and Joan, daughter of King John. 1002, 1003, 1009

Dauyd (Dafydd) (2) Son of Gruffudd ap Llywelyn ap Iorwerth and brother of Llywelyn, the last native Prince of Wales. 1016, 1063

Deheuwyr Men of the South. 801

Dewi St. David, patron saint of Wales. 683, 687, 777, 796

Diermit There are two kings of this name: Diarmait mac Énna mac Diarmait mac Máil-na-mBó (d. 1072) and Diarmait mac Énna mac Murchad mac Diarmait mac Máil-na-mBó (d. 1117). 771

Dunavt (Dunawd) Dinabutius, the boy playing with Myrddin when he is discovred by Gwrtheyrn's emissaries. 201, 202

Dyuric/Dyuryc (Dyfrig) The archbishop who crowns Arthur. 362, 369, 425

Ebrict One of Medrod's Saxon allies. 546

Ebryct urenhin Llychlyn Scandinavian king, one of Arthur's allies in battle against Medrawd. 549

Edelstan First Saxon king to hold sway over the whole of Britain; died 939 A.D. 574

Edmwnt Second son of Henry III, 1245–1296. 1049

Edward (1) Edward the Confessor, King of England 1042–66. 714

Edward (vab Henri) (2) King Edward I of England, 1239–1307. 1022, 1032, 1041, 1048, 1055

Eigyr (Eigr) Wife of Gorlois Earl of Cornwall, daughter of Amlawdd Wledig; ravished by Uthr Pen Dragon; mother of King Arthur. 286, 314, 316, 330, 350

Elaes One of Medrod's Saxon allies. 546

Emreis Wledic Son of Custennyn Fendigaid (Custennyn the Blessed). 102, 392

Emyr Llydav (Emyr Llydaw) Father of Howel, King of Brittany. 474

Eneas Yscvydwyn (Ysgwydwyn) Aeneas of the White Shield, the common ancestor of the Britons and the Romans; flees from Troy with his son Ascanius after its defeat by the Greeks; sails to Italy and is received honourably by king Latinus but King Turnus is jealous of him; Aeneas does battle with Turnus, defeats him, seizes his kingdom and wins Lavinia daughter of Latinus as his wife; on his death he is succeeded by his son Ascanius. 1, 4, 6, 8

Essyllt Daughter of king of Germany, beloved by Locrinus (see below). 67, 71, 76, 80

Ewein (Owain) Gwynedd, the best known of Gruffudd ap Cynan's sons, 1100–1170. 737

Ewein vab Edwin (Owain fab Edwin) Father-in-law of Gruffudd ap Cynan. 730

Franges Frances, daughter of Picot of Sai, born 1070, one of the Norman lords who settled in Wales after the conquest; married to Cadwgawn ap Bleddyn and mother of Gruffydd ap Cadwgawn, Lord of Nannau. 696

Fychteit Picts 483, 547

Gerald Known as Gerald of Windsor, steward of Pembroke Castle and husband of Nest, daughter of Rhys ap Tewdwr. 606, 615, 617, 626, 639, 648, 657

Gillamvri One of Medrod's Irish allies. 546

Gillapatric One of Medrod's Irish allies. 546

Gillari One of Medrod's Irish allies. 547

Gillassor One of Medrod's Irish allies. 547

Gilys See Brewys.

Gorlois Earl of Cornwall, husband of Eigr (see above). 286. 300. 303, 311, 335, 336

Gortheyrn Gortheneu/Gwrtheyrn Gwrthenau Earl of Gwent and Ergyng and Yeuas; seizes the kingship of Britain after the assassination of Custennyn; fears revenge of Constans's brothers, Emrys Wledig and Uthr Pen Dragon, and of the Picts for his summary execution of Constans's assassins; accepts offer of help to defend himself from the Saxon princes Hengist and Horsa; rewards them with land; marries Rhonwen daughter of Hengist and bequeaths Kent as her dowry; is deposed by his son Gwerthefyr, who drives the Saxons away; recovers his throne after Rhonwen poisons Gwerthefyr; invites the Saxons back again but is soon overshadowed; flees to Wales; tries to erect a fortress in Eryri but what is built during the day collapses by the following morning; magicians advise him that only the blood of a fatherless boy will bind the cement. Myrddin (see below) is discovered and solves the problem of the collapsing walls. 104*n*., 116, 122, 126, 128, 132

Gruffud ap Gwennwynwyn (Gruffudd ap Gwenwynwyn) Fights on King Edward I's side against Llywelyn ap Gruffudd; died c. 1286 (see Rosser Mortymer below). 1067–8

Gruffud vab Kenan (Gruffudd fab Cynan) c. 1055–1137; Dublin-born heir to the throne of Gwynedd; the only Welsh prince whose biography has survived.

(See Introduction xxxiii–xxxvii and text ll. 714–866). 715, 720, 722, 729, 740, 757

Gruffud vab Llywelyn (Gruffudd fab Llywelyn) Natural son of Llywelyn ap Iorwerth by Tangwystl, daughter of Llywarch Goch o Rhos; born sometime before Llywelyn's marriage to Joan in 1206 and died 1244. 1012, 1015

Gucharki Wydel (Wyddel) G. the Irishman; possibly a mercenary soldier, who kills Trahaearn in the Battle of Mynydd Carn. 823

Guendoleu (Gwenddolau) Daughter of Corineus, wife of Locrinus (see below). 66, 73, 75, 76, 79

Guenhvyuar (Gwenhwyfar) Arthur's queen; rasied by Cadwr, earl of Cernyw (Cornwall); has an adulterous relationship with Medrod; ends her days as a nun in the church of Julius the Martyr. 397, 471, 498

Guenlliant (Gwenllian) Daughter of Gruffudd ap Cynan by one of his mistresses (*HW*, ii 417) and wife of Gruffudd ap Rhys ap Tewdwr; named in *BS*, 134 as mother of Madog ap Cadwgan. 737

Guertheuyr Uendigeit (Gwerthefyr Fendigaid) One of Gwrtheyrn's sons by Rhonwen. 168

Gugavn (Gwgawn) son of Merwyd, one of three envoys sent by Gruffudd ap Cynan to negotiate with the men of Môn and Arfon (Anglesey and Caernarfon) 758

Gvrgant (Gwrgant) Earl of Kent, whose earldom was given without his knowledge as a gift to Hengist in return for his daughter's hand in marriage. 165

Gwalchmei (Gwalchmai) Son of Lleu fab Cynfarch and Anna; brother of Medrod. 394

Gwalchmei uab Guyar (Gwalchmai fab Gwyar) Arthur's nephew. 489

Gwallter Walter, High Sheriff of Gloucester, c.1065–1129. 658

Gwallter Maryscal Walter Marshal, 5th Earl of Pembroke (1199–1245), sent to fortify the castle at Cardigan. 1006

Gwrtheyrn Gwrtheneu see **Gortheyrn Gortheneu**.

Gwenhvyssyon Men of Gwent. 789

Gwenwynwyn o Bowys Son of Owain Cyfeiliog; helped Llywelyn ap Iorwerth in his struggle against King John. 915

Gwilym Jeuang see Brewys (2)

Gwladus Daughter of Rhiwallon, mother of Nest, cousin of Cadwgan ap Bleddyn. 609

Gwydel (Gwyddel) m. Irishman; pl. **Gwydyl** (Gwyddyl) 484, 547, 689, 773, 799, 811, 860

Gwyndit Men of Gwynedd. 800, 812

Hauren (Hafren) Daughter of Locrinus and Esyllt; drowned in river Hafren

(Severn) which is named after her. 72, 81

Hector Son of Priam, King of Troy, and Hecuba; the bravest of the Trojan heroes; dragged three times around Troy by Achilles; one of the famous men to whom the Lord Rhys is likened. 896

Heingyst (Hengist) Saxon prince; lands in Kent with his brother Hors; received by Gwrtheyrn and helps him defeat the Picts; is given Kent on the marriage of his daughter, Rhonwen, to Gwrtheyrn. 139, 141, 160, 480, 591

Helenus uab Pryaf Son of Priam, King of Troy; defeated by Pyrr uab Achel (Pyrrhus, son of Achilles), in the siege of Troy; his descendants are held captive by Pandrasus, King of Greece. 28

Henri King Henry I of England, c.1068–1135. 632, 641

Henri King Henry III of England, 1207–1272. 978, 1004, 1041, 1048

Herkwlff Hercules, son of Jupiter and Alcmena. In Greek mythology he is the son of Zeus and Alcmene, a mortal; he is proverbial for his great strength and performs many deeds of valour, always triumphing over evil. He is most famous for the Twelve Labours which he undertakes as a penance for killing his wife and children in a fit of madness. On his death he ascends to the heavens and is the only mortal to be rasied to the same level as the Olympian gods. One of the famous men to whom the Lord Rhys is likened. 894

Himing One of Medrod's Saxon allies. 546

Howel uab Emyr Llydav (Hywel fab Emyr Llydaw) King of Brittany, cousin and ally of Arthur. 473–4

Howel ap Gruffud ap Edneved (Hywel ap Gruffudd ap Ednyfed) Leads Edward I's fleet in his final struggle against Llywelyn ap Gruffudd. Grandson of Ednyfed Fychan, a court official who served three generations of the house of Gwynedd; died 1246. 1057–8

Hu yarll Caer (Huw iarll Caer) *alias* Hugh d'Avranches and Hugh the Fat. Given large grants of land by William the Conqueror in return for his support; became First Earl of Chester in 1070; spent most of his time fighting his Welsh neighbours and subdued a good part of north Wales; d. 1107. 766

Humyr *Humber rex Hunorum*, King of the Huns; attacks Albanactus and his people are compelled to flee to Locrinus. Humyr is killed on the banks of the river Humber to which he gives his name. 64

Hors Saxon prince; lands in Kent; received by Gwrtheyrn and helps him defeat the Picts. (See Heingist). 480, 591

Hywel Son of Ednyfed; Bishop of St Asaph. 996

Hywel vab Grufud ap Kynan (Hywel fab Gruffudd ap Cynan). Helps Llywelyn ap Iorwerth in his struggle against King John. 915

Ideon (Iddewon) Jews 861

Iessu Grist Jesus Christ 604

Ieuan/Jeuan vrenhin Lloegyr King John of England, 1166–1216, whose natural daughter Joan was given in a dynastic marriage to Llywelyn the Great. 912, 949, 1003

Ini Nephew of Cadwaladr the Blessed and cousin of Ifor. 565

Iosue fab Nun (Joshua fab Nwn) The man chosen to lead the Israelites into Canaan on the death of Moses. There is no record of national mourning on his death. 861–2.

Ithael Son of Rhirid ap Bleddyn; incited by Richard, Bishop of London to avenge the injury done to Gerald of Windsor. 640, 666, 697

Iuor uab Alan/Catwaladyr (Ifor fab Alan/Cadwaladr) Son of Cadwaladr the Blessed; also referred to as Iuor vab Alan, King of Britanny in MS Pen. 20. Has been identified with Ini of Wessex, who married Aethelburh and who is said to have gone to Rome. See *BT* (*Pen. 20 trans.*) 565, 584

Iulius/Julius Verthyr Julius the Martyr; a church in York was dedicated to him. 414, 501

Jeuan see **Ieuan**.

Jon Joan, natural daughter of King John and wife of Llywelyn ap Iorwerth, sometimes known as Siwan. 994, 1002

Jon see **Brewys**

Jorr[werth] Abbot of Tal y Llychau 941

Jurdan o Dindagol Castellan of Tintagol whose image is assumed by Wlffin on the night of Eigr's seduction. 337, 344,

Latinus King of Italy; welcomes Aeneas to his kingdom. 7

Lauynya (Lavinia) Daughter of Latinus; wife of Aeneas. 7, 12

Locrinus Son of Brutus; rules over Lloegr (England) as his share of his inheritance; falls in love with Esyllt but is forced to marry Gwenddolau, daughter of Corineus. On his father-in-law's death, he deserts Gwenddolau in favour of Esyllt, whom he has kept protected in an underground room in London; Gwenddolau leads a rebellion against them and Locrinus is killed; Gwenddolau assumes power and drowns Esyllt and her daughter Hafren (Severn) in the river which bears her name. 56, 59, 65, 66, 78, 79

Lleu uab Kynuarch (Lleu fab Cynfarch) Loth, brother of Urien and Arawn; compensated by Arthur for the loss of his territories to the Saxons; married to Anna, sister of Arthur and mother of Medrod. 388, 391

Llud (Lludd) Eldest son of Beli Mawr and brother of Caswallon; renames the capital Caer Ludd, which became corrupted to Llundein; is buried near a gateway named Porth Llud in Welsh and Ludysgat (Ludgate) in English. 84, 92

Llywarch vab Trahaearn Assigned as accomplice to Madoc and Ithel, the two sons of Rhiryd ap Bleddyn (1049–1307), King of Powys, who are sent by Richard, Bishop of London to avenge the rape of Nest by Ywein ap Cadwgan (Owain ap Cadwgan); his brothers were killed by Owain. 650, 666

Llywelyn ap Gruffud (Gruffudd) *c.* 1223–1282; grandson of Llywelyn ap Iorwerth (the Great) and the last native prince of Wales. 1012, 1016, 1017, 1025, 1028, 1054

Llywelyn vab Jorwerth *c.* 1173–1240; prince of Gwynedd and eventually over most of Wales; known as Llywelyn the Great. 910, 913, 918, 930, 932, 941

Madavc (1) (Madog) Son of Locrinus and Gwenddolau; fostered by his grandfather Corineus. 73

Madavc (2) (Madog) Son of Rhiryd ap Bleddyn; incited by Richard, Bishop of London to avenge the injury done to Gerald of Windsor. 640, 666, 697

Madoc vab Gruffud Maelawr (Madog fab Gruffudd Maelor) Helps Llywelyn ap Iorwerth in his struggle against King John. 916

Maelgwn Son of the Lord Rhys; helps Llywelyn ap Iorwerth in his struggle against King John 917.

Manogan Digueillus/Cliguellus. Ruler of Britain; succeeded by his son Beli Mawr. 83

Maredud Great grandfather of Cadwgawn ap Bledynt (see above). 611

Maredud vab Rotpert o Gedewein (Maredudd fab Robert o Gedewain) Helps Llywelyn ap Iorwerth in his struggle against King John. 916

Maredud vab Ryderch (Maredudd fab Rhydderch) Offers protection to those who fled to Ystrad Tywi in the aftermath of Uchdryd's quest for vengeance on Owain ap Cadwgan. (See Ywein below). 663

Maredud vab Rys Gryg (Maredudd fab Rhys Grug) Helps Llywelyn ap Gruffudd to win Perfeddwlad and is granted land around Builth as a reward. 1029, 1033, 1034, 1039

Maredud vab Ywein (ap Gruffudd) (Maredudd fab Owain ap Gruffudd) In return for aiding Llywelyn ap Gruffudd, he is given King Edward's lands in Ceredigion. 1032

Maryret (Maryred) Daughter of Gruffudd ap Cynan, married to Ieuan ap Caradog and mother of Howel ap Ieuan, Lord of Arwystli, whom Owain Gwynedd attacked in 1162. 738

Marvret Daughter of Llywelyn the Great; married to Jon Brewys (see above). 973

Medravt (Medrod) Son of Lleu fab Cynfarch and Anna; Arthur's nephew; seizes Arthur's crown and has an adulterous relationship with Gwenhwyfar. 394. 470, 476, 482, 493, 495

Meilir m. Riwallaun (Meilir m. Rhiwallon) Killed in the battle of Mynydd Carn. 790

Meir Vyry, Y Wynnuydic Feir The Virgin Mary. 557, 564, 997

Meiryavn Son of Merwyd, one of three envoys sent by Gruffudd ap Cynan to negotiate with the men of Môn and Arfon (Anglesey and Caernarfon).758

Merwyd o Leyn Named in *EWGT*, p . 117 under the variant Meurig as father of Asser, Gwgant and Meirion (see above). 758

Meugant Magician who advises Gwrtheyrn on *incubi* and Myrddin. 223, 224

Meuryc (Meurig) King of Dyfed and sword bearer at the ceremony in Caer Lleon. 430

Mvrcard (Mvrchath) Muirchertach Ua Briain (*c*.1050–*c*. 1119), High King of Ireland, son of Toirdelbach Ua Briain and great-gradnson of Brian Bóruma. 689, 746

Myrdin (Myrddin) Merlinus. Wonderchild, son of a nun, daughter of king of Dyfed, and an *incubus*; saves himself from death by solving the mystery of the disappearing foundations; makes many prophecies and assists Uthr Pen Dragon to ravish Eigr and beget Arthur. 201, 202, 206, 211, 213, 233

Nordmannyeyt (Normaniaid) Norman cross-bowmen, who had served Caradog mab Gruffudd in his attack on Rhys ap Tewdwr. 790, 844

Nest Daughter of Rhys ap Tewdwr, last king of Deheubarth, and wife of Gerald of Windsor; her beauty was proverbial and she is known as 'Helen of Wales', because of her abduction by Owain son of Cadwgan; she had many lovers including Henry I and is said to have produced at least seventeen children; one of her grandchildren was Giraldus Cambrensis (Gerald of Wales). 605, 609, 615, 622, 625, 627

Nestor In Greek mythology he is the eldest of the Greek kings in the Trojan war; well known for his diplomacy, interceding in the quarrels of his fellow warriors and advising moderation. One of the famous men to whom the Lord Rhys is likened. 895

Nynnyav (Nyniaw) Youngest son of Beli Mawr. 85

Nun See **Iosue.**

Owein Son of Cadwgan; see **Ywein.**

Owein uab Vryen (Owain fab Urien) Prince of Rheged in the north, said to have been eulogised by Taliesin, an early British poet of the post-Roman period. 490

Padarn Eponymous founder of St. Padarn's Church, Llanbadarn, nr. Aberystwyth. 687

Pandrasus King of Greece; enslaves descendants of Helenus, son of Priam of Troy, who are rescued by Brutus. 29

Pasken One of Gwrtheyrn's sons by Rhonwen. 168

Paris Trojan prince; it was his abduction of Helen, wife of the Greek prince

Menelaus, that provoked the Trojan War. One of the famous men to whom the Lord Rhys is likened. 897

Pedyr (Pedr) Peter the Apostle. 209

Pigot o Saisis See **Franges** above. 697

Powyswyr Men of Powys. 790

Pryaf Priam King of Troy, common ancestor of Romans and Britons. 29

Pyrr uab Achel Pyrrhus son of Achilles; after the Trojan War he captures Helenus and several other Trojans, and keeps them in slavery in revenge for his father's death. 29

Ragnell Daughter of Afloedd and mother of Gruffudd ap Cynan. 718

Rainillt Daughter of Gruffudd ap Cynan and mother of Cadwallon ap Madoc ap Idnerth ap Kadwgon ab Elystan, *EWGT* 104. 738

Reinallt see **Brewys**

Richyard Bishop of London and King Henry I's steward at Shrewsbury; incites Ithel and Madoc, sons of Rhiryd ap Bleddyn to avenge the injury done to Gerald of Windsor. 638, 694

Riryd ap Bleddyn Father of Ithel and Madoc, who avange the injury done to Gerald of Windsor. 640, 698

Riwallawn (Rhiwallon) Son of Cynfyn, great grandfather of Nest, uncle of Cadwgawn ap Bledynt. 610

Robert Rudlan A powerful Norman baron who wished to establish himself as ruler of Gwynedd, close relative of Hugh of Chester. 765

Ronwen (Rhonwen) Daughter of Hengist/Heingist (see above), married to Gortheyrn Gortheneu. 140

Rosser Mortymer Roger Mortimer; together with Gruffudd ap Gwenwynwyn was responsible for the death of Llywelyn ap Gruffudd, the last native Prince of Wales, at Builth in 1282. 1067

Rotpert esgob Bangor Robert Bishop of Bangor was captured by Llywelyn ap Iorwerth but later ransomed for 200 falcons. 928

Rutyl The Rutuli, legendary Italic tribe. 5, 6

Rys Nephew of Maredyd vab Rys (see above). 1033

Rys ap Gruffud (1) (Rhys ap Gruffudd) 1132–97; commonly known as the Lord Rhys, last powerful Prince of Deheubarth, see text ll. 867–909; grandson of Rhys ap Tewdwr (see below). 867, 872, 874, 881, 884, 917, 938–9

Rys Ieuanc ap Gruffudd (2) (Rhys ap Gruffudd) Grandson of the Lord Rhys. Together with his brother Owain/Ywein, he refuses to make peace with King John, although all the other princes of Wales had done so. Helps Llywelyn ap Iorwerth in his struggle with Reginald de Breos and acts as mediator between the citizens of Brecon and Llywelyn ap Iorwerth; died 1222. 917, 939, 956, 963

Rys ap/m. Teudwr (Rhys ap/mab Tewdwr) Father of Nest (see above); Prince in south Wales from 1079 till his death in 1093; would have been a powerful lord when Gruffudd ap Cynan was in exile, but in the text he is portrayed as being vastly inferior. 606 776, 778, 782, 794, 805

Rys Gryg (Rhys Gryg) Also referred to as Rhys Fychan; sent to force Rhys and Owain, sons of Gruffudd ap Rhys to yield or drive them from the kingdom; given custody of Seinhenydd castle. 971, 972

Saesson Saxons, English people 170, 174, 265, 364, 382, 390

Samson Biblical character, who was deprived of his strength when his locks were shorn by his wife Delilah. One of the famous men to whom the Lord Rhys is likened. 896

Selinx Saxon prince invited by Medrod to help him in his struggle against Arthur. 477

Selyf Solomon, son of the biblical King David, proverbial for his wisdom. One of the famous men to whom the Lord Rhys is likened. 897

Sergius The pope who beatified Cadwaladr Fendigaid (the Blessed). 560

Sussanna Daughter of Gruffudd ap Cynan and wife of Madog ap Maredudd. 738

Syluyus (Silvius) Son of Ascanius, grandson of Aeneas; has an affair with Lavinia's niece; she has a son by him but dies in childbirth; the son is named Brutus. 11

Symeon archdiagon Archdeacon at Clynnog, one of the most important churches in Wales during the Middle Ages. Is present at the deathbed of Gruffudd ap Cynan. 849

Teneuan (Tenefan) Tenvantius; son of Lludd; became earl of Cornwall on his father's death; succeeded Caswallon as ruler of Britain. Brother of Auarvy (Afarwy). 92

Terdelach Probably Toirrdelbach ua Briain, grandson of Brian Ború. 714*n*.

Trahaearn vab Caradauc (Trahaearn fab Caradog) Unlawful ruler of Gwynedd; his rule is challenged by Gruffudd ap Cynan; his grand-daughter, Gwladus, is married to Owain Gwynedd. 754, 791, 821

Turn Turnus, King of the Rutuli; is killed in battle by Aeneas. 5, 6

Tydeus Son of Aeneas, the Trojan War hero and Periboea; father of Diomedes. 895

Uryen uab Kynuarch (Urien fab Cynfarch) Brother of Arawn and Lleu; compensated by Arthur for the loss of his territories to the Saxons; Lord of Rheged, said to have been eulogised by Taliesin, an early British poet of the post-Roman period. 388, 394

Uthyr see **Vthyr**

Vchdryd ap Edwin (Uchdryd ap Edwin) Accompanies Llywarch son of Trahayarn on his mission to avenge the rape of Nest. 651, 653, 662, 666, 668, 677, 678

Vlffin/Vlffyn o Ryt Garadavc (Wlffin o Ryd Caradog) Companion of Uthr Pen Dragon; transformed into Jurdan o Dindagol (see above) to help Uthr Pen Dragon seduce Eigr. 314, 319, 325, 337, 343

Vlixes In Greek mythology he is the son of Laertes, king of Ithaca. After the Trojan war he spends twenty years trying to return home but is thwarted in his attempts by Poseidon and by others such as Calypso, Circe and the Sirens. He is also known as Odysseus and his adventures are the subject of Homer's *Odyssey*. One of the famous men to whom the Lord Rhys is likened. 897

Vthur/Uthyr Pen Dragon Son of Custennyn and father of Arthur. He and his brother, Aurelius Ambrosius, return from Brittany to avenge the deaths of their father and brother at the hands of Gwrtheyrn (Vortigern). When Aurelius suffers a treacherous death at the hands of the Saxons, Uthr Pen Dragon succeeds him and celebrates his accession to the throne of Britain with a feast in London at Eastertide. Subsequently, through the magic of Merlin, he seduces Eigr, wife of Gorlois, Earl of Cornwall, from which union Arthur is born. 102, 313, 360, 363, 365, 393

Yscotyeit Medrod's allies against Arthur. 483, 547

Ywein (Owain) Son of Cadwgan ap Bleddyn; rapes Nest, the wife of Gerald de Windsor (see above), steward of Pembroke Castle; died 1116. 603, 605, 629, 635, 639, 645

Ywein Gwyned (Owain Gwynedd) Ruler of Gwynedd from 1137 until his death in 1170. 1000

Ywein (Owain) **ap Gruffudd** Son of the Lord Rhys's son Gruffudd. 939, 956

Ywein Goch (Owain Goch) Son of Gruffudd ap Llywelyn ap Iorwerth; together with his brother Llywelyn he succeeded his uncle Dafydd ap Llywelyn, who died without issue in 1246. 1012, 1016

INDEX OF PLACE NAMES

Colomcell a ficticious area of Dublin, name taken from *Columcille*, a 6th century
saint 716*n*.
Conwy town in Caernarvonshire 926
Kroes Oswallt (Croesoswallt) Oswestry 953
Kymry/Kemry (Cymru) Wales 62, 178, 753, 776, 779, 785

Deheubarth early Welsh kingdom in south west Wales; came into existence
in 920 when Hywel Dda combined the former kingdoms of Dyfed and
Seisyllwg 881
Denmarc Denmark 550, 810, 860
Dulyn Dublin 715, 719
Dymolt, Castell *castellum Dimilioc* (*GM* §137.472) Near the village of Pendoggett,
about 5 and a half miles south west of Tintagel is an emcampment named
Tregeare Rounds and is known locally as Castle Dameliock (*HKB* 206)
308
Dunavt (Dunawd) 64*n*.
Dygannwy Deganwy 920
Dyued/Dyuet Dyfed 208, 430, 656

Eifft, Yr (Aifft) Egypt 854
Ergyng in Herefordshire 105*n*.
Eryri Snowdonia 184, 919, 927
Ess Ssex Essex 601
Evirwic York 595
Eydal (Eidal) Italy 2, 4, 7, 26

Freinc/Freing (Ffrianc) France 272, 474, 878

Germania Germany 138, 365, 477, 481
Groec (Groeg) Greece 28, 29, 40, 42, 43
Gwent county in south east Wales, situated between the rivers Usk, Wye and
Monnow 104
Gwent Uch Coet, Gwent Is Coet two cantrefs which form the land of Gwent
789
Gulat Uorgant (Gwlad Forgan) Glamorgan 406
Gwhyr (Gwyr) Gower 966
Gwyned/Gvyned Gwynedd in north west Wales 430, 715, 718, 755, 840, 844

Hauren (Hafren) River Severn 61
Hay Hay on Wye 952
Henford (Henffordd) Hereford 943, 950
Humyr Humber 368, 479

Jorck York 595

Leaws Lewes in East Sussex 1044
Lincol Lincoln 175
Lodoneis Londonesia 392
London 594
Ludysgat Ludsgate 91
Llannbadarn Llanbadarn 681
Llanndewivreui Llanddewibrefi 683
Llandefit (Llandyfái) Lamphey 942*n.*
Llanngaenten Llanganten 1065
Llangyuc Llangiwg 967
Lloegyr (Lloegr) England 60, 574, 589, 592, 596
Llundein (Llundain) London 68, 87, 90, 97, 118, 120
Llychlyn Scandinavia 549
Llydaw/Llydav Britanny 585

Maelenyd Maelienydd 655, 661
Maeshyueid (Maesyfed) Radnor 952
Meirionnyd 1031
Menei Menai 1059
Menyd Carn (Mynydd Carn) site of battle fought in 1081 between Gruffudd ap
  Cynan and Rhys ap Tewdwr against Trahaearn ap Caradog and Caradog
  ap Gruffydd; the location has not been precisely identified, but is thought
  to be in Pembrokeshire 836*n.*
Mon Anglesey 691, 757, 800, 919, 1057, 1058
Morgannvc (Morgannwg) Glamorgan 789
Mynheu (Mynnau) Alps 468
Mynyd (Mynydd) **Ambri** Mount Ambrius, possibly Amesbury, near Salisbury
  599*n.*
Mynyd (Mynydd) **Du** Black Mountain 966
Mynyv (Mynyw) St David's 775, 777, 942

Northamtvn Northampton 486

Peruedwlat (Perfeddwlad) lit. ˊMiddle Country 919*n.*, 936, 1029
Powys county in mid Wales 603, 629, 693, 698, 712, 755
Porth Cleis (Clais) about a mile south west of St Davids, where the river Alun
  flows into the sea. *Cleis* is possibly an archaic gen. of *clas*, 'cloister,
  monastery'; the meaning is 'Gateway of the Monastery' (see *MPW* 107).
  774.
Porthlarc Porthlarg, Waterford 772
Porth Llud (Lludd) Ludsgate 91
Prydein (Prydain) Britain 57, 84, 157, 172, 384, 385

Reget Rheged, ancient British kingdom 395
Rudlan Rhuddlan 765, 1057

ABBREVIATIONS

AC	*Annales Cambriae.*
Add.	Additional.
BBCS	*Bulletin of the Board of Celtic Studies.*
BD	Brut Dingestow Court manuscript.
BD	*Brut Dingestow* selections in this edition.
BL	British Library.
BR	*Breudwyt Ronabwy, allan o'r Llyfr coch o Hergest*, (ed.) Melville Richards (Cardiff, 1948).
BrD	*Brut Dingestow*, ed. Henry Lewis (Cardiff, 1942).
BS	Brenhinedd y Saesson.
BS	*Brenhinedd y Saesson*, ed. Thomas Jones (Cardiff, 1971).
BT	Brut y Tywysogyon.
BT	*Brut y Tywysogyon* selections in this edition.
BT (*Pen. 20*)	*Brut y Tywysogyon Peniarth MS. 20*, ed. Thomas Jones (Cardiff, 1941).
BT (*Pen. 20 trans.*)	*Brut y Tywysogyon or The Chronicle of the Princes, Peniarth MS. 20*, ed. Thomas Jones, (Cardiff, 1952).
BT (*RB*)	*Brut y Tywysogyon (Red Book of Hergest Version)*, ed. Thomas Jones (Cardiff, 1955).
CBT	*Cyfres Beirdd y Tywysogion* (Poets of the Princes Series).
CL	'Old and Middle Welsh', Martin J. Ball and Nicole Müller (eds.). *The Celtic Languages* 2nd edition (London and New York, 2010).
CMCS	*Cambridge/Cambrian Medieval Celtic Studies.*
CW	*Cronica de Wallia.*
ed(s).	editor(s), edited by.
EWGT	*Early Welsh Genealogical Tracts*, ed. P.C. Bartrum, (Cardiff, 1946).
ex.	example.
GM	*Geoffrey of Monmouth, The History of the Kings of Britain. An Edition and Translation of De Gestis Britonum [Historia Regum Britanniae]*, ed. Michael D. Reeve, trans. Neil Wright (Woodbridge, 2007).
GMW	*A Grammar of Middle Welsh*, ed. D. Simon Evans, (Dublin, 1964).
GPC	*Geiriadur Prifysgol Cymru. A Dictionary of the Welsh Language* (Cardiff, 1950–2002).
GPC²	*Geiriadur Prifysgol Cymru. A Dictionary of the Welsh Language* (2nd edn., Cardiff, 2003–.
H1, H2	Havod Manuscripts 1 and 2.
HB	Historia Brittonum.

HGK	Historia Gruffud vab Kenan.
HGK	*Historia Gruffud vab Kenan* selections in this edition.
HGrK	*Historia Gruffud vab Kenan,* ed. D. Simon Evans (Cardiff, 1977).
HRB	Historia Regum Britanniae.
L&S	Charlton C. Lewis and Charles Short, *A Latin Dictionary* (Oxford, 1958).
Llı	Llanstephan manuscript 1.
MA	*The Myvyrian Archaiology of Wales,* eds. Owen Jones, Edward Williams and William Owen [Pughe] (2nd edn. Denbigh, 1870).
MPW	*A Mediaeval Prince of Wales. The Life of Gruffudd ap Cynan,* ed. D. Simon Evans (Felinfach, 1990).
MS(S)	Manuscript(s).
NLW	National Library of Wales.
Pen. 20	Peniarth 20 manuscript.
PKM	*Pedeir Keinc y Mabinogi,* ed. Ifor Williams (Cardiff, 1930).
RB	Red Book of Hergest.
RC	*Revue Celtique.*
SW	*The Syntax of Welsh,* Borsley, Robert D. et al. (eds.), (Cambridge, 2007).
TBRB	*The Text of the Bruts from the Red Book of Hergest,* ed. John Rhŷs and J. Gwenogvryn Evans (Oxford, 1890).
trans.	translation/translator(s)/translated by.
VGC	*Vita Griffini Filii Conani. The Medieval Life of Gruffudd ap Cynan* ed. Paul Russell (Cardiff, 2005).
YBH	*Selections from Ystorya Bown o Hamtwn,* ed. Erich Poppe and Regine Reck (Cardiff, 2009).
YBY	*Y Bibyl Ynghymraec,* ed. Thomas Jones (Cardiff, 1940).

BIBLIOGRAPHY

ANDERSON, KATHARINE, '*Urth Noe e Tat*. The Question of Fosterage in High Medieval Wales', *North American Journal of Welsh Studies*, 4 (2004), 1–11.

BARTRUM, P. C., *A Welsh Classical Dictionary* (Aberystwyth, 1993).

BEDE, *The Ecclesiastical History of the English People*, (ed.) Bertram Colgrave and R. A. B. Mynors (Oxford, 1969).

BALL, MARTIN J. and MÜLLER, NICOLE (eds.), *The Celtic Languages*, (2nd edition, London and New York, 2010).

BORSLEY, ROBERT D. ET AL. (eds.), *The Syntax of Welsh* (Cambridge, 2007).

BOETHIUS, *The Consolation of Philosophy*, trans. V. E.Watts (Harmonsworth, 1969).

BRAMLEY, KATHLEEN ANN ET AL. (eds.), *Gwaith Llywelyn Fardd I ac eraill o feirdd y ddeuddegfed ganrif* (Cyfres Beirdd y Tywysogion 2, Cardiff, 1994).

BREEZE, ANDREW, 'Celtic etymologies for Old English *cursung* 'curse', *gafeluc*.'javelin', *staer* 'history', *syrce* 'coat of mail', and Middle English *clog(ge)* 'block, wooden shoe', *cokkunge* 'striving', *tirven* 'to flay', *warroke* 'hunchback', *Notes and queries,* Vol no. 40 (1993), 287–97.

Brill's New Pauly. Encyclopedia of the Ancient World (Leiden, 2004).

BROMWICH, RACHEL (ed.), *Trioedd Ynys Prydein. The Triads of the Island of Britain* (3rd edition, Cardiff, 2006).

BROMWICH, RACHEL and D. SIMON EVANS (eds.), *Culhwch and Olwen. An edition and study of the oldest Arthurian tale* (Cardiff, 1992).

CARTWRIGHT, JANE, (ed.), *Celtic Hagiography and Saints' Cults*, (Cardiff, 2003).

CHADWICK, H. MUNRO, *Origin of the English Nation* (Cambridge, 1907).

—— ET AL. (eds.) *Studies in Early British History* (Cambridge, 1954).

CHADWICK, NORA K., 'Bretwalda. Gwledig. Vortigern', *BBCS* 19 (1961), 225–30.

CHARLES-EDWARDS, T. M., *Early Irish and Welsh Kinship* (Oxford, 1993).

—— 'Honour and Status in some Prose Tales', *Ériu* 29 (1978), 121–41.

CICERO, *Brutus*, ed. G. L. Henrickson and H. M. Hubbell (London, 1971).

—— *Epistolae ad Familiares*, ed. W. Glynn Williams, (Cambridge, Mass., and London, England, 1990).

—— *Pro Milone, In Pisone, Pro Scauro, Pro Fonteio, Pro Rabirio Postumo, Pro Marcello, Pro Ligario, Pro Rege Deiotaro*, ed. Harry Caplan, trans. Neville Hunter Watts (Cambridge, Mass., 1994).

—— *The Verrine Orations II* , ed. T. E. Page (London and Cambridge, Mass., 1935).

CRICK, JULIA C., *The Historia Regum Britannie of Geoffrey of Monmouth, III: A Summary Catalogue of the Manuscripts* (Cambridge, 1989).

DAVIES, JOHN and OTHERS (eds.), *The Welsh Academy Encyclopaedia of Wales* (Cardiff, 2008).

DAVIES, R. R., *Conquest, Coexistence, and Change: Wales 1063–1415* (Oxford and Cardiff, 1987).

DAVIES, SIONED (trans.), *The Mabinogion* (Oxford, 2007).

DAY, JENNY, ' "Ongyr gwyr gwedi gwyro a heyrn ar naid": dwy agwedd ar frwydro a gwaywffyn yng ngherddi Beirdd y Tywysogion,' *Dwned*, 14 (2008), 11–46.

DUFFY, SEAN, 'Ostmen, Irish and Welsh in the eleventh century', *Peritia* 9 (1995), 378–96.

——'The 1169 invasion as a turning point in Irish-Welsh relations', *Britain and Ireland 900–1300: Insular responses to Medieval European Change*, ed. B. Smith (Cambridge, 1999), 98–113.

DUMVILLE, DAVID N., 'Nennius and the *Historia Brittonum*', *Studia Celtica* 10/11 (1975/6), 78–95.

——(ed.), *The Historia Brittonum. The 'Vatican Recension'* (Cambridge, 1985).

ELLIS, HENRY (ed.), *Register and Chronicle of Aberconway from the Harleian MS 3725* (London, 1847).

EVANS, D. SIMON, *A Grammar of Middle Welsh* (Dublin, 1964).

——(ed.), *A Mediaeval Prince of Wales. The Life of Gruffudd ap Cynan* (Felinfach, 1990).

——(ed.), *Historia Gruffud vab Kenan* (Cardiff, 1977).

FEDERICO, SYLVIA, *New Troy, Fantasies of Empire in the Late Middle Ages* (Minneapolis, 2003).

FLANAGAN, MARIE THERESE, '*Historia Gruffud vab Kenan* and the origins of Balrothery', *CMCS* 28 (Winter, 1994), 71–94.

GEOFFREY OF MONMOUTH, *The History of the Kings of Britain*, trans. Lewis Thorpe (Harmondsworth, 1988).

——, *The History of the Kings of Britain. An Edition and Translation of De Gestis Britonum [Historia Regum Britanniae]*, ed. Michael D. Reeve, trans. Neil Wright (Woodbridge, 2007).

——, *The Historia Regum Britanniae of Geoffrey of Monmouth* ed. Acton Griscom with a literal translation of the Welsh manuscript no. LXI of Jesus College, Oxford, by Robert Ellis Jones (London, 1929).

——*Vita Merlini Gaufridi de Monemuta*, trans. Basil Clark (Cardiff, 1973).

GERALD OF WALES, *The Journey through Wales. The Description of Wales*, trans. Lewis Thorpe (Harmondsworth, 1980).

GROOMS, CHRIS, *The Giants of Wales: Cewri Cymru* (Lewiston, 1993).

JACOB HAMMER (ed.) *Geoffrey of Monmouth, Historia Regum Britanniae. A variant version edited from Manuscripts* by (Cambridge, Mass., 1951).

HANNING, ROBERT W., *The Vision of History in Early Britain* (New York and London, 1966).

HUWS, DANIEL, *Medieval Welsh Manuscripts* (Aberystwyth, 2002).

ISAAC, G.R., 'A note on the name of Ireland in Irish and Welsh' *Ériu* 59, 2009, 49–55.

ISIDORE OF SEVILLE, *The Etymologies of Isidore of Seville*, trans. STEPHEN A. BARNEY, W. J. LEWIS, J. A. BEACH and OLIVER BERGHOF (Cambridge, 2006).

JACKSON, K. H., 'Once again Arthur's battles', *Modern Philology*, 43 (1945–6), 44–57.

JANKULAK, KAREN, *Geoffrey of Monmouth* (Cardiff, 2010).

JARMAN, A. O. H., *Sieffre o Fynwy. Geoffrey of Monmouth* (Cardiff, 1966).

——and E. D. JONES (eds.), *Llyfr Du Caerfyrddin* (Cardiff, 1982).

——and GWILYM REES HUGHES (eds.), *A Guide to Welsh Literature*, Vol. 1 (Swansea, 1992).

JENKINS, DAFYDD (ed.), *Llyfr Colan* (Cardiff, 1963).

——(trans.), *The Law of Hywel Dda* (Llandysul, 2000).

JENKINS, DAFYDD and MORFYDD E. OWEN (eds.), *The Welsh Law of Women* (Cardiff, 1980).

JONES, A., *The History of Gruffydd ap Cynan* (Manchester, 1910).

JONES, NERYS ANN, 'The Mynydd Carn "Prophecy": A Reassessment', *CMCS* 38 (Winter 1999), 78–81.

—— and ANN PARRY OWEN (eds.), *Gwaith Cynddelw Brydydd Mawr*, Vol. 2 (Cyfres Beirdd y Tywysogion 4, Cardiff, 1995).

—— and MORFYDD E. OWEN, 'Twelfth-century Welsh Hagiography', *Celtic Hagiography and Saints' Cults*, ed. Jane Cartwright (Cardiff, 2003), 45–76.

JONES, OWEN, EDWARD WILLIAMS and WILLIAM OWEN [PUGHE] (eds.), *Myvyrian Archaiology of Wales* (second edition, Denbigh, 1870).

JONES, THOMAS (ed.), *Brenhinedd y Saesson* (Cardiff, 1971).

—— *Brut y Tywysogyon or The Chronicle of the Princes, Peniarth MS. 20* (Cardiff, 1952).

—— *Brut y Tywysogyon Peniarth MS. 20* (Cardiff, 1941).

—— *Brut y Tywysogyon (Red Book of Hergest Version)*, (Cardiff, 1955).

—— *Cronica de Wallia and Other Documents from Exeter Cathedral Library MS. 3514*. Reprinted with indexes, from *B* xii. (November, 1946), 27–44.

—— (ed.), *Gerallt Gymro* (Cardiff, 1938).

—— 'Historical Writing in Medieval Welsh', *Scottish Studies*, 12 (1968), 15–27.

—— (ed.), *Y Bibyl Ynghymraec* (Cardiff, 1940).

—— (ed.), *Ystoryaeu Seint Greal* (Cardiff, 1992).

KOCH, JOHN (ed.), *Celtic Culture. A Historical Encyclopaedia* (5 vols., Santa Barbara, Denver, Oxford, 2006).

LEWIS, HENRY (ed.), *Brut Dingestow* (Cardiff, 1942).

LIVY, *Books I-II*, trans. B. O. Foster (Cambridge, Mass., 1952).

LLOYD, JOHN EDWARD, *A History of Wales from the Earliest Times to the Edwardian Conquest* (2 vols., London, 1939).

—— *The Welsh Chronicles* (Proceedings of the British Academy, Vol. 14) (London, 1928).

LOOMIS, R. S. (ed.), *Arthurian Literature in the Middle Ages* (Oxford, 1959).

LUARD, HENRY RICHARD (ed.), *Annales Monastici*, 5 Vols. (London, 1864–9).

MAC CANA, PROINSIAS, 'An Old Nominal Relative Sentence in Welsh', *Celtica* 7 (1966), 91–115.

MARTIN, C. T. (ed.), *Registrum Epistolarum Johannis Peckham* (London, 1884).

MAUND, K. L. (ed.), *Gruffudd ap Cynan: a collaborative biography* (Woodbridge, 1996).

—— *Ireland, Wales and England in the Eleventh Century* (Woodbridge, 1991).

MAUND, KARI, *Princess Nest of Wales. Seductress of the English* (Stroud, 2007).

—— *The Welsh Kings: warriors, warlords and princes* (Stroud, 2006).

MORGAN, T. J., *Y Treigladau a'u Cystrawen* (Cardiff, 1989).

MORRIS, JOHN (ed.), *Nennius, British History and the Welsh Annals* (London and Chichester, 1980).

MORRIS-JONES, JOHN, *A Welsh Grammar* (Oxford, 1930).

Ó CATHASAIGH, TOMÁS, 'The sister's son in early Irish literature', *Peritia* 5 (1986), 128–60.

O'CONNOR, RALPH, 'History or Fiction? Truth-claims and defensive narrators in Icelandic romance-sagas', *Mediaeval Scandinavia*, 15 (2005), 101–69.

Ó'CORRÁIN, DONNCHADH, 'Historical Need and Literary Narrative', *Proceedings of the Seventh International Congress of Celtic Studies* ed. D. Ellis Evans, John G. Griffith and E. M. Jope (Oxford, 1986), 141–58.

Ó CRÓINÍN, DÁIBHÍ, *Early Medieval Ireland 400–1200* (London & New York, 1995).

O'DONOVAN, JOHN (ed.), *Annála Rioghachta Éireann*, 7 vols. (Dublin, 1848–51).

O'RAHILLY, CECILE (ed.), *Táin Bó Cúailnge from the Book of Leinster* (Dublin, 1967).

OWEN, GEORGE, *The Description of Pembrokeshire*, ed. Henry Owen (London, 1892).

OWEN, HYWEL WYN and RICHARD MORGAN (eds.), *Dictionary of the Place-names of Wales* (Llandysul, 2007).

OWENS, B. G., *Y Fersiynau Cymraeg o Dares Phrygius, eu Tarddiad, eu Nodweddion a'u Cydberthynas* (Unpublished M.A. thesis, University of Wales, Aberystwyth, 1951).

PADEL, O. J., *Arthur in Medieval Welsh Literature* (Cardiff, 2000).

—— 'Geoffrey of Monmouth and Cornwall', *CMCS* 8 (Winter 1984), 1–28.

—— 'Geoffrey of Monmouth and the development of the Merlin legend', *CMCS* 51 (Summer 2006), 37–65.

PARRY, J. J. (ed.), *Brut y Brenhinedd, Cotton Cleopatra Version* (Cambridge, Mass., 1937).

—— 'The Welsh texts of Geoffrey of Monmouth', *Speculum*, 5 (1930), pp. 424–30.

—— and R. A. CALDWELL, 'Geoffrey of Monmouth', *Arthurian Literature in the Middle Ages*, ed R.S.Loomis (Oxford, 1959), 72–93.

PARRY, THOMAS (ed.), *The Oxford Book of Welsh Verse* (Oxford, 1987).

—— *A History of Welsh Literature*, trans. Idris Bell (Oxford, 1955).

POPPE, ERICH, 'The evidence of narrative prose', *The Cambridge History of Literary Criticism*, Vol. 2, The Middle Ages, ed. A. Minnis and I. Johnson (Cambridge, 2005), 302–09.

—— *Of Cycles and Other Critical Matters. Some Issues in Medieval Irish Literary History and Criticism* (Cambridge, 2008).

—— [Review of RUSSELL, *Vita Griffini Filii Conani*], *Studia Celtica* 41 (2007), 261–64.

—— and REGINE RECK (eds.), *Selections from Ystorya Bown o Hamtwn* (Cardiff, 2009).

QUINTILIAN, *The Orator's Education*, ed., Donald A. Russell (5 vols., Cambridge, Mass., London, 2001).

RHŶS, JOHN and J. GWENOGVRYN EVANS (eds.), *The Text of the Bruts from the Red Book of Hergest* (Oxford, 1890).

ROBERTS, BRYNLEY F. (ed.) *Brut Tysilio* (Swansea, 1980).

—— (ed.), *Brut y Brenhinedd Llanstephan MS. 1 Version* (Dublin, 1984).

—— (ed.) *Cyfranc Lludd a Llefelys* (Dublin, 1975).

—— 'Ystoria', *BBCS*, 26 (1974–76), 13–20.

ROBERTS, S. E., *The Legal Triads of Medieval Wales* (Cardiff, 2007).

ROSS, A. S. C., 'Hengist's watchword', *English and Germanic Studies* 2 (1948–9), 81–101.

Rowley, Richard (trans.), *Historia Brittonum. The History of Britons attributed to Nennius* (Lampeter, 2005).

Russell, Paul (ed.), *Vita Griffini Filii Conani. The Medieval Life of Gruffudd ap Cynan* (Cardiff, 2005).

—— 'What did Medieval Scribes Do? The scribe of the Dingestow Court Manuscript', *CMCS* 37 (Summer 1999), 79–96.

Seneca, *Tragedies* II, ed. Jeffrey Henderson (Cambridge. Mass. and London England, 2004).

Smith, J. Beverley, *Llywelyn ap Gruffudd, Prince of Wales* (Cardiff, 1998).

—— *The Sense of History in Medieval Wales* (Aberystwyth, 1989).

—— 'Historical Writing in Medieval Wales: The Composition of *Brenhinedd y Saesson*, *Studia Celtica* XLII (2008), 55–86.

Stenton, F. M., *Anglo-Saxon England* (Oxford, 1943).

Stephens, Meic (ed.), *The New Companion to the Literature of Wales* (Cardiff, 1998).

Stephenson, David, *The Aberconwy Chronicle* (Cambridge, 2002).

Stokes, Whitley (ed.), 'The Annals of Tigernach', *Revue Celtique* 17 (1896), 6–33, 119–263, 337–420.

Swanton, M. J., *The Spearheads of the Anglo-Saxon Settlements* (London, 1973).

Thomas, Peter Wynn, 'Cysylltiadau Daearyddol Chwedlau Odo', *Ysgrifau Beirniadol* 19, ed. J. E. C. Williams (Denbigh, 1993), 59–85.

—— '(GWNAETH): Newidyn Arddulliol yn y Cyfnod Canol', in *Cyfoeth y Testun*: *Ysgrifau ar Lenyddiaeth Gymraeg yr Oesoedd Canol*, ed. Iestyn Daniel et al. (Cardiff, 2003), 252–80.

—— 'Middle Welsh Dialects: Problems and Perspectives', *BBCS* 40 (1993), 17–50.

Thomas, R. J., *Enwau Afonydd a Nentydd Cymru* Vol. 1 (Cardiff, 1938).

Thomson, Derick S. (ed.), *Branwen Uerch Lyr* (Dublin, 1968).

Thomson, R. L. (ed.), *Pwyll Pendeuic Dyuet* (Dublin, 1957).

Thornton, David, 'The Genealogy of Gruffudd ap Cynan', *Gruffudd ap Cynan: a collaborative biography*, ed. K.L. Maund (Woodbridge, 1996), 79–108.

Thucydides, *The Peleponnesian War,* ed. Walter Blanco and Jennifer Tolbert Roberts (New York, London 1998).

Toner, Gregory, 'The Ulster Cycle: Historiography of Fiction?', *CMCS* 40 (Winter 2000), 1–20.

Watkin, Morgan (ed.), *Ystorya Bown de Hamtwn* (Caerdydd 1958).

Watkins, T. Arwyn, 'Yr Arddodiad HG. (*h*)*i, in*; CC. *y* (= yn), *yn*', *BBCS* 17 (1957), 137- 58.

Wiliam, Aled Rhys, *Llyfr Iorwerth* (Cardiff, 1960).

Williams, G. J. and E. D. Jones (eds.), *Gramadegau'r Penceirddiaid* (Cardiff, 1934).

Williams, Ifor (ed.), *Armes Prydein. The Prophecy of Britain from the Book of Taliesin,* English Version by Rachel Bromwich (Dublin, 1972).

—— (ed.), *Canu Aneirin* (Cardiff, 1938).

—— (ed.), *Pedeir Keinc y Mabinogi* (Cardiff, 1930).

—— *Enwau Lleoedd* (Lerpwl, 1962).

Williams, J. E. Caerwyn, 'Meilyr Brydydd and Gruffudd ap Cynan', *Gruffudd ap Cynan: a collaborative biography*, ed. K.L. Maund (Woodbridge, 1996), 165–86.

—— *The Court Poet of Medieval Wales. An Essay* (Lampeter, 1997).

——and others (eds), *Gwaith Meilir Brydydd a'i Ddisgynyddion* (Cyfres Beirdd y Tywysogion 1, Cardiff, 1994).

Williams, Patricia (ed.), *Kedymdeithyas Amlyn ac Amic* (Cardiff, 1982).

Williams, Stephen, J. (ed.), *Ffordd y Brawd Odrig* (Cardiff, 1929).

——and Enoch Powell (eds), *Llyfr Blegywryd* (Cardiff, 1942).

Willis, David, 'Old and Middle Welsh' *The Celtic Languages*, ed. Martin J. Ball and Nicole Müller (2nd edition, London and New York, 2010), 117–60.

Wright, Neil (ed.), *Historia Regum Brittannie. First Variant Version* (Cambridge, 1988).

——*The Historia Regum Britannie of Geoffrey of Monmouth,* I: *A Single-manuscript Edition from Bern, Burgerbibliothek, MS 568* (Cambridge, 1984).

www.asnc.cam.ac.uk/publications/hughes.htm (Accessed 20.3.2012).

www.maryjones.us/ctexts/merlini.html (Accessed 20.3.2012).

www.theoi.com/Text/DaresPhrygius.html (Accessed 20.3.2012).

www.ingramcontent.com/pod-product-compliance
Lightning Source LLC
Chambersburg PA
CBHW072354030726
47505CB00014B/1827